Collaboration Strategy

To Pam and Rich
with best wishes,

Felix

Collaboration Strategy

How to Get What You Want from
Employees, Suppliers and
Business Partners

By Felix Barber and Michael Goold

B L O O M S B U R Y
LONDON • NEW DELHI • NEW YORK • SYDNEY

First published in the United Kingdom in 2014

Copyright © Felix Barber and Michael Goold, 2014

Bloomsbury Publishing Plc
50 Bedford Square
London
WC1B 3DP

www.bloomsbury.com

London, New Delhi, New York, and Sydney

A CIP record for this book is available from the British Library.
ISBN: 9-781-4729-1202-2

MIX
Paper from
responsible sources
FSC® C020471

Design by Fiona Pike, Pike Design, Winchester
Typeset by Hewer Text UK Ltd, Edinburgh
Printed and bound in the United Kingdom by CPI Group (UK) Ltd, Croydon CR0 4YY

Contents

Acknowledgements

This book emphasizes the importance of collaboration to business success. And, consistent with this view, we have benefitted greatly from the assistance of many collaborators in our work on it.

To research the book, in addition to an extensive search of the relevant literature and press, we carried out nearly 200 in person interviews in North America – Canada and the US – and in Western Europe – Austria, France, Germany, Ireland, the Netherlands, Switzerland, and the UK. We would like to thank the managers from leading companies across a wide range of industries – for example, airlines, banks, computer manufacturers, dairy producers, engineering and construction firms, insurance, film production, oil exploration and development, pharmaceuticals, software, retailing, telecommunications, and utilities – and across a wide range of ownership forms – for example, cooperatives, family firms, foundations, franchisers, government authorities, partnerships, private equity funds, and public companies – who helped us with our research and provided valuable insights into how they were able to get what they wanted from their employees, suppliers and other business partners.

Associates at work, past and present, have contributed ideas and constructive criticism throughout the long research process. Above all we are grateful to our colleagues at the Ashridge Strategic Management Centre and the Heads of Strategy from the companies in the Ashridge Collaborative Strategy Network. They provided extensive assistance in many meetings and informal discussions in developing the framework and process we describe in the book for deciding how to set up business activities for success. Alumni and current employees of The Boston Consulting Group have provided invaluable help in giving and organizing interviews for us. CEAMS, a Swiss institutional asset management firm where one of the authors is a Director, deserve a special mention as their staff invested many weeks of effort in helping us test particular hypotheses using their proprietary databases.

Writing and publishing the book have taken almost as much time and effort as researching it. Therefore we'd like to thank our agent Peter Bernstein, who has provided encouragement, support and shrewd comments, John Landry, who helped to make the book much more readable through his expert editorial advice, and Alana Clogan, Rosie Bick and Suzi Williamson at Bloomsbury for managing the publishing process for us. We would also like to thank Michelle Moore for handling the graphics for the book.

Last but not least we thank our families for their unflagging support over the best part of a decade that it took to complete this project.

Chapter 1

The Challenge of Getting Work Done for You

The greatest concern for most business owners and CEOs, what keeps them awake at night, is often not their strategy – how to create a compelling customer offer or how to outsmart the competition – it's how to get people to make that strategy actually happen.

Implementation has become a pervasive problem in recent years, with many companies struggling to motivate their employees to deliver on value-creating strategies. Investment banks have constructed bonuses for talented bankers to motivate them to maximize profits without taking excessive risks – and the financial crisis of 2008 came about partly because these efforts fell short. Less well known is that most of the big prescription drug companies have been failing to develop the new products that their strategies depend on.[1] A PriceWaterhouse Coopers report[2] concluded that 'the industry is investing twice as much in R&D as it was a decade ago to produce two-fifths of the new medicines it then produced.' Research and development employees have evidently not been as productive as their companies had hoped in coming up with new drugs. Getting your employees to do what you want in order to implement your strategy has become a critical management challenge.

What's more, it's not even enough to get your employees to do what you want. Your suppliers must be on board as well. Companies have come to rely heavily on outside contractors and other external partners to realize key aspects of their strategy. As outsourcing becomes possible for more business tasks and processes, companies are finding success by focusing on just a few areas in-house. It's often better to contract out to a variety of specialists, who benefit from economies of scale, than to reproduce those skills in-house. But many companies have yet to master these new relationships. A study of 240 large outsourcing contracts in Europe and the US,[3] for example, found that two-thirds unravelled before the contract's full term.

Large projects seem to cause many of the most acute problems. A recent study[4] found that one in six major IT projects cost more than twice as much as expected. And governments and major corporate clients have almost come to expect delays and cost overruns on large construction jobs where many parties are working together. For example, the Scottish Parliament building in Edinburgh was budgeted at £40 million, cost 10 times that and took twice as long to complete.[5] In the United States, the city of Boston's 'Big Dig' project to move a highway segment underground cost double its initial price tag of $7 billion.[6]

The root cause of implementation problems

Whether working with employees or with external suppliers, companies are increasingly stumbling with implementing strategy. But why is this happening? And how can we address it?

Getting work done for you is straightforward enough in routine activities where you can clearly specify the outputs you want from suppliers and easily direct and control the work of employees. Problems arise when specialized suppliers and employees are undertaking non-routine tasks, such as product development and marketing, or carrying out complex projects. This is precisely where you'll struggle to specify just what output is required, or to direct and control – and your strategy may not play out.

Specialization per se is not the problem. After all, companies have moved in this direction with great success, at least since the famous pin factory in Adam Smith's *Wealth of Nations*. One inexperienced man working alone, Smith says, can make fewer than 20 pins a day. But a small factory with specialized division of tasks between 10 men can produce 40,000 pins per day, or in other words 200 times the output per man.

In Smith's pin factory of the 1770s, however, the workers' tasks are routine with easily measurable outputs. The manager of the pin factory can readily direct and control his employees, and, if dissatisfied, he can hire and train new workers. Relationships with suppliers, such as makers of brass wire for example, are also easy to handle. The manager can specify the type and quality of wire, inspect the wire on delivery, and he will pay only if he gets what he has ordered. When choosing which people and companies to work with, the manager can decide simply on the basis of who is best able to get the work done. There is little need to worry about motivation, since he can specify precisely what he wants and make continued employment or supply relationships dependent on getting it.

Today, specialization still creates few problems provided suppliers and employees are carrying out routine tasks. Indeed, companies are pushing ever harder to concentrate solely on those activities where they are competitively advantaged, and outsource the rest to specialist suppliers. The Internet has slashed the cost of finding low-cost suppliers and has greatly facilitated communicating with them about what is wanted. For Apple and other leading electronics companies, for example, it has become easier and easier to outsource routine production tasks to low-cost manufacturers in the developing world.

But in an increasingly knowledge- and service-based economy, non-routine activities are growing in importance. Adding value in a business is more about designing, developing, marketing, buying and selling, and less about producing and delivering standard products and services. The share of US employment in non-routine occupations has grown steadily from 40 per cent in 1976 to 60 per cent in 2012.[7] Non-routine activities are now the norm.

Getting employees to trade financial derivatives or research and develop new pharmaceutical drugs, getting external contractors to design and install a new IT system or move a highway segment, is a far cry from manufacturing pins. Managers can no longer specify precisely what they want done. They often know less about the activity at hand than their specialist partners, and readily grant them autonomy so they can use their judgement and creativity. In non-routine activities, where you cannot specify precisely *what* you want done, specialization can create problems in getting things done.

To choose the employees and suppliers you want to work with, it is not enough to know if you have chosen the most able people and companies to help you. Since you can't tell them exactly what you want from them, you have to rely on their ongoing discretion and trust their decisions. So you have to set things up in such a way that you will gain their motivation to accomplish what you want. By 'motivation' we mean not just their willingness to work hard, but also their commitment to the results you seek.

This difficulty with sufficiently specifying the output you want from partners – whether contractors or employees – is the root cause of many implementation problems. If you and your partners are not clear about what you want done, it will be difficult to set up an agreement to get what you want, and hard to be sure you are getting favourable terms. Take, for example, what happens when you try to get a good deal from the emergency plumbing service you call out to fix a major leak, or from the computer services company that comes to sort out dire problems with your PC. You want the problems fixed fast, but you do not know what needs to be done. As a result, you're vulnerable to shoddy workmanship, incompetence and overcharging. Similar problems, writ large, afflict companies when they can't tell suppliers or employees what to do.

Specification challenges lead to two other kinds of problems. These arise particularly with suppliers but can also occur with employees. Firstly, if you aren't ready to define what you want when you set out the contract, your suppliers may easily gain bargaining power – which means they can demand more of the value they help you generate than you want to give them. Suppose you are a fashion retailer relying on outside manufacturers to produce your garments. You would like to place your order close to the time of sale, when your product is in keeping with the current fashion trends. But if you wait that long, capacity with the capable manufacturers will be booked out. So you reserve some manufacturing capacity before the season starts without placing specific orders. When you come to place specific orders during the season, the manufacturer has gained a negotiating advantage. You can't get a competitive bid for the garments because you are committed to your supplier, and you may not know enough about the manufacturing process to be sure how much the work should cost.

Secondly, if the problem is not about timing but instead about your basic inability to define what you want – and only a partner can help you with the specifications – your partner may have an awkward conflict of interest. She may pursue goals that follow her own interests rather than yours, so the work fails to generate the value expected. Let's say you are a consumer products maker relying heavily on marketing to build up your brand. You hire an advertising agency to develop creative media placements. Based on only the most general guidelines from you (the specification problem), the talented members of the agency come up with a highly original message. More concerned about winning ad industry awards than attracting customers, they convince you (in your ignorance) to make this message the centrepiece of your media campaign. Their creativity in fact does win an award, but it makes much less of an impression with your intended audience of potential customers.

These two dangers can play off each other. Suppose you've hired a consulting firm to help you evaluate a potential acquisition. If you go ahead with the deal, you're likely to go on to hire that same firm to help carry out the post-merger integration. The consulting firm starts with a strong bias to recommend for the move. Even if the acquisition creates little value for your company, it should create value for the firm. You can remove the consultants' conflict of interest if you make it clear you will work with a different firm to do the post-merger integration. However, the firm that helps you evaluate the acquisition will learn so much about you and the target that you may not want to switch.

With these non-routine tasks, you must think much harder about how to set things up so that people and companies are not only able but also motivated to implement your strategy. Essentially, you must design a basis of working together, or 'collaboration,' with your employees and suppliers that will get them to do what you want. *or coming up with a better objective.*

Overcoming the specification problem

Most executives and entrepreneurs at least implicitly understand the pitfalls in setting up to get work done. But as the examples at the beginning of the chapter testify, they often struggle to deal with them.

Sometimes the solution just takes a little more work. Fashion retailers overcome their timing problem by combining the two-stage ordering with a greater in-house expertise on manufacturing costs. They reserve factory capacity well in advance, and then place specific orders with a better sense of what they should be paying. They are still stuck with the supplier with the reserved capacity, but they show more knowledge during the negotiations. That gives them leverage because suppliers are keen not to lose the next season's orders.

Changing the way you set up activities to improve motivation

But when specification challenges are severe, fixing them may require fundamental changes in the design of your business. And this is where executives often get in trouble because they make sequential decisions about what they want done, the people and companies to help them do it, and agreements to motivate these people and companies to do what they want. If they can't find agreements that work, they're stuck. A sequential approach to deciding how to get the work done is limiting. Motivating partners often means going beyond contract adjustments or newfangled compensation plans – or the kind of engaged leadership that's often the buzz in organizational circles. The best solution may require going back and reconsidering the number and mix of people and companies to do the work, or perhaps changing your business strategy and what you want done for you.

Even the creative performance incentives that companies have devised in recent decades sometimes won't solve a motivation problem. Performance incentives are indeed a way to motivate employees when you can't direct and control their effort, or to motivate suppliers when you can't define their output in advance. But powerful performance incentives can introduce awkward conflicts of interest. Getting round these awkward conflicts of interest and making performance incentives work often requires some quite far-reaching changes in other aspects of how you set up to do business.

For example, in response to the declining R&D productivity in pharmaceuticals, some pharma companies tried to introduce performance incentives for key R&D employees. But the difficulty they faced was that it takes such a long time to reliably measure results – developing a new drug and demonstrating its safety and efficacy can involve a decade of work. To measure performance faster, one company decided to reward the number of candidate drugs passing through to the next phase of clinical trials – an early indicator of overall success. The incentive certainly had an impact: more candidate drugs did pass through to the next phase of trials. However, a higher than usual percentage of these drugs ended up with problems of safety or efficacy. Most of them failed later, and therefore more expensively, than they would have without the incentives. If you reward progress towards a goal instead of full achievement, then managers will be tempted, consciously or unconsciously, to manipulate the metrics.

Instead of tinkering with employees' rewards, pharma companies have had more success by going back and rethinking who should be doing the work. Many of them have outsourced some of their R&D work to venture capital-backed firms that were small and focused enough to be able to motivate R&D managers by giving them options or a share of the equity. The price at which these firms are bought out – typically every three to five years – helps to measure their managers' performance more objectively.[8] Some pharma firms have now outsourced so much of their R&D that they have effectively changed their strategy. They have decided that their competitive advantage now lies more in their ability to select and manage a network of external research and development partners – and in their marketing and distribution prowess – than in basic R&D.

Recasting motivational challenges will give you a much wider range of tactics for getting what you want done. You can modify your strategy or the help you want to implement it. A bank that can't control its deal-makers, perhaps, should refocus on less risky parts of the business or should work on more effectively hedging risky deals. A soft-drinks manufacturer that wants a customized plastic bottle and cap should outsource the production but should also invest to own the moulds for the bottle and the cap. This way the supplier doesn't gain bargaining power when the manufacturer wants to re-order, as the supplier will not own critical assets for doing the work.

You can also change the number and mix of people and companies you get to do the work. This may let you avoid awkward conflicts of interest or retain bargaining power. Banks can build up an independent risk-management staff to prevent excessive risk-taking by dealmakers with powerful performance incentives and who face awkward conflicts because they share in profits but not in losses. Manufacturers can involve several suppliers in producing the same part; 'second sourc-ing' is a common ploy to maintain competitive pressure and hence bargaining power. You can also use a similar ploy within a company, as a consulting firm does when it encourages its partners to team up to serve clients. A client served by several consulting partners has a relationship with the consulting firm, not merely with a particular individual and it becomes more difficult for partners that leave the consulting firm to take their clients with them.

If you are prepared to make more commitments to the people and companies you work with, that may also help motivate them to do what you want. Properly motivating people and companies means offering an agreement that works for them as well as for you. Take a large IT project, for example. The systems integrator you want to hire may be reluctant to give you a fixed-price commitment for installing and roll-ing out the system because they are concerned that your own in-house team will not provide the support they need. In order to get the price you want, you may need to make detailed commitments about the support they will get from your IT department.

Entrepreneurs and executives need to move beyond considering incen-tives – or leadership alone – as the solution to motivational problems. There is plenty of room for creativity in designing rewards to motivate and get commitment from partners carrying out non-routine tasks. But to address deep-seated problems, as the examples above suggest, there are more levers you can pull.

Business partners sharing entrepreneurial responsibility

For the most difficult tasks you may need to pull many levers at once: changing the help you want in implementing your strategy, changing the type and number of people and companies you want help from, and changing the agreements you set up with them. Thus, you are likely to find yourself in quite a different type of working relationship. The people and companies you work with are no longer traditional employ-ees or suppliers; they have become business partners sharing with you in decision-making, risks and rewards and often providing critical assets for the business.

For example, when big pharmaceutical companies work with small research firms to develop new drugs, both sides bring technology and know-how critical to project success. Different parties may take the lead in different phases of the drug development process – in the early phase perhaps the small firm, in later phases, the big company – and both sides share in the revenues from the drug once it is registered for sale. The big pharmaceutical company and the small research firm are partners.

We can go further here. The venture-capital fund that owns a majority of the small research firm and the top managers that run it are partners too. The managers own a minority share of the firm and take many critical decisions. The venture-capital fund that owns the research firm is itself a partnership between financial investors who provide the risk capital, and a venture-capital firm that takes the decisions about how to invest it – both share in the profits. And the venture-capital firm that invests the money is itself a management partnership.

Even if the task you want to accomplish is not as skilled and complex as coming up with a new prescription drug, you may find yourself in a similar position if you want to specialize to get the best possible return on your investment of time and money. A hamburger and fries, even if they taste a lot better, may be a far cry in their development complexity from a prescription drug, but if you are a small entrepreneur seeking to own and operate a hamburger restaurant, you are unlikely to want to develop the restaurant brand and concept yourself. Instead, you'll want to take a franchise from one of the big chains such as McDonalds or Burger King. You and your franchisor will be business partners. You can't set up a traditional 'supplier' relationship with the franchisor because you don't know how you want the brand and the restaurant menu to develop over the life of your restaurant investment. Instead you will reward the franchisor and align your interests by sharing the revenues from your hamburger restaurant.

As non-routine tasks become the norm, employees and suppliers who share entrepreneurial responsibility with you in the business – providing critical resources, taking and implementing critical decisions, and carrying business risks – are also becoming common. And when they share entrepreneurial responsibilities with you, they will often share in the business rewards. They become, effectively, co-owners in the business or the assets you jointly work to develop.

Collaboration designs of this kind are becoming prevalent across a wide range of industries and for a wide range of tasks. We list some of the most popular collaboration designs in Figure 1.1. There are a multitude of other designs with no names tailor-made to fit the needs of particular business situations.

Figure 1.1 Sharing entrepreneurial responsibility with business partners is now common

Example of collaboration designs	Examples of their applications
• Development Alliances	• Pharmaceutical development
• Pain/gain sharing Alliances (projects)	• Engineering, construction, mining
• Framework Alliances (relationships)	• Utilities, infrastructure
• Network Alliances	• Airlines
• Venture capital	• Biotech, hi-tech
• Private equity	• Undermanaged basic businesses
• Franchising	• Hotels, restaurants, services
• Licensing	• Luxury goods, hi-tech
• Production sharing contracts	• Oil exploration and production
• Risk and revenue sharing partnerships	• Aerospace (jet engines)
• Public Private Partnerships	• Infrastructure, public services
• Open source communities	• Software, information platforms

Whether or not the people or companies who do the work are sharing in the business income, if you are asking them to carry out non-routine tasks for you or to provide critical assets – such as a brand and concept – for the business, there is always an element of 'partnering' involved. If you are relying on employees to take critical business decisions, then they are not just human resources or 'human capital'. They are sharing in the entrepreneurial responsibility for the business outcome. You must make sure they have no awkward conflicts of interest. Similarly, if your suppliers are investing to provide critical assets for the business, you must make sure you can motivate them to let you use those assets on favourable terms.

We call these non-routine employees and suppliers 'partners', partly in order to have a single term of reference, but also to make the point that people and companies you might once have treated as an afterthought may increasingly justify a more partner-oriented approach. When you think hard about how to motivate them to do the work, and not just about whether they have the ability, you will often take a quite different approach to setting up business activities. We look at many examples of what this means throughout the book. And to give you a flavour, we start right away with a construction project below.

Getting an airport terminal built

Let's look in detail at the kind of troublesome building project mentioned at the beginning of the chapter. Suppose I head up construction for an airport management company, and I'm charged with putting up a new terminal. Architects submit designs for the new terminal, but the most attractive design, which also maximizes the site's retail potential, is technically highly complex to construct. It will be a challenge to build it on time and at a cost that will give a good return on investment. I have no experience supervising the construction of anything so complex. Having heard about the Scottish Parliament fiasco, I'm worried. I try to use my influence to support a simpler design, but I'm overruled.

Now I have to make the chosen design work. I consider getting the architects to provide further details on the specifications in order to submit the construction work to competitive bids. That way I should get favourable terms for the construction and a fixed price that transfers the risk to the contractors. But can I trust the bids I get? The project is so complex that the work will take years and there will likely be many changes to the specifications. Contractors will be tempted to submit a low bid to win the business, but then negotiate hard for higher fees for the inevitable modifications along the way. And can I trust the architects? They sound convincing about the new technology involved in construction, but will it really work? And couldn't some aspects of what they are proposing be simplified to get the same result for lower cost?

I would like to get the engineering and construction firms that are actually going to be responsible for the construction involved earlier in finalizing the specifications. But they will be reluctant to invest a lot of time in understanding the project without a contract in hand. If I want to select the prime contractors at an early stage, though, I won't know enough to properly put the project out to competitive bid.

I could pay the prime contractors' time and expenses instead of a fixed fee. But on a time-and-expenses contract the contractors have little incentive to keep costs down. I could work hard to manage costs when supervising the construction, but I'm not sure of my abilities or my colleagues' to do this if the contractors don't start with a strong incentive to perform. And if the contract doesn't tie everything down beforehand, I'll open the door to changes in specifications from my colleagues elsewhere in the company with different ideas about the new terminal.

I need to find a middle way, something that gets me the help I need before finalizing the design, while also aligning my interests with the contractors'. I look further into selecting the prime contractors early, but with a twist. Instead of paying their time and expenses, we use our knowledge from the design phase to agree on a definite target cost for the work. Not only will the costs be clearer to both parties, but the contractors will have had time to get reliable bids from subcontractors. There will certainly be some changes to specifications during construction anyway. But maybe I can persuade the contractors that only material changes to specifications will count for the purpose of modifying the target costs. I make a note to myself to consider how I can agree with the contractors on what will be considered 'material'.

Beyond that, I can try to persuade the contractors to share the 'pain-and-gain' from coming in above or below the target costs. Not only do they have a further incentive to keep costs low during construction, but they are less likely to charge aggressively for these material changes to specifications. I now have the same incentive – which I can use to discourage my colleagues from costly specification changes, or to encourage them to agree to opportunities for cost reduction that we discover along the way. If the terminal comes in over budget, the contractor swallows half of the overrun, but if it ends under budget then the contractor gets half the savings. After all, we use target bonuses inside the company with employees. Why not a similar approach with the contractors?

Once the target costs are set, both my colleagues and the prime contractors will have fully aligned interests and powerful incentives to work efficiently. That sounds good, but I am still concerned about how the target costs are set. If the prime contractors are left to come up with the target costs, then I am letting them write themselves a blank check. I don't trust the architects or my in-house team to assess if we are getting a good deal. So I decide to take on an additional engineering firm as an advisor, to go over the target costings with a sharp pencil and check that I am getting value for money.

This is beginning to feel like a way of setting up collaboration that will resolve the difficult problems that I know I will face. I will get commitment and alignment on favourable terms. Certainly there are some difficult trade-offs – I lose the marketplace discipline of competitive bids, and I will need to work harder to manage the project. But for this project I think I have made the right decisions.

What we've just described is a simplified version of a 'pain and gain sharing alliance,' an approach that's attracting growing interest in Europe and else-where. We discuss it at length in Chapter 4, and it reflects the kind of creative collaboration we champion in this book.

The need for an integrated framework

We argue that companies looking to implement strategy should start early in considering how to motivate their partners. But conventional approaches to strategy development discourage companies from doing this. Strategy development focuses on achieving competitive advantage, which is equated with having strong market positions, patented technologies, greater process expertise, large scale plants and other valuable resources under the company's control. The conventional approach is to assume that people are 'human resources' that can also be controlled. Competitive advantage is not equated with setting up activities in a way that makes it easier to use available resources to good effect. In the conventional approach, that is something to think about later.

Integrating considerations of motivating partners upfront into strategy development involves some difficult trade-offs. If you engage additional partners to help direct and motivate others, there will be additional costs. If you invest to do the work in-house to limit problems of conflicts of interest and lack of bargaining power with external contractors, you will require more capital to do business. If you outsource the work to better motivate and create more value, you may find your contractor will capture the lion's share of the rewards and not your own company. Executives and managers need a framework that helps them ask the right questions, think more flexibly about the type and mix of partners to work with, make the right trade-offs and test whether they have set up to successfully implement their strategy. They need what we call in this book a 'collaboration strategy', that is to say a clear view of how to set things up so that you will get what you want from your employees, suppliers and other business partners.

To help executives to develop a collaboration strategy , we have developed a systematic framework for diagnosing potential problems in setting up collaboration (see Figure 1.2.) If you are able to anticipate possible problems before you start to work together, you are much more likely to be able to solve them.

Figure 1.2 The 10 requirements for profitable collaboration

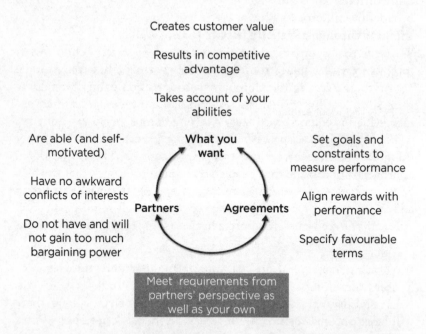

The framework addresses all three major aspects of setting up the work: deciding what you want help in doing; selecting the partners; and devising the partner agreements. For each aspect, the framework forces the entrepreneur or the executive in charge to ask if the set-up meets three key requirements. The arrows connecting each aspect go in both direc-tions, because the framework calls for an iterative, not sequential proc-ess. The tenth and final requirement, at the bottom, calls for making sure these arrangements fit your partners' needs as well as your own. We explain this framework and how to use it in Chapter 2, in the context of discussing a collaboration strategy for working with external contrac-tors on a large IT project.

If you meet all the 10 requirements, you will have set up profitable collaboration with your partners, so you can use the framework to test and refine what you propose to do. By using each aspect of the framework, leaders can fine-tune their choices of partners and agree-ments and accept trade-offs – or resort to creative thinking such as sharing business income and ownership or taking the strategy in a quite different direction. The framework is the central element in the broader overall process, shown below (Figure 1.3) that we propose for thinking through collaboration strategy.

Figure 1.3 The process for developing a collaboration design

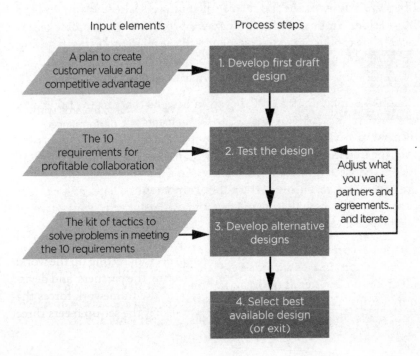

Before you can use the collaboration framework, you need a draft collaboration design: you must define what you want to do and the partners and agreements you will work with to get it done. We discuss how to come up with a first draft collaboration design in Chapter 3, looking in more detail at the example of setting up a chain of fast-food restaurants. We show that the best collaboration design involves balancing considerations of market and competitive strategy, ability and motivation.

The focus of Chapters 4 to 7 is on developing tactics to deal with the main problems that can occur in setting up collaboration – all based on detailed industry case studies. We discuss problems and solutions across a wide range of industries including engineering and construction, consumer brands, retail chains, utilities, software, telecommunications, banking and pharmaceuticals.

Chapter 4 focuses on working with external suppliers. Chapter 5 addresses the special case of monopoly power, when a supplier may gain excessive bargaining power with a whole industry. Chapter 6 focuses on tactics when working with employees generally, while Chapter 7 addresses the special case of employees who work on R&D or innovation. The discussions in Chapters 4 to 7 allow us to pull together a complete toolkit of tactics for solving all the main problems in setting up collaboration with employees, suppliers and other business partners – an invaluable aid in developing alternative collaboration designs.

Chapters 8 and 9 look at collaboration designs that create opportunities and solve problems by explicitly sharing business income and ownership. In Chapter 8, we look at how private equity creates opportunities for investors – but above all for managers – by sharing business income between investors and managers in a way that solves the corporate governance problems of the public company. In Chapter 9 we take a broader look at how sharing income and ownership with your partners can help you get the work done.

Chapter 10 brings together our main ideas on how to set up profitable collaboration and how to achieve a collaboration advantage. It also identifies the big trends in collaboration that we have observed and the implications for strategy and competitive advantage. Lastly, it draws out broader implications for individuals, governments and society.

To conclude the book, we add a special summary guide to the design process we propose for setting up collaboration, explaining the four steps in the process along with the key tactics – with references to the chapters that discuss each of these. This summary adds no new ideas to the book; we offer it as a refresher for those who have read the book and want to try out the process themselves.

The growing specialization of companies and employees is surely a great benefit to business, generating more value for customers than earlier generations would have thought possible. Adam Smith's division of labour continues to boost productivity, aided by advances in strategy that help companies leverage their resources by focusing on those activities they do best and outsourcing the rest.

But as companies push specialization further in non-routine activities, problems of direction and motivation are overwhelming traditional management approaches – and causing major problems in implementing strategy. The framework we propose for setting up collaboration integrates issues of direction and motivation of partners into the development of strategy, and so will nip these problems in the bud. Companies that follow the process laid out in this book to devise their collaboration strategies will ensure that the business strategies they pursue will be much easier to implement – and will yield a good deal more value.

---

[1] After a long period of poor performance, there are some recent signs of improvement as we will discuss in Chapter 7.

[2] PriceWaterhouseCoopers. 'Pharma 2020: The Vision. Which Path Will You Take?, 2007.

[3] Simon Caulkin. 'Out of house, out of mind – and out of pocket'. *The Observer*, 13th May 2007.

[4] Alexander Budzier and Bent Flyvbjerg. *Double Whammy – How ICT Projects are Fooled by Randomness and Screwed by Political Intent*. Working Paper, Saïd Business School, University of Oxford, August 2011.

[5] Ian Swanson. *Hard task of nailing down costs of building*, Evening News, Scotland, 30th June 2008.

[6] Robert W. Poole, Jr. and Peter Samuel. *Transportation Mega-Projects and Risk*. Reason Foundation Policy Brief 97, February 2011.

[7] Stefania Albanesi, Victoria Gregory, Christina Patterson, and Ayşegül Şahin. 'Is Job Polarization holding back the labor market?' Liberty Street Economics, Federal Reserve Bank of New York, 27th March 2013. Available at http://libertystreeteconomics.newyorkfed.org/2013/03/is-job-polarization-holding-back-

the-labor-market.html downloaded 18th November 2013. Data based on US Census Bureau, Current Population Survey.

8   Of course, a more open approach to R&D has the additional benefit that pharma companies are more flexible in offering the work to whoever has the best ability to get it done.

Chapter 2

The Requirements for Success

It's time to start putting our process into action. This chapter focuses on the second step in our process, where we show how to test a proposed collaboration design to see if it will work. You must meet 10 success requirements. These requirements cover what you want, the partners you work with and the agreements you put in place to motivate them. For successful collaboration, you must meet all the requirements from your partners' perspective as well as your own. You want, of course, to capture a good share of the business income but the results should be satisfactory for all parties. The 10 success requirements we discuss are at the heart of the book, so it's essential to understand what they are, why we have chosen them, and how they can be helpful in increasing your chances of setting up profitable collaboration. We'll use a common corporate challenge – installing an ERP system – to do that.

An Enterprise Resource Planning (ERP) system is an information platform that links separate information systems in a company so they can share data. By integrating accounting, financial reporting, supply chain management, manufacturing, human resources, and other systems, companies can better understand the ramifications, say, of adding a new product to the mix. An ERP system can boost productivity in many ways, which is why most large companies now have one, so the collaboration challenges we describe should be familiar to many readers.

However, after thousands of ERP installations over several decades, most of these projects still don't run smoothly. A 2013 survey of 172 companies installing an ERP system[1] found that more than one in six went at least 50 per cent over budget, more than one in three took over 50 per cent longer to complete than expected, and over half failed to achieve 50 per cent of the benefits expected. And such broad surveys as this one, looking mainly at installations of smaller systems, probably fail to capture the full scale of the problems in large global companies rolling out a system across countries and continents. One global manufacturer we talked to was just starting its third attempt at installing a single global ERP system. It had already spent over $500 million, around

10 per cent of the company's annual revenue, without any easily measurable benefit.

What makes designing and installing an ERP system so difficult? The technology is not the problem. ERP systems use standard software, and after so many adoptions the technology is quite mature. The trouble lies in configuring and customizing the software to fit the specifics of your business processes. Since the software is not infinitely flexible, you will also need to modify at least some of your business processes to fit the dictates of the software. It may take months of design work to adapt the software to your business processes and your business processes to the software. Then it may take several years to install and roll out the new software and processes across diverse multinational operations.

Given all this complexity – affecting all areas of the organization – you will inevitably have to work hard to gain agreement on what needs to be done. Then you need to make sure that the people designing and installing the system are able and motivated to do it on favourable terms for you.

Managing an ERP project involves setting up the internal team and any relationships with outside contractors. Since we intend the ERP example to illustrate general collaboration problems, we'll keep it simple and focus on challenges with the IT contractors that usually do most of the work. We'll assume that, like most company CEOs, you would like to delegate extensively and rely heavily on contractors. There are more than enough problems here to illustrate the wide range of possibilities.

The 10 requirements for success can help you identify likely collaboration problems. Once you have a clear view of the problems in meeting the 10 requirements, you can often quickly find an alternative collaboration design that will do a better job. Once we have laid out the 10 requirements, we'll briefly consider how you can use them to solve problems or at least minimize their impact.

Generating the 10 requirements for profitable collaboration: three big choices

To set up collaboration, you must make three sets of choices: about what you want, about partners and about agreements (Figure 2.1). A simple, intuitive view of what setting up collaboration entails is as follows: what you want is to create value for your company; the partners you work with, whether employees or contractors, should be well able to provide the help you want do that; and the agreements you set up, whether legally binding contracts or informal management agreements, should motivate your partners to provide the help you want. But let's look at what it takes to set up profitable collaboration in a bit more detail.

Figure 2.1 Requirements for setting up profitable collaboration (simple view)

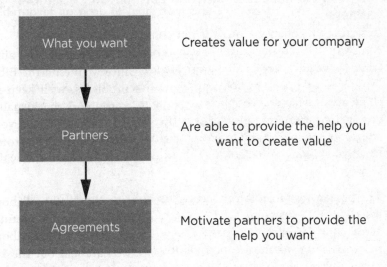

What you want — Creates value for your company

Partners — Are able to provide the help you want to create value

Agreements — Motivate partners to provide the help you want

What you want

To create value for your company, you must think hard about your company, its business strategy and its strengths. But what is less obvious is that, to get what you want, you must also think hard about yourself and your own personal abilities.

Customer value and competitive advantage

When you consider how to create value for your company – and of course gather facts and information about this – you should address both how you will create customer value that leads to revenue, and how you will achieve a competitive advantage so that you can make a profit.[2]

From this perspective, justifying an investment in an ERP system as part of your business strategy is often straightforward enough. An ERP system has the potential to help you both create more value for customers and build competitive advantage. If you are, say, a food or a fashion retailer, an ERP system can help you with product replenishment from a central warehouse to your stores and from your suppliers to the warehouse. If you can improve the replenishment process thanks to better, faster, more integrated information, you can reduce out-of-stocks and generate more revenues, and you can do so with lower inventories, reducing your costs.

You have the needed abilities to get what you want from partners

In setting up collaboration, it is not enough to think about how 'the company' will create value for customers in a way that results in competitive advantage. Companies are legal entities and don't do any work; it is real people of flesh and blood that do the work. You need to think about what real people must do to make the strategy happen. If you are the person responsible for setting up collaboration, the strategy you adopt must, first and foremost, include consideration of your own personal abilities. You can worry about finding good partners for your strategy later.

The person responsible for setting up collaboration to design and install an ERP system is the CEO. An ERP system impacts processes across all parts of the company. It requires a large project team with participation from most functions and business units. It represents a major investment. Yet, as CEO, you have quite a burden in taking responsibility for implementing a large ERP project. You are probably not an IT or an ERP expert. You are not well qualified to take on the responsibility of getting the project implemented. You will need help, not just in doing the work but also in setting up collaboration to get it done.

If, as CEO, you decide, despite your lack of relevant experience, to press ahead with a large ERP project, you will probably want to delegate as much responsibility for it as quickly as possible. But that won't be easy. A large ERP project will be a one-of-a-kind for your company. The current Chief Information Officer (CIO) and the staff in your IT department may not be well qualified to direct and control the work either. And to design and install the system, the CIO will need the support of line managers who don't report to him. So the CIO may not have enough power to get things done if you, as CEO, are not sufficiently engaged.

In the course of researching the book, we talked to a number of large, well-respected companies where the CEO had quickly delegated responsibility for a large ERP project, usually to the CIO. It was a common thing to do. But these companies seldom succeeded. They often needed a 'restart' of the project work months or even years into the project; the CIO, the members of the internal project team and external partners were replaced and costs and time to complete often ran double what was expected. In each case the CEO had not understood enough about the project such that he or she would be in a position to delegate successfully.

One discussion was particularly revealing, and it happened at a company where the ERP installation seemed to be a success story. We spoke to the CIO in a €1.5 billion global manufacturing company where the CIO reported to the Chief Financial Officer (CFO) and the CFO had taken overall responsibility for the ERP installation. The CIO was full of praise for the CFO's work in actively overseeing and supervising the project. So we asked the CIO if he could arrange for us to talk to the CFO to get his perspective directly. No, this would not be possible. Why not? Well, the CFO had recently been fired by the CEO. Why was that? For his handling of the ERP project. And why was that? The project had overrun by nearly 300 per cent. We were now quite confused. The CIO explained that, in his view, the project had indeed been a success and completed for a quite reasonable cost. But the CFO had deliberately put in an extremely low budget for the project. He didn't think the CEO would give the go ahead for any higher sum. Here we see what happens when the CEO does not have enough understanding of the projects he has delegated: this CEO did not appreciate what sort of budget the ERP project needed, and he subsequently made bad decisions about it.

If you are responsible for getting something done, you do not need to – and you normally should not – do all the work yourself. But you must have the ability and time to define what you want done, select the right partners, and put in place agreements that motivate them to do it. This may seem like an obvious requirement to set up successful collaboration but it is frequently not met.

Partners

To collaborate successfully, you should work with partners who are able to provide the help you want. But it is not just about ability. You also need to consider any awkward conflicts of interest and problems with bargaining power that may arise when working with different types of partner.

Ability

Work of any complexity usually requires a variety of abilities. Typically you need a mix of skills and partners.

Successfully designing and installing an ERP system requires a sizeable internal team. To make use of a standard ERP system and services from an external IT consultant or systems integrator, you need to be able to describe your own business activities and the information you want to support each activity. So you need know-how on the team about your own current internal information systems and processes.

Most companies rely heavily on an external IT contractor both to design their ERP system and to manage its installation. They usually don't have enough available and qualified people in their internal IT department to do all the work. And they seldom want to hire the many additional people with specialist expertise that would be needed to do the work in-house for a one-off project. Nor does company strategy require you to do the work in-house to build competitive advantage. The ERP system itself should become a source of competitive advantage for the company. But you are not planning to build competitive advantage in designing and installing ERP systems.

Awkward conflicts of interest

You face a conflict of interest with almost anyone you want to work for you. Most people would rather play a round of golf or go to the movies than work. But you can eliminate this initial conflict of interest quite effectively once you agree to pay people to spend their time working for you. Payment makes the work worthwhile and, when committed to spending their time working for you, most people are interested in doing a good job.

Sometimes, however, you face conflicts of interest that don't go away simply because you are paying someone – what we call awkward conflicts of interest. If you ask a manager to evaluate an acquisition of a new business, and she is in line to become CEO of the business if you acquire it, then she has an inherent conflict in helping you. Recommending against the acquisition may be the right thing for the company but she loses her chance of an exciting new job. The CFO who put in a low budget for the IT project also had this kind of conflict, stemming from his desire for the project to go ahead. But assuming he didn't want to be fired, his action was naïve as well as dishonest.

If you want the same IT contractor to help you design and then install the system, the contractor has an interest in proposing a design with an ambitious scope and suggesting a generous budget for the installation. The more man-hours the firm proposes you put in the installation budget, the more income it stands to receive for helping you install the system. A design with an ambitious scope, that requires a generous installation budget, is in the contractor's interests, but probably not in yours. This is an awkward conflict of interest.

With external contractors there are even simpler but still awkward conflicts of interest to watch out for. One interviewee told us that, after a number of months of work on their ERP project, the contractor started pulling key staff off to work on an assignment for another company where they had just won a competitive bid. Their new client had insisted on interviewing individual consultants and writing their names into the contract. The contractor then transferred some of the best staff from our interviewee's ERP project to the new assignment and replaced them with consultants with less experience.

Awkward conflicts of interest tend to be most pronounced on large one-off projects working with contractors with whom you do not have a long-term relationship. If you can hold out the prospect of a continuing long-term relationship subject to good performance, that will help to align interests. In the context of a long-term relationship, you have sanctions available if the contractor is not able or behaves unprofessionally. Unfortunately, an ERP project is a major one-off effort and it is difficult to remove awkward conflicts of interest by promising follow-on work.

Bargaining power

It's no use working with a partner who can help you to create a lot of value if you don't have the bargaining power to capture a good share of that value. The contractor best able to help you may, for example, have a near monopoly position in the special kind of ERP system you need.

These sorts of bargaining power problems may seem clear initially when you start to negotiate, but other bargaining power problems may not be. For most kinds of ERP systems there are plenty of IT contractors to choose from, so you can get a good deal. But until you have worked with the contractor to specify the system's design, you don't know what scope of project you want, so you can't meaningfully negotiate a fixed price for the whole project upfront. After the design and planning phase of an ERP project you may be able to specify what you want the contractor to do in sufficient detail to set up a robust contract to get it, but by then you lack competitive pressure; the IT contractor has acquired know-how about your systems and processes and built relationships in your organization. Switching to another firm for installation will be costly.

Self-motivation

You may think we 'lay it on a bit thick' in pointing out these motivational problems. Most service providers do indeed have a sense of professionalism, which means that they will have a genuine concern for their clients' interests. Aside from the formal agreement you set up with them, they are self-motivated to do a good job for you. You are certainly more likely to collaborate successfully with partners who have a strong professional self-motivation to act in your interests.

Yet there are plenty of temptations for an IT contractor, especially when their commercial interests are not aligned with yours and they have a strong bargaining position. As the Germans are fond of saying, 'Trust is good, control is better;'[3] you would prefer to have a robust and motivating agreement that will underpin the contractor's professional self-motivation.

Agreements

A legal contract or an informal management agreement can motivate your partners through rewards. In a commercial business, the rewards you offer are primarily financial. We generally accept that external suppliers or contractors will be motivated by the money you offer. But in discussing employee motivation, it is common to hear that it is 'not about the money'.

Certainly, employees are not motivated only by money; sometimes money plays almost no role. New York City firemen surely didn't climb up the twin towers on 9/11 for the money; they did it to save lives. However, undeniably money and other tangible rewards such as promotion and career prospects, which later translate into money (and power) in the organization, usually do play a critical role. In a recent survey by Deloitte, employees ranked compensation, promotion prospects and job security as the most important drivers of employee departure and retention, ahead of trust in the leadership or support and recognition from supervisors or managers.[4]

We don't wish to downplay the importance of other approaches to motivating employees and other partners. But it is a lot easier to motivate your partners if you can match tangible rewards to what you want your partners to do. And tangible rewards are the subject of agreements. So in defining the requirements for good agreements, we focus on these.

Setting goals and constraints to measure performance

To align your partners' rewards with their performance in doing what you want, you must be able to specify what you want done and then measure if it gets done. You must be able to set goals for your partner's output – or for the business income, the revenue or profit that you want to achieve from it. And you may wish to set constraints on how your partner goes about achieving the goals you set – such as insisting that the staff assigned to the project all have previous experience on similar projects and will not be rotated off onto another project without your permission.[5]

If you can communicate what you want done and measure if it gets done, you can agree to pay only if your goals and constraints are met. That should motivate your partner to do what you want. The harder it is to set goals and constraints and measure their fulfilment, the more you will struggle to motivate your partner. That is true regardless of whether you are working with employees or external contractors.

It is difficult to set goals for your partner if you don't know how productively your partner can work. But you can get around this problem by paying for performance: you pay the seamstress per garment sewn or the salesperson per dollar of revenue generated.

You will face a trickier problem in setting goals if you want help from a partner in deciding what to do. For example, you will give your IT contractor a great deal of direction in laying out what you want the ERP system to accomplish, but you must leave the contractor room for creativity in deciding exactly how to go about the work – which software modules to use, how to structure the integration, and so on. You can't prescribe the precise output you want, otherwise you wouldn't need a design phase in the project at all – you could go straight to implementation and roll out.

After the design phase, once you have an installation plan, you should be able to specify what you want done in sufficient detail to set up a robust contract and agree a fixed price. But that may not be so easy. The scope and specifications of what you want done are still not precise. You have configured and customized the system to your needs, but as you install and roll out to new countries, you are not quite sure what changes may be needed to take account of local requirements. You or the design contractor may have overlooked something, or circumstances may change and some changes to scope may be needed.

When you can't set robust goals and constraints, you face the awkward conflicts of interest and bargaining power problems mentioned above. In the design phase, the contractor may be tempted to propose an ambitious scope and an inflated budget for installation. During installation and roll out, the contractor may not push forward speedily to complete the work. Because you weren't able to set up a robust contract, you lack sanctions to put pressure on them to perform and to keep them from taking advantage of you.

Aligning rewards with performance

Aligning rewards with performance requires being able to address negative performance, for example, if your partner destroys value for your company. Incentivising performance is not just about rewarding good work. To discourage partners from potentially destructive behaviour, you should include financial penalties in the contract. If you can offer your partner rewards for creating value but can't punish them when they destroy it then your partner may take too many risks.

Big 'systems integrators' that handle ERP projects should be willing to carry at least some of the responsibility to cover any damages caused by their work. Smaller contractors may not and with employees it is often simply not possible, as financial firms discovered in the recent crisis.

Specifying favourable terms

Not only do you want to properly motivate your partners, but you also want the work done on good terms for you. When working with contractors, you can often determine favourable terms through competitive bidding. But for the installation, you may have a strong bias to continue with the design contractor that has invested in learning about your systems. There will be no effective competition. You may be able to negotiate favourable terms nevertheless. But if your internal team is weak, you will not know enough about how much it should cost to install the system. In that case you just won't be able to negotiate effectively. The CEO who fired his CFO is only an extreme example of corporate reality.

Meet the requirements from your partner's perspective

It takes two to tango; to motivate a partner to enter into an agreement with you, the agreement you set up needs to be a good one, not just for you but also for your partner. This is especially important if your partner will need help from you or other partners to get the work done.

So once you have a design for the ERP system and a plan for the ERP installation, ideally you want to get a fixed price for the installation work. But many companies find it difficult to persuade their contractor to commit to installing the system for a fixed price. To carry out the installation work as planned, the contractor depends on you to request only a limited number of modifications. They also depend on you providing in-house staff to assist them – staff from both your central IT department and all the countries getting the new system. Convincing the contractor that you will fulfil your side of the bargain is critical in persuading the contractor to commit to doing what you want for a good price.

Testing and improving the likelihood of profitable collaboration

Now that we have explored the three big choices for profitable collaboration – what you want, partners and agreements – and the challenges that go hand-in-hand with them, we can lay out 10 key requirements for successful collaboration (shown in Figure 2.2), again using the example of the ERP project. There are three requirements for each choice, plus the final requirement that you meet all these nine from your partner's perspective as well as your own. We have displayed them in a circle because there are often linkages and difficult trade-offs to be made between meeting the requirements related to what you want, partners and agreements.

Figure 2.2 Requirements for setting up profitable collaboration

Creates value for customers

Results in competitive advantage

Takes account of your abilities

Are able (and self-motivated)

Have no awkward conflicts of interests

Do not have and will not gain too much bargaining power

What you want

Partners   **Agreements**

Set goals and constraints to measure performance

Align rewards with performance

Specify favourable terms

Meet requirements from partners' perspective as well as your own

Figure 2.2 provides a most useful test of the likelihood that any collaboration will achieve the results you want. If you meet all these requirements, you will be set up for success. In addition, you must also consider how the relationship will develop over time. Your partner may be sweetness and light when first competing for your business but later on they may gain bargaining power and become difficult to deal with.

Our list of requirements is quite short and simple – as any practical decision framework for managers must be. There is a good reason why Moses came down from the mountain with 10 commandments and not 52! But it raises many issues that are not included in the initial simple view of requirements shown in Figure 2.1, and these are critical additional issues that managers often don't consider sufficiently.

As a manager, when your collaboration set-up doesn't meet the requirements of the project, you have to use your skills to compensate: you must work with contractors that have awkward conflicts of interest and have become difficult to substitute; you must motivate employees whose rewards do not depend solely on doing what you want. More often than not, the strain imposed on your management and leadership skills will be too great.

Figure 2.3 highlights the ways we've described in which ERP projects can fall short of the 10 requirements. If the CEO and the CIO have not addressed these failings, they will not be in their managerial comfort zone, nor even their learning zone. They will be in the panic zone.[6] The panic zone is not a good place to be.

In order to avoid the panic zone, you cannot rely on your management skills to solve collaboration problems once the project is underway. You must work hard, before the project starts, to set up collaboration to increase your chances of success. That way you will be able to identify the dangers and adjust your collaboration strategy to develop better agreements, change your partners, or even modify what you want from partners before it's too late.

Figure 2.3 ERP project: problems in meeting the success requirements

Responsible person, CEO, not able to tell if the project has been set up for success

Internal team likely to lack needed abilities in sufficient quantity

IT contractor that designs and then installs has awkward conflict of interest and may gain bargaining power

What you want

Partners

Agreements

Impossible to precisely define output goals before design work complete and difficult even after that

Insufficient expertise to specify favourable terms

IT contractor dependent on company internal team

What you want: raising your level of involvement

As CEO, you lacked experience in setting up and managing large ERP projects – so you planned to transfer as much responsibility and take as much help as you possibly could. But now you see the pitfalls: you cannot reliably transfer responsibility for the decisions needed to set up collaboration; you must be able to choose whom to work with, and you must set up agreements with them; and if the agreements you set up require you to monitor and control the work to be sure of getting what you want, you must be able to do that too.

If you lack experience, then you will need to devote more time and effort, not less. But you do have options to slightly reduce your work-load. You can take on a personal advisor, separate from the manager, someone who has the experience to help you set up the project and monitor progress and to whom you can delegate responsibility for the project.

If you are not convinced that raising your involvement will sufficiently reduce the risks in the project, perhaps you should move more slowly or even not all. A new ERP system will be valuable but there are surely other ways of creating value in the business and, with your background, these may be easier to implement. If you are running the company, the right strategy for the company depends on your abilities.

Partners: adjusting the mix

Let's assume you decide to go ahead with the project. Your internal IT function lacked capacity and experience to run the ERP project, so you planned to rely heavily on support from an external IT contractor. But that IT contractor faces awkward conflicts of interest and you know they will gain bargaining power in the course of the project as their team becomes increasingly difficult to substitute.

A stronger in-house team

To address these problems, you can invest to build a stronger in-house project team. Your employees, unlike a contractor, have no direct financial interest in proposing an ambitious scope for the new system or an inflated budget to install it. They have the chance of long-term employment with you if they do a good job. Individual employees should also be easier to substitute in the course of the project than an entire team from an external IT contractor. Employees still have conflicts of interest. But on the whole, a stronger internal team will both mitigate awkward conflicts of interest and give you more bargaining power.

Separate contractors for the design and installation phases

You can also reduce awkward conflicts of interest with the contractor by taking on separate contractors for the different phases of the work. If design contractors don't expect to install the system, they have no awkward conflict of interest in specifying the scope and budget for installation.

But as we noted above, there are trade-offs. The same contractor may have the best ability to help you in both phases of the work, especially if experience in installing ERP systems is valuable in designing them, or the team gains know-how in the design phase that will be valuable in implementation and roll out. Working with the same contractor also avoids any duplication of effort and costs of transition across phases.

Using the same contractor may also make it easier to get the installation work done for a fixed fee and transfer project risk to the contractor

– which may be quite valuable to you. A contractor that has done the design work will better understand the design and know what it will take to install it in different countries. They will also have a sense of your company staff, how competent they are and how difficult it will be to work with them during the installation phase. Their risks in installing the system for a fixed price should therefore be much lower than if they were coming in fresh.

There is no simple answer to how to make this particular trade-off. It depends, for example, on how well you think your internal team can assess whether the contractor has appropriately scoped and priced the installation.

Professionalism of the contractor

It also depends on your contractor's professionalism. You would do well to screen the contractor as thoroughly for their history of professionalism as for their ability.

A second opinion

If the same contractor will do the design and the installation, the CIO may want to take an additional external advisor with benchmarks on similar projects to review the scope and budget for installation.

Agreements: separate contracts for design and installation

Putting in place a robust agreement to motivate your partner to do what you want is the central problem in setting up collaboration. Given all the advantages explained above, it is likely that you will want to work with the same contractor for design and installation, but you can make gains here by not allowing the contractor to presume that you will. You will be in a far better position if you can convince the contractor that continued collaboration is subject to good performance and a competitive bid for the installation.

As a result, even if you fully intend to stay on with the contractor, you need to set up clearly separate contracts for the design and installation phases of the work. Separate contracts also make sense in principle because your concerns are different in these two phases: they involve different types of information and so you may want different types of contracts altogether. First, the design phase involves so much uncertainty that you cannot precisely specify the desired output. So a contract for the design will describe in broad terms what you want, and will state that you will pay the contractor for budgeted resource capacity on the basis of time and expenses and not for a fixed fee. As most of the costs for ERP projects are in the installation across the company, your risks from a time- and expense-based contract are (fortunately) not so great when it comes to design. Your main concern should be whether the contractor does a high quality job in specifying the design and planning the installation work. A strong internal team – and perhaps some additional external advice – will help you direct and assess the contractor's work. Selecting an able and highly-professional contractor will be critical. Second, you will want to avoid a time- and expense-based contract for installation. But even in this phase, there will still be many open issues to be resolved, so contractors will be reluctant to agree to a fixed price.

Partner's perspective: making upfront commitments

In order to convince a contractor to accept a fixed price, even the contractor that produced the design, you will need to make some commitments. ERP installations depend as much on the client organization's cooperation as on the skill of the contractor. The client must provide internal resources and decide on key questions in a timely way.

Understanding this dynamic helped a multinational insurer, where we spoke with a member of the team managing the project for the company, persuade their ERP contractor to offer a fixed price. After the design phase, the client opened up the installation phase of the project to competitive bids. But none of the new companies asked to bid were willing to go with a fixed price. The contractor for the design was also reluctant, even having configured and customized the software, and specified and budgeted the installation. To persuade this contractor, the client contractually committed to take timely decisions in the course of the installation, to ensure the availability of suitably qualified client-side people, and to restrict requests for modifications to an agreed number per quarter. A personal advisor to the CEO had suggested this approach.[7] Both parties made compromises. The insurance company fixed a target cost for the installation from the estimated hours to be worked and daily rates. Bills were to be sent quarterly. If the company failed to keep their side of the bargain, the IT contractor could propose triggering an event. 'Triggering an event' would allow the contractor to charge more hours and a substantially higher overhead rate for that quarter. If the client did not agree to the triggering, the contractor would still be able to charge higher overheads for the quarter, albeit not at the same high level as if the client had agreed. If the contractor proposed triggering an event, the company could avoid the additional charges only by discussing and resolving the problem with the contractor. The contract stipulated that discussions to resolve these problems were to be between top managers from the client and the contractor. These discussions had to take place at short notice, because the client was contractually obliged to accept or decline a proposed triggered event – and if declined, suggest a remedy – within a brief period.

This governance aspect of the contract, which both sides took seriously because of the money involved, proved most helpful. The contractor proposed triggering a number of events early on, but rarely did so later. After experiencing a few such discussions, the client team did everything they could to avoid further proposals for triggering events, as these entailed not just extra costs but also forced their superiors to get involved. This was inconvenient and unpleasant for everyone at the company, as it showed that the client and contractor project teams were not able to sort out problems themselves. The teams learned to agree on minor changes and resolved minor differences on their own.

The installation took place in six countries and on two continents. But aside from a small extra cost for the early triggered events, it came in on time and on budget, which is rare for an ERP project of this scope.

Conclusions

Figure 2.4 summarizes these elements of a solution to the problems in setting up an ERP project, especially those to do with the contractor.

Figure 2.4 ERP project: elements of a possible solution to problems

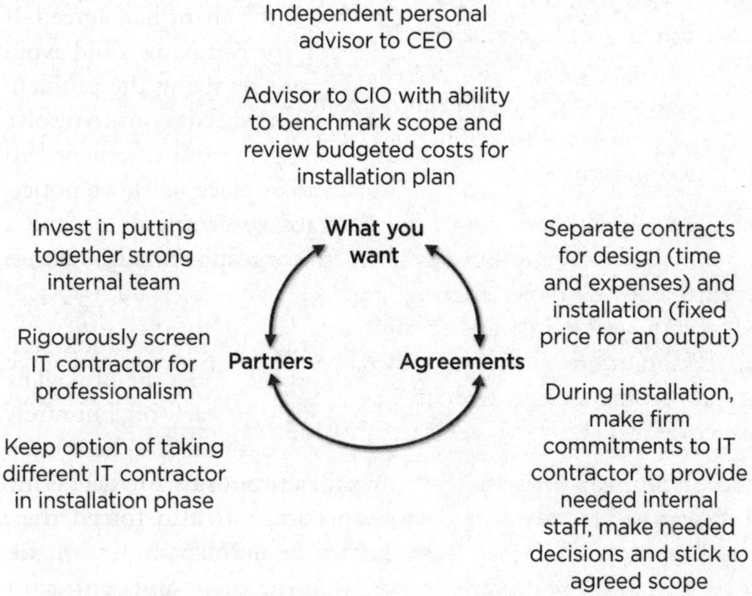

Independent personal
advisor to CEO

Advisor to CIO with ability
to benchmark scope and
review budgeted costs for
installation plan

Invest in putting
together strong
internal team

**What you
want**

Separate contracts
for design (time
and expenses) and
installation (fixed
price for an output)

Rigourously screen
IT contractor for
professionalism

Partners

Agreements

During installation,
make firm
commitments to IT

Keep option of taking
different IT contractor
in installation phase

contractor to provide
needed internal
staff, make needed
decisions and stick to
agreed scope

ERP installations illustrate the underlying challenge in setting up collaboration in an increasingly specialized business world with more non-routine tasks. Executives must take responsibility for getting work done when they lack the know-how to personally supervise important aspects of the work, and when they can't precisely define the output they want. The temptation in this uncomfortable situation is to hand over responsibility as quickly and as fully as possible – to get the monkey off your back. But if you know little about what you want done, you must invest heavily to set collaboration up for success.

To avoid landing in the panic zone, you should meet the 10 requirements we have laid out. These requirements are not rocket science, but at times even the smart executive will overlook a few of them.

Some requirements get overlooked more often than others. To get what you want, you must think not only about what is good for your company but also about your own personal skills and abilities. In choosing partners you must consider not just if they are able to do what you want, but also if they will have awkward conflicts of interest or gain bargaining power with you. When setting up agreements, remember that you can lose out not only by lacking bargaining power, but also by not investing enough to learn how much the work should cost. And if you are struggling to get a commitment from a partner to produce the output you want, what is lacking may be your commitment to support your partner in return.

Developing a collaboration strategy often involves difficult trade-offs. And as collaboration is essentially about relationships between people, the right trade-offs depend strongly on who you are, whom you are working with, and the details of your situation. When it is difficult to set up collaboration, choices about what you want, partners and agreements all become interdependent. There are no standard answers, and the process for making choices is iterative, not sequential.

We chose a problem with a fairly straightforward solution to get started and later we will tackle more complex problems. But first, let's take a step back and consider how to come up with an initial draft of a collaboration design in the first place.

---

[1] Panorama Consulting Group. '2013 ERP report'. <www.panorama-consulting.com>.

[2] We will look in more detail in the next chapter at how your strategy influences not only what you want but also the type of partners you want to work with and the type of agreements you want to set up with them.

[3] 'Vertrauen ist gut, Kontrolle ist besser' ('Trust is good, control is better') is a particularly common saying in Germany and usually attributed to Vladimir Lenin, although he was not always a reliable guide.

[4] Deloitte Consulting LLP. 'Talent Edge 2020: Building the recovery together – What talent expects and how leaders are responding'. April 2011.

[5] It's common to suppose that if you contract to pay for resource capacity you need to control the

progress of the work to make sure you get what you want; but that if you contract to pay for the output of the work and buy a product, you do not. Surely, if you are paying for a product, it should be enough to check the product on delivery to see if it is what you ordered? In fact, if you want to impose constraints on how the product is produced, you must control the progress of the work even if you are paying for a product to be produced for you. As consumer demand places more constraints on how products are made, companies and governments are more frequently being called to account because they have paid insufficient attention in observing production constraints. For example, the German government and major German food retailers came under pressure recently when it was discovered that 'free range' eggs, for which consumers were prepared to pay premium prices, were in fact often being produced in fully caged farms.

6 'Comfort zone', 'learning zone', 'panic zone', are terms that are now fairly widely used. They were first introduced in Tom Senninger's book, *Abenteuer leiten – in Abenteuern lernen: Methodenset zur Planung und Leitung kooperativer Lerngemeinschaften für Training und Teamentwicklung in Schule, Jugendarbeit und Betrieb.* *(Leading adventures – learning in adventures: a set of methods for planning and leading cooperative learning communities in schools, youth work and business)* Münster: Ökotopia Verlag (Press), 2000.

7 Not, incidentally, one of the authors.

Chapter 3

Setting Up for Success

In Chapter 2 we tested a draft design for setting up profitable collaboration. But what if you must come up with the initial draft? Here, we'll work systematically from a few strategic choices to come up with a draft design, using the example of a chain of fast-food restaurants.

In deciding what you want from partners, your market and competitive strategy is the starting point. You aim to maximize the return on your investment of time and money by focusing on whatever it is that you are competitively advantaged at doing. To make this work, you must transfer responsibility to able partners for doing everything else necessary to deliver a valuable customer offer. However, you may find you can't define well enough what you want these partners to do in order to properly transfer responsibility to them, or you may, for other reasons, be unable to motivate them to do what you want. That's where the 10 requirements come in. As in the ERP system example, we'll test our first draft to make sure we address not just customer value and competitive advantage, but all the other requirements, and in particular partners' motivation. We'll also suggest modifications to overcome the problems. We'll explore how successful fast-food chains – McDonald's, Burger King, Subway, Starbucks – actually do set up collaboration in order to address these challenges. What might at first appear to be subtle differences among market segments and approaches to building advantage can translate into substantial differences in collaboration design. Along the way we'll address a major decision in setting up collaboration: whether to do the work in-house or outsource it. We'll provide a simple, powerful framework for this decision.

How market and competitive strategy drives collaboration

Developing your business strategy involves deciding how to create customer value and where to focus your investment of time and money. To get the best return, you will want to focus on activities where you can build competitive advantage, rather than be dragged down by the many other activities necessary to create customer value but which other people and companies are better placed to carry out. Following this simple principle takes you a long way in deciding how you would like to set up collaboration.

The customer offer determines what needs to get done

Market and competitive strategy starts with the offer to customers; from there you can determine the necessary assets and human resources, the activities to be carried out and, as a result, the risks involved. Figure 3.1 shows these details for a typical fast-food chain. To establish a successful fast-food chain you need a brand and concept, real estate, equipment, fixtures, fittings and supplies. You must operate the restaurants, purchase the supplies and continually develop the brand and concept.

Unlike installing an ERP system, which almost always involves hiring an outside IT systems integrator, these activities require some judgement calls about the type of partners to work with. Should you employ your own staff to manage and work in the restaurants, for example, or rely on an external partner to operate the facilities? We have left out a great many activities in the value chain that we assume you will outsource, from growing the vegetables served to making the paint to cover the store walls.

Figure 3.1 The customer offer determines what it takes to do

What it takes in a fast-food restaurant chain

- Brand and concept (Assets)
- Brand and concept development (HR and activities)
- Restaurant management (HR and activities)
- Cooking and service (HR and activities)
- Real estate (Assets)
- Kitchen equipment, signage, seating and decor (Assets)
- Supplies (Assets)
- Purchasing supplies (HR and activities)

Competitive advantage determines what to outsource

As consulting firms and business academics have long pointed out, competitive advantage drives what you should do in-house and what you should outsource. You will want to take responsibility for those activities where you have an advantage, while transferring responsibility for all other activities to an able external partner.[1] These choices can be explained using a simple matrix, shown in Figure 3.2, the 'classic' outsourcing framework.[2]

In effect, both axes in the framework ask questions about competitive advantage. The vertical axis asks about your company's current ability to do the work compared to external partners – your current competitive advantage. The horizontal axis asks whether the activity is 'core to the business' or, in other words, important to competitive advantage. Asking whether the activity is core to the business is therefore tantamount to asking: 'Where do we most want to have advantaged ability in-house as part of our strategy?'

If you have an advantaged ability to get the work done and the work is core to your business, you should take responsibility for getting the work done. You will want to own the necessary assets and carry out the work yourself or, more likely, hire and supervise employees to do it. If you don't have an advantaged ability for the work and it isn't core to your business, you should outsource it to a supplier.

Figure 3.2 'Classic' framework links strategy and in-/outsourcing decision

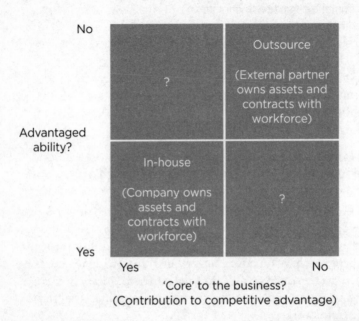

'Core' to the business?
(Contribution to competitive advantage)

If you have a competitive advantage where your business strategy says you don't need it, or you lack one where you do need it, your aims and your abilities are mismatched and you face a potentially difficult choice of what to do. Should you outsource less critical activities, even if you have advantage in carrying them out? Should you in-source vital activities, even if today you lack advantage and will need to build it? The classic outsourcing framework provides limited guidance on how to make these difficult choices. But it initiates a process of reflection or – conveniently for the firms that developed this framework – a consulting project that helps you to decide where you need to try to maintain or build advantage. But the key issue remains to decide where you intend to have competitive advantage in the future. (For a way to break out of this binary choice that previews our later argument, see the textbox, 'A middle ground between owning and outsourcing.')

A middle ground between owning and outsourcing

A ready example of the top left quadrant in Figure 3.2 can be found in fast-food chains from the perspective not of the chain owner, but the franchisees. To compete, they need a strong brand and concept. But developing these assets is expensive, and makes sense only for restaurant chains with many more stores than any single franchisee could muster. They cannot afford to develop the brand and concept, but they cannot simply buy them from an outsourcer either. So they go for a middle ground: licensing the brand and concept from a company that does have the scale (or potential scale) to develop these assets.

Franchising is neither owning nor outsourcing, but something else: a way to gain an asset (or capability) with a scope of use broader than that of your own business. It gives you exclusive use of the asset, but limits you in a variety of ways – after all, you are not the owner.

For franchisees, the limitations start with territory, but continue into other areas we discuss in this chapter. When you have limited rights, you also have limited advantage. Once you understand the rights you want, you can decide limited rights are enough or you need to expand the scope of your business in order to afford full control of the assets. The decision involves difficult trade-offs, as we can illustrate with an example from the grocery industry.

Tesco is the UK's leading food retailer. Their 'Clubcard' has made an important contribution to their growth and profitability. Customers use this card with their purchases, and Tesco uses the data to personalize direct marketing offers and thereby generate additional sales and margin. To mine the data, Tesco relies on support from Dunnhumby, a specialist data-mining firm. Dunnhumby works for a range of retailers and consumer brand companies, a scale that enables Dunnhumby to move faster down the experience curve of how to use customer data for marketing. But Dunnhumby does not work for Tesco's direct competitors, so Tesco can build competitive advantage based on Dunnhumby's experience.

In effect, Tesco decided it needed exclusive use of the data-mining capability in food retailing in the UK, but not in some other types of business. But how best to guarantee the limited exclusivity needed? A contract can fulfil a need for exclusivity in the short term in a focused way. But Tesco could not know enough about what services they would want in the long term from

Dunnhumby to set up a contract that would protect their interests for the longer term. Their solution has been to take a controlling equity stake in Dunnhumby – at the price of making an investment that is not exclusively focused on their own retailing business. When Dunnhumby did their initial work for Tesco in 1994, it was a small independent company. But Tesco could see the enormous potential for building competitive advantage in their business from having exclusive use of Dunnhumby's capability, so they began to acquire shares in the company a year later. They further increased their stake in 2006.[3]

If you know where you intend to have competitive advantage, it is easy enough to work out what to do. Suppose you own a chain of hamburger restaurants and are considering whether to manufacture the cooking equipment in-house or to outsource the work.[4] Unless you think cooking equipment is a competitive differentiator for restaurants – and you can stand out only by making this equipment yourself – you will not see cooking equipment as core to your business.[5] So you would outsource the manufacture of this equipment and expect your supplier to handle all the activities needed to make it according to your specifications.[6]

Competitive advantage also largely determines agreements with partners

In simple cases, you can extend the logic of the 'classic' outsourcing framework to decide on the type of agreements you want to have with partners. Ideally, your external partners will take on all the responsibilities for doing the work outside of your competitive advantage – including any business risks involved in doing the work. If you want to transfer the risk involved in manufacturing broilers, you'll want to pay your equipment manufacturer simply a fixed price per broiler with penalty clauses for non-performance, instead of paying for the time and expenses involved in the manufacture of the broiler.

By contrast, you'll want a different arrangement for developing the brand and concept. You'll want to pay for the time and expense involved, in this case by hiring employees to do this work. You'll carry the risks involved in the development work if you do this, but with your competitive advantage in getting the work done, you should be able to make a profit more than sufficient to cover the risks you take on.

Pulling all this together, there is a rather easy link between where you intend to have competitive advantage and your collaboration strategy. It is shown in Figure 3.3.

Figure 3.3 Competitive advantage and collaboration strategy

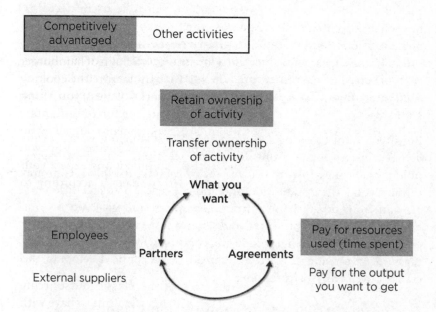

As we saw with the ERP systems, however, there is a catch. In order to transfer risk and responsibility for doing the work, you must be able to sufficiently define the output you want. This should not be difficult if you are running a chain of hamburger restaurants and want to buy additional units of a broiler of a type you have bought before. But for non-routine tasks such as designing a new broiler, you may lack the information to set up agreements that effectively transfer risk and responsibility for delivering what you want to a partner. You will then need to go beyond considerations of who is most able to do the work and integrate motivational issues to finally decide how to set up collaboration. We sketched out how to do this for ERP systems in Chapter 2, and we look at how to manage similar problems in setting up collaboration between franchisors and franchisees further below.

A first draft design for fast-food restaurants based on competitive advantage

Before we look at how to bridge the gap, let's first see how far considerations of competitive advantage will take us in deciding how to set up collaboration – across the full range of activities – for a chain of fast-food restaurants. Every restaurant in a chain poses unique challenges. Some locations are more attractive to customers than others. The customer mix and what customers want to buy at each location is a little different. The ease of recruiting appropriate staff varies.

But if you want to set up a chain, you will probably not want to gain competitive advantage from doing an exceptional job of managing unique challenges. Instead you will seek advantage in what is common to the chain – the restaurant brand and concept. These will differentiate you from other chains, attract customers, and give you process advantages in cooking the food and serving customers. A large number of restaurants with a single brand and concept will give you scale advantages in advertising and let you spread the costs of developing the concept over a high sales volume.

Partners: employees, suppliers, and franchisees

Since brand and concept are key competitive resources, you will want to own them. That will give you unrestricted and exclusive use of them in maximizing your profitability. You will also want to build a competitively advantaged ability to innovate and enhance the value of the brand and concept over time. So you will want to develop the brand and concept in-house. In practice this means having a strong in-house team that will help you further develop the menu and also the cooking and service processes that drive the value of a fast-food concept. But you don't need to do everything yourself here. You can comfortably outsource aspects of your brand, such as your advertising campaigns.

After all, you aren't looking to compete on your ability to create advertising content.

What about actually operating the restaurants in the chain? Because these do vary so much across locations, you will prefer to leave the operations to outside partners who hire and pay for staff to do the work. Let them focus on the challenges specific to each location. You can do that by licensing your brand and concept. You need only require that the operator's investments, menu and work processes fit the brand and concept. Because the way that restaurants are managed will greatly influence their performance, it's logical for operators to take on the risks as well. In short, you should license your brand and concept to partners, franchisees, who invest in and manage the restaurants. This is indeed what most fast-food chains do, with some important exceptions that we'll discuss later in this chapter.

However, following this logic, you won't want to outsource everything about operations. There is skill involved in seeking out good suppliers, as well as substantial scale effects in purchasing. So instead of having franchisees handle their own supply chains, you are likely to want to hire specialist employees to manage the purchasing process. Interestingly, though, many fast-food chains don't do this. Instead, they leave purchasing of supplies to franchisees. We'll also look at why they do this later.

Figure 3.4 shows the implications of this view of how to build competitive advantage for how you want to obtain the resources needed in the business and for what you would like to in- and outsource. It also shows the type of contracts you would like to set up with partners following the simple competitive-advantage-related logic we outlined above.

The value of focus

Franchising enables you to outsource much of the investment of money and time in setting up a chain and focus just on those assets and activities that offer the greatest potential for competitive advantage. As the brand and concept owner, you can leverage your investment of money and time in the business. Chains such as Burger King, Dairy Queen and Kentucky Fried Chicken have used this approach to become large and successful businesses.

Figure 3.4 Competitive advantage drives which resources you own and contract for

Resources needed to create customer value	Basis for advantage?	Own? Contract for? Rely on partner?	What to contract to pay for?
Brand and concept (Assets)	Yes	Own	No payment (create brand)
Brand and concept development (HR)	Yes	Contract with employees	Employees' time spent
Restaurant management (HR)	No	Contract with franchisee	Restaurant output
Cooking and service (HR)	No	Rely on franchisee	
Real estate (Assets)	No	Rely on franchisee	
Kitchen, signage and seating (Assets)	No	Rely on franchisee	
Supplies (Assets)	Yes	Own	Output of supplies
Purchasing supplies (HR)	Yes	Contract with employees	Employees' time spent

Subway, the 'submarine' sandwich chain, has taken outsourcing to an extreme, partly because its founders have preferred to maintain full ownership of the business. An entrepreneur's resources, both money and time, are more tightly constrained than a public company's.[7] Besides franchising all of its stores,[8] Doctor's Associates, Subway's parent company,[9] even outsources the recruiting of new franchisees.[10] Franchisees also purchase their supplies through a cooperative that they own[11] and, via a trust into which they pay advertising contributions,[12] steer the advertising, even national campaigns focused on the brand itself.

Nevertheless, Subway has now overtaken McDonald's as the chain with the most US fast-food outlets[13] (though not in total revenue), and its founders are now billionaires.[14] Their financial success shows the high value of focusing your money and time strictly on those assets and activities that contribute to competitive advantage. Thinking through what is essential, and then basing your collaboration set-up on it, can pay high dividends.

Limits to outsourcing

Of course, the elements of your competitive advantage are not quite that straightforward. Advantage can arise from links between quite different business activities, across the value chain or in serving separate customer groups and markets. More important, carrying out a business activity requires taking on several different responsibilities, and different parties may have more advantage when taking these on. These complexities may induce you to keep some in-house activities that you would otherwise outsource. They can also create difficulties in setting up motivating agreements.

Links between different business activities

Within the value chain, a variety of reasons may lead you to operate at least a few restaurants yourself. To convince potential franchisees, you will want to have a few stores running successfully as proof of concept. Even once you're well established, it helps to have some stores you can use as a 'laboratory' to test new ideas and learn what makes the brand tick. You may also want to train and test prospective franchisees by having them work in your stores. And indeed, most chains work with a mix of owned and franchised stores.[15] Smaller chains tend to have more owned stores in relation to franchised stores than larger ones. McDonald's owns and operates about 10 per cent of the stores in their chain. Even Doctor's Associates had 16 stores before starting to franchise Subway.[16]

Unbundling responsibilities for a single business activity

Owning and running a business involves taking on three different entrepreneurial responsibilities: obtaining the use of the necessary assets and human resources, taking and implementing decisions to get the work done, and providing the capital to carry the business risks. This is also true for each of the individual activities or value-chain steps in a business. So far, we have lumped all three responsibilities together in assessing competitive advantage. But with some activities you may be competitively advantaged in taking on only one or two of the three entrepreneurial responsibilities.

In this case, our outsourcing logic suggests 'unbundling' responsibilities and setting up collaboration to assign responsibilities to those who are best at fulfilling them. In fast food, you would like your franchisees to do everything related to setting up an individual restaurant. But the individuals best qualified to run restaurants might well lack the risk capital needed. In the UK over half of McDonald's franchisees are former McDonald's employees.[17] Former employees should be good at managing restaurants, but they rarely start with the personal wealth to invest in a lease and in fixtures and fittings for an outlet. A freestanding hamburger restaurant typically costs well over a million dollars.

McDonald's gets around this problem by taking back some of the franchisee's entrepreneurial responsibilities. Unlike most franchisors, McDonald's typically owns or leases the properties needed for the restaurants itself, and then sublets them to franchisees. It also helps franchisees finance the acquisition of other needed restaurant assets. Over the past decade, half of McDonald's new franchisees in the US have obtained their franchise this way.[18]

When McDonald's franchisees hire employees and manage the stores, McDonald's Corporation provides much of the risk capital, and each takes on just those entrepreneurial responsibilities for which they are best qualified. This specialization is attractive. Each party exploits their competitive advantage. On the other hand, when different parties are advantaged in taking on different entrepreneurial responsibilities for the same business activity, there is no longer a simple answer to the question of how to set up motivating agreements between them.

When entrepreneurial responsibilities for the same business activity are shared, one approach to motivate your partner is to share the business rewards from the activity. You can share revenues or share profits with your partner. McDonald's franchisees pay McDonald's Corporation a percentage of their restaurant revenues as rent for the stores, and that works well to reward McDonald's Corporation for providing risk finance for the store leases. However, as we discuss further below, while sharing business income helps to align parties' interests, it sometimes falls short. And there are many different ways of setting up income-sharing agreements. So, when entrepreneurial responsibilities are shared, collaboration design becomes more complex. There is no longer a simple answer. You must use the 10 requirements to test alternative designs and make the trade-offs.

Factoring in partner motivation with the 10 requirements

After thinking through the implications of how you want to build competitive advantage, you should now have most of the elements of a first draft collaboration design. But you may have found you lack the information to set up simple agreements to effectively transfer responsibility to contractors. Or considerations of competitive advantage suggest you unbundle and share entrepreneurial responsibilities with a partner for an activity, and you don't know how to share the business rewards in order to align your interests.

In that case, your draft may need to be changed; you don't know if you can motivate your chosen partners to do what you want. Customer value and competitive advantage are the place to start in deciding how to set up collaboration. But to finish the job you need to know how to motivate your partners. That is what the classic outsourcing framework ignores, and what we emphasize in the book as critical to develop a successful collaboration strategy. So it's time for the next step in our overall process, using the 10 requirements to complete and test the draft, while focusing on motivational issues (see Figure 3.5).

Partners . . .

While competitive advantage determines the broad type of partners to work with – external franchisees rather than in-house employees – it has little to say about how many franchisees to work with. Do you work with one franchisee for each restaurant, or allow each franchisee to own a number of different restaurants? If the latter, how quickly do you allow franchisees to amass their portfolio?

Figure 3.5 The 10 success requirements: motivational requirements not met?

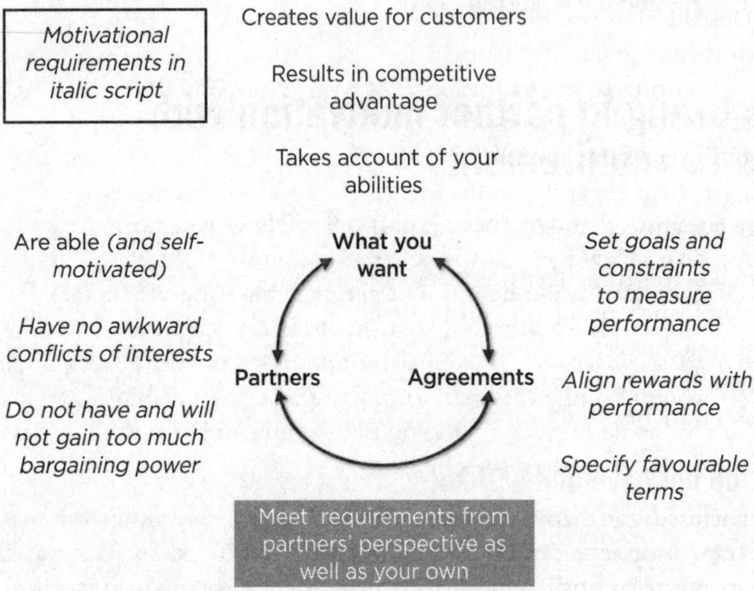

Motivational requirements in italic script

Creates value for customers

Results in competitive advantage

Takes account of your abilities

Are able (and self-motivated)

Have no awkward conflicts of interests

Do not have and will not gain too much bargaining power

What you want

Partners

Agreements

Set goals and constraints to measure performance

Align rewards with performance

Specify favourable terms

Meet requirements from partners' perspective as well as your own

... are able and self-motivated

There should be no serious problems in finding people who are able to run restaurants as franchisees, and who have a personal interest in doing so. But if you hold out the possibility of multiple franchises, you will increase their motivation to work with you, as opposed to another chain. Many franchisees take on numerous stores from a single franchisor, and franchisors generally prefer this as well. The average for McDonald's is five stores per franchisee.[19]

... have no awkward conflicts of interest

Multiple franchising can both reduce and increase the chance of awkward conflicts of interest, especially when it comes to whether to franchise stores one at a time or to franchise whole territories all at one go. All-at-one-go helps to reduce conflicts between franchisees. A franchisee that starts with many stores in a large territory will be less concerned that other franchisees will open stores and cannibalize his sales. But the franchisee's size may create awkward conflicts with the franchisor, not to mention the fact that it may give the franchisee too much bargaining power.

McDonald's has traditionally franchised stores one at a time. This has given them a greater measure of control over their franchisees. A franchisee wanting to gain additional franchises must do a good job and strictly follow the McDonalds concept in the initial outlet. The founders of Burger King, by contrast, franchised large territories all at once. This let them expand rapidly. But they struggled to ensure that these large franchisees consistently executed on the concept.[20]

With a better franchising agreement, as well as new, stronger franchising laws, such problems can be avoided. Burger King still has many large franchisees, and the largest US franchisee, Carrols Corporation,[21] owns and operates over 570 outlets.[22] But franchising stores one by one gives a franchisor additional control over franchisees' behaviour.

... do not have and will not gain too much bargaining power

A franchisee with many stores may gain too much bargaining power with the franchisor at the end of the franchise period. The franchisee could use its portfolio of sites to start up a new chain or switch to a rival. In practice, this risk is quite limited, at least in fast-food restaurants, as there are plenty of potential locations for new stores.

This risk is more important in some other forms of franchising such as soft drinks, for example, where bottling plants, distribution networks, control over other brands and established business-to-business relationships give franchisees more bargaining power than retail locations for fast food. Unlike franchisees, bottlers' investments in site leases, equipment, signage and decor don't have clearly limited lives that match a contract period. This gives a bottler for Coke or Pepsi, for example, the freedom to switch to a rival brand and, while rare, this does happen. Take the Cisneros Group in Venezuela, who had $400 million in revenues and 85 per cent share of the soda business, 40 per cent with Pepsi and 45 per cent with other brands. In 1996, Coke bought half of Cisneros and the group immediately switched allegiance to Coke, which at the time had only a 10 per cent share. Pepsi's share in the market dropped to zero for a year until it signed up another bottler.[23]

Agreements . . .

You want to transfer to your franchisees the responsibility for investing in and managing the restaurants, and for the risks involved with the operation. But you don't have the information to easily set up an agreement with franchisees to fully transfer this responsibility. You face problems in setting goals and constraints to measure performance, in aligning rewards with performance, and in specifying favourable terms.

. . . set goals and constraints to measure performance

In order to work with you, a franchisee needs to make a number of long-term investments: sign a long-term lease on a location, build-out the site, and acquire the kitchen equipment, seating, signage and décor. These investments are largely valuable only for a restaurant using your brand and concept. A nice pair of McDonald's arches is of no use to a Burger King franchisee. In order to persuade prospective partners to sign on, you need to give them a contract that will last the full useful life of the investments. However, you can't set goals for the outputs you want from your franchisee's work over this period. And consequently you can't fully transfer the responsibility for owning and operating the restaurants in return for a fixed-fee licensing payment.

Let's look at this issue in a bit more detail. If you knew what the menu and prices would be for the next year, you could set goals for the output you want from your franchisee's work and set up a contract to get it. You could pay your franchisee a fixed price per unit of each menu item produced and sold. But such an agreement would give you (too much) bargaining power with your franchisee. Your franchisee would have made a substantial capital investment specifically to work with you before agreeing the terms and conditions on which you will pay her and she would not expect to be able to agree favourable payment terms for producing the menu items you want. Of course, if you could fix the menu and the prices for the full life of the contract, you and your franchisee could avoid this problem. But neither of you know how the business and the menu will evolve and so setting such terms is impossible.

Instead of you paying your franchisee a fixed price per unit of each menu item produced and sold, perhaps your franchisee could pay you a fixed price for the use of your brand and concept for the life of the franchise contract? However, if a franchisee agrees, upfront, to pay you a fixed price for the use of your brand and concept, that removes your incentive to further develop the brand and concept to meet franchisees' evolving needs. From the franchisee's perspective, it does not align (your) rewards with (your) performance. It might do if franchisees could set goals for the new menu items or advertising campaigns they wanted from you. They could then make their payment conditional on you delivering this more specific output. But franchisees don't know what menu and what advertising they want from you over the long life of their franchise investments.[24]

An income-sharing agreement between franchisor and franchisee, to share revenues from the stores, helps get around these problems. This is the third basic payment option for getting work done, shown in Figure 3.6. It complements the two other options: paying your partner for the resources you need to get the work done, and paying your partner for the output you want from the work. For franchisees, paying the franchisor for the use of the brand and concept with a share of their sales revenues prevents the franchisor gaining excess bargaining power with them in negotiating terms and conditions. How revenues will be shared between franchisor and franchisee can be determined before the franchisee invests and becomes locked in to working with the franchisor. And sharing in the franchisees' revenues also helps motivate the franchisor to invest in the brand and concept to grow franchisee sales. As we shall discuss further in Chapter 9, income-sharing agreements are often useful where you share responsibilities with your partners in a way that makes your results mutually dependent over an extended period of time.

. . . align rewards with performance

An income-sharing agreement can be very helpful in getting around any motivation problems you might otherwise face if paying for resources or paying for an output. But there are many types of income-sharing agreement, and you need to choose one that closely aligns your partner's interests with yours. In fast-food franchising, sharing sales revenues can, in most respects, do a good enough job of aligning interests. It perhaps does a better job than sharing profits, as cost control in the restaurants is largely up to franchisees. Fast-food chains commonly pay the franchisor 4–5 per cent of sales revenue for the use of the brand and concept.

Figure 3.6 Sharing business income is the third basic payment option

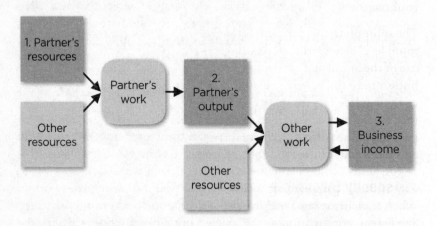

Goals set as basis for payment: 1. receive resources *(when you have competitive advantage)*, 2. receive an output *(when your partner has competitive advantage)*, 3. receive business income *(when you and your partner both have competitive advantage but in taking on different responsibilities for getting the work done).*

Sharing revenues instead of profits also limits a potentially serious problem in measuring franchisee performance. Franchisees and their family members may themselves work in the business and receipts may be taken in cash, making it easy to hide some revenues and much more substantially understate profits. A franchisor would find it difficult to measure the profits achieved by each of a large number of small franchise businesses.

Yet the revenue-sharing model does lead to one awkward conflict of interest. Franchisors are responsible for national or regional brand advertising, and they may be tempted to under spend. Less advertising would mean lower sales, but the drop off in sales, translated into lower franchise fees, would be less than the franchisor's savings on ad spending. If you halve advertising, your franchisees' sales will probably not, at least in the short term, fall by 50 per cent. Franchisees' profits, by contrast, are likely to fall much more than their sales – given their substantial fixed costs as a result of their restaurant investments. They will be concerned that franchisors maintain an adequate level of brand advertising. So how can you, as franchisor, design an agreement that meets the requirements from your franchisee's perspective as well as your own?

The solution to this problem is that most franchise contracts fix a minimum level of advertising spending. On top of the basic franchise fee for use of the brand and concept, many franchisees make an explicit contribution to brand advertising – costing them an additional 3–5 per cent of their sales. The franchisor may manage the brand advertising, but the franchisor is constrained to spend at least what the franchisees have paid for. The success of restaurant franchising suggests that this approach does quite a good job of aligning interests.

. . . specify favourable terms

When franchisors and franchisees negotiate the terms of the franchise agreement, competition in the market should help both parties make an acceptable return. But that may not be the case when a chain launches and the value of its brand and concept are not yet clear.

In the early days of fast-food chains, franchises were not perceived as very valuable. Why pay a lot to use someone else's brand and concept? You could probably go it alone. Franchisors were able to charge only 1–2 per cent of sales for the use of their brand and concept. To make franchising pay, early franchisors would give out large territories to single franchisees and invest little in supporting and controlling them. This was the approach taken by Burger King. As a consequence they faced difficulties with the quality and image of the brand.

If, alternatively, a franchisor invested to support and control franchisees and limited them to just a few stores, they got a better quality and reputation, but struggled to make a profit on the low franchise fee. McDonald's took this approach. But by financing franchisees' real estate investment and charging franchisees a rental based on their store revenues – a creative tactic for collaboration – McDonald's nevertheless made a good profit.[25] The revenue-based rental enabled them to earn more income from the success of their stores, justifying the substantial investment in supporting and controlling franchisees.

Meeting requirements from your partners' perspective

Sharing the business income, and specifying minimum spending on advertising, satisfies many of the requirements from your partners' perspective. But if you purchase the supplies needed in the restaurants and sell them to franchisees, the franchisees could suffer.

As described in Figure 3.4, buying supplies and selling them to franchisees is a source of competitive advantage for you. But you and the franchisee aren't likely to be able to agree on terms to pay for the supplies before the franchisee makes restaurant investments. You will want to negotiate and modify terms over time. However, again, that gives you too much bargaining power with franchisees in negotiating the price of supplies.

To avoid this conflict, most big fast-food franchisors tend not to purchase supplies. Franchisees of McDonald's, Burger King and Subway all purchase direct from suppliers or specialized distributors. The latter two have set up franchisee cooperatives to organize purchasing.[26] McDonald's organizes purchasing on behalf of franchisees, but the purchase transaction between suppliers and franchisees is direct.[27]

Why Starbucks owns rather than franchises its stores

In some cases, competitive advantage will dictate an arrangement that makes it difficult to satisfy franchisees' concerns. You may prefer to bring activities in-house, despite the reduced efficiency. What may seem like small differences between businesses can make a big difference to the best way to set up collaboration – once you factor in partners' motivation. In contrast to most restaurant chains, Starbucks, the leading global coffeehouse chain, generally owns and operates its stores.

Supplies are not central to competitive advantage in service-driven retailing such as fast food. The brand and service concept are the keys to success. But for an upscale coffee-house chain like Starbucks, the quality of the coffee is a differentiator and purchasing coffee on the global market is a core competence. Were Starbucks to retain the responsibility for purchasing coffee but franchise its stores, it would be difficult for franchisees to ensure they get favourable terms on the supplies.

Another problem for franchisees would be Starbucks' strategic preference for a dense network. Starbucks seeks to be a 'third place', somewhere other than home or work, where customers will visit regularly. So stores may be across the street or around the corner from each other, as customers don't want to travel for a latte. It may make sense for Starbucks to open stores in close proximity to existing ones even if the new stores cannibalize existing stores' revenues. But if franchisees owned the existing stores, they wouldn't want new stores right next to theirs. It is easier to build a dense network of stores if you own and manage them.

Thinking beyond conflicts with franchisees, Starbucks' strategy requires employees to identify closely with the franchisor. The baristas who prepare and serve the coffee in a Starbucks store play an important role in building the Starbucks brand. Starbucks refer to all their employees as 'partners'. In contrast to service staff in most fast-food chains, they are expected to build customer relationships. To make Starbucks an attractive place to have a coffee, it helps if baristas feel that it is a great place to work. Starbucks offers all their employees a wide range of benefits including health coverage, matching contributions to a 401K-pension plan and a stock equity reward plan.[28] It would be difficult to offer such direct motivational benefits if baristas were employed by franchisees.

For all these reasons we can see that Starbucks Corporation's business strategy is less well suited to working with external franchise partners. The company owns the large majority of their stores – with impressive results. Starbucks' example shows that the right collaboration design needs to be carefully tailored to the specifics of your strategy and your partners' motivations.

Factoring in motivation: summary

Considerations of competitive advantage influence, but should not fully determine, an effective collaboration design. Figure 3.7 shows some of the ways that motivation matters, both motivation for your partners and your own motivation as a fast-food restaurant corporation.

Competitive advantage would have you focus entirely on the branding and store concept. You would pay partners a fixed fee for investing in and managing the restaurants the way you want, while you benefit fully from the upside of the business. But to motivate partners to make store investments, you have to franchise your brand and store concept to restaurant owners and share income with them. Motivational concerns will also define how you share income with them. Ideally, you would share profits, but as we have seen, franchisees could then be motivated to under-report their revenue and their costs. So you go for the simpler metric of revenues.

Motivational considerations also affect your choice of the number of partners to work with. Franchisees are better motivated if they can have multiple sites. So you want to allow large franchisees – but not so large that they gain a critical mass with bargaining power over you. And to meet franchisees' requirements, you need to accept some important limitations on the activities you engage in. Strategically, you could purchase the restaurant supplies so you can gain economies of scale and ensure a fit with the brand. But franchisees won't like this because they will be locked in to purchasing from you with no opportunity to negotiate favourable terms. So you'll have to allow the franchisees to purchase supplies directly. If you are not prepared to relinquish responsibility for purchasing because it is a core competence for your strategy, then you may need to give up on the idea of franchising altogether and run the stores yourself – the opposite of what initial considerations of competitive advantage suggested.

Figure 3.7 Filling in gaps and modifying the first draft collaboration design

Conclusions

The conventional wisdom on business strategy – focus on your strengths – is indeed a good starting point for designing collaboration. You should take responsibility for areas where you have a competitive advantage, and transfer responsibility to suppliers for everything else. The fast-food industry shows how a focused approach can reduce your investment of money and time and powerfully leverage your returns.

Yet it also shows the limits of the simple principle of strategic focus. Motivational considerations may lead you to stray far from a first draft design that allocates business responsibilities to whoever is best able to take them on. It is not just agreements that are affected. The mix of partners, and the mix of what you do in-house vs. what you outsource, may also change. Coming up with a first draft collaboration design based on market and competitive strategy is a good way to get started. But it is crucial to test your design to see if it meets the 10 requirements, and adjust it where necessary to set up for profitable and sustainable collaboration.

---

[1] Usually, only an external partner can take on the full responsibility for getting the work done including obtaining the use of any assets and human resources needed, taking and implementing decisions to get the work done and, critically, carrying any risks involved in producing the output you want from the work.

[2] For example, according to a presentation to the Ashridge Strategic Management Centre Research Committee by Marcus Alexander on 13th December 1995, these included frameworks by Andersen Consulting, P-E Consulting, Simon Smith of Capital Strategies, Tom Auwers and Dirk Deschoolmeester of Vlerick School of Management, J. B. Quinn and F.G. Hilmer in Sloan Management Review of Summer 1994 and quite a number more. A more recent version of a very similar framework is provided in Ronan McIvor, 'The influence of capability considerations on the outsourcing decision: the case of a manufacturing company.' *International Journal of Production Research*, Vol. 48, No. 17, 1 September 2010, 5031–5052.

[3] See, for example, Elizabeth Rigby, 'Eyes in the till: Every time a Clubcard owner goes shopping at Tesco, more information is added to what is probably the biggest collection of up-to-date personal data in the UK. So should we be worrying about a Big Brother at the checkout – or celebrating an astounding achievement in sales and market analysis?' *Financial Times Weekend Magazine* – Technology Special, 11 November 2006 and <http://www.dunnhumby.com/us/about-us-history-of-success>. Downloaded 29th October 2012.

[4] Interestingly, the leading hamburger chains mostly started out with close relationships to equipment manufacturers. Burger Chef, one of the early leaders in the business, design was even founded and

owned by an equipment manufacturer, General Equipment Corporation, that saw owning a chain of hamburger restaurants as a valuable way of marketing and selling their own patented flame broiler. See <http://jsfburgerchef.homestead.com/BurgerChefHistory.html>. Downloaded 11th April 2013.

[5] Dave Edgerton and Jim McLamore, who co-founded Burger King, designed their own broiler through frustration at the poor functioning of the ones they had bought. But they still went out and outsourced the manufacture of the new equipment. See Bill Carlino. 'BK co-founder McLamore dead at 70 (Burger King Corp.'s James W. McLamore dies of lung cancer)'. *Nation's Restaurant News*, 19th August 1996.

[6] Even equipment manufacturers could follow this logic. Like Apple, which focussed on product development and marketing while outsourcing the actual production.

[7] In principle, a public company is less constrained in pursuing opportunities by the requirement that the strategy should leave the company doing what it does well rather than an entrepreneur. The skills and the risk-taking capacity of a public company are less limited. The company owns the assets and holds the contracts. But the decisions are taken by the board of directors and the management. The board and the management can be changed if they are not making the right decisions. The risks are taken by the shareholders. The shareholders can be asked to provide additional equity if this is needed to pursue opportunities. New shareholders can invest. In practice, however, a public company should also address the question of 'how do we get to there from here?' Whoever is responsible for making decisions on behalf of the company is unlikely to voluntarily step down if they don't have the right decision-making abilities. They have an awkward conflict of interest; they want to keep their job. And the ability to raise new equity finance is not unlimited.

[8] Most fast-food chains own and operate a substantial number of stores. We describe why they do this below. Subway originally owned some stores, see <http://www.subway.com/subwayroot/about_us/history.aspx> (downloaded 14th April 2013) but now franchises them all, see http://www.qsrmagazine.com/reports/qsr50-2013-sandwich-segment-breakdown (downloaded 27th January 2014).

[9] So named because of the PhD qualification in physics of Peter Buck, one of Subway's two founders.

[10] To Subway development agents.

[11] The Independent Purchasing Cooperative Inc.

[12] The Subway Franchisee Advertising Fund Trust (SFAFT). However, note that Doctors Associates have recently moved to be able to take greater control, see, for example, <http://www.bluemaumau.org/8951/subway_gains_control_600m_advertising_trust>. Downloaded 15th September 2013.

[13] Julie Jargon. 'Subway Runs Past McDonald's Chain'. *The Wall Street Journal*, 8th March 2011

[14] See <http://www.forbes.com/profile/fred-deluca/ and http://www.forbes.com/profile/peter-buck/>.

[15] See, for example, Jeffrey L. Bradach. *Franchise Organizations*. Harvard Business School Press, 1998.

[16] <http://www.subway.com/subwayroot/about_us/history.aspx>. Downloaded 14th April 2013.

[17] McDonald's Franchise Brochure, McDonald's Corporation 2011.

[18] Steve Gerhardt, Dan Dudley, and Samuel Hazen. 'Franchising and the Impact of McDonald's.' *Proceedings of the ASBBS*, Volume 18, Number 1, pp. 493–500, February 2011.

[19] Angus Loten. 'Franchising; The Big Get Bigger; When awarding new outlets, restaurant chains are giving preference to franchisees who already own a bunch'. *The Wall Street Journal* Online, 18th May 2012.

[20] <http://www.answers.com/topic/burger-king>. Downloaded 8th May 2013.

[21] Burger King Worldwide Inc 10k 2012, page 6.

[22] <http://www.carrols.com/burgerking/>. Downloaded 8th May 2013.

[23] Glenn Collins, 'How Venezuela Is Becoming Coca-Cola Country', *New York Times*, 21st August 1996 and Constance Hays, 'Coke and Pepsi Fight a Turf War in Venezuela', *New York Times*, 18th December 1998.

[24] A further argument against franchisees agreeing to pay a lump sum for the rights to your brand and concept is that franchisees may not be competitively advantaged in taking the risks involved in a large fixed investment to work with you, additional to their investment in the lease, equipment, fixtures and fittings.

[25] John F. Love. 'McDonald's: Silent partner spots way for McDonald's to turn profit'. *Houston Chronicle*, 19th November 1986.

[26] Restaurant Services, Inc. for Burger King and the independent Purchasing Cooperative, Inc. for Subway.

[27] London Economics. *McDonald's economic footprint in Europe*. October 2011.

[28] Starbucks Pay and Benefits, Starbucks Coffee Company 2012.

Chapter 4

Tactics for Collaboration with Suppliers

The next four chapters take on problems with collaboration in a variety of settings. We'll use the 10 requirements framework to identify these problems and describe tactics that companies use to deal with them. We'll also use the framework to suggest a few new tactics. For each kind of problem we'll generate a summary list of tactics.

This chapter looks at working with external suppliers. Our focus is not on buying standard products, as these are routine exchanges with few difficulties. We focus on custom orders, where you are likely to face problems in *setting* sufficiently precise *goals* for the *output*, which means you'll struggle to establish a contract that's robust enough to let you pay only if you get what you want.

Different common situations pose different problems

Problems may arise simply because you have not devoted enough attention to specifying the output you want from your supplier's work. Once you realize this, the solution is straightforward – you must devote more time and effort to the specifications. But often it isn't possible to provide sufficient details in advance, or perhaps doing so would interfere with implementing your strategy. Here it is useful to distinguish three different situations.

Not ready to decide what you want

First, you may need to choose a supplier and place an order before you are ready to set the output goals for the supplier's work. You could do a better job of specifying what you want later when you have more information but you can still can go ahead and place an order anyway.

However, you then run the risk that what you order is not what you want and does not create *customer value*. Alternatively, you could first reserve the production capacity you need with a supplier and wait until you know what you want before you tell your supplier what output to produce. But by the time you know what you want, you may have no alternative but to use that supplier, who thereby *gains bargaining power* with you and you won't be able to *specify favourable terms* for the output.

You want help deciding what you want

In the second situation, you may need a supplier's help to decide on the output you want. But you are then faced with a fundamental problem in *setting goals*: you can't devise a robust contract to get the output you want when determining that output is part of what you want the supplier to do.

You want help deciding what you want, and then doing it

The third situation is more complicated: it involves two-stage projects where you first settle on a design, and then you execute that design. You need a supplier's help in both stages, and you want to work with the same supplier for both. This situation offers the most opportunities for creative contracting. You face all the problems in the first two situations, and the additional one that your contractor has an *awkward conflict of interest* with you in helping set the goals for the execution phase.

The problems meeting the 10 requirements

Figure 4.1 illustrates these problems. They are a subset of the 10 requirements that we laid out in Chapter 2. Using examples from fashion retailing, automobile manufacture, consumer brands, large engineering and construction projects, government contracting and utilities, we now discuss tactics to mitigate them.[1]

Figure 4.1 Working with suppliers: common problems we focus on in this chapter

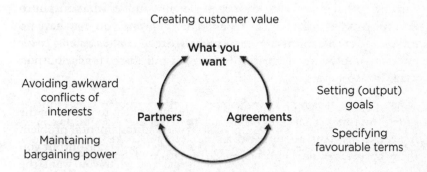

Creating customer value

What you want

Avoiding awkward conflicts of interests

Maintaining bargaining power

Partners

Agreements

Setting (output) goals

Specifying favourable terms

Not ready to decide what you want

If you are not ready to decide what you want done when you choose a supplier, you risk either customer value (by contracting in advance) or favourable terms (by delaying decisions on the output). Industry contracting practices have shifted substantially in order to make better trade-offs in meeting these two requirements for profitable collaboration, as we can see in the fashion and automotive industries.

Fashion retail

Many fashion chains and department stores used to place specific orders, or 'output contracts', for garments long before the start of the selling season. This enabled them to negotiate hard to get low prices from competing manufacturers. But it also meant they had to make early decisions about their product range to ensure available capacity with the best manufacturers. To fully specify orders, retailers had to make up their minds about the details of their product range as much as a year in advance, well before the season's fashion winners became clear. This left them, in season, in a situation where they were out-of-stock of popular garments and forced them to make high markdowns to clear slow-moving items.

Difficulties in creating customer value

For many years, retailers tended to see these problems of high out-of-stocks and high markdowns as caused by their own inability to predict demand sufficiently far in advance. Garment manufacturers did what fashion retailers asked them to do. They competed to get retailers' orders and then delivered them as promised. So retailers devoted their efforts to improving their capability to predict fashion trends. But they made little progress.

It has proved easier to solve fashion retailers' problems by reducing order lead times. That gives them time to detect and respond to emerging consumer demand, rather than predicting it. To reduce lead times, many apparel retailers have changed the nature of the agreements they set up with garment manufacturers. They first reserve capacity with manufacturers, and then later, just before the season starts, determine and order the specific garments they want – models, colours and sizes. They also use the capacity they reserve to be able to introduce new models and restock in season.

Reserving capacity does a good job of reducing markdowns and out-of-stocks. But shifting from output contracts to capacity contracts gets in the way of other requirements for profitable collaboration. When the retailer and garment manufacturer come to negotiate the price for specific garments, the retailer can no longer rely on competition between garment manufacturers to make sure of getting a good deal. It's too late to reserve capacity elsewhere, so the manufacturer has *gained bargaining power*. Regardless of bargaining power considerations, a retailer without competitive bids will likely lack sufficient information about garment manufacturing costs to be able to specify favourable terms on his own.

Maintaining bargaining power

So the problem has shifted from creating customer value to preserving *bargaining power*. Figure 4.2 shows a list of tactics to prevent a partner gaining bargaining power. We will discuss these tactics in the course of the chapter.[2]

Figure 4.2 Tactics to prevent your partner gaining bargaining power

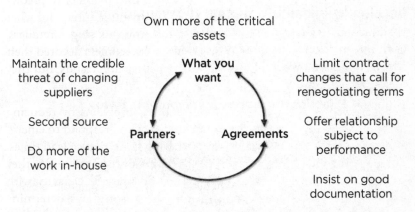

Own more of the critical assets

Maintain the credible threat of changing suppliers

What you want

Limit contract changes that call for renegotiating terms

Second source

Partners

Agreements

Offer relationship subject to performance

Do more of the work in-house

Insist on good documentation

Fashion retailers have more bargaining power than they might realize. They can *credibly threaten to change suppliers*. Manufacturers may have leverage in negotiating terms for the specifics of the garment, but they also seek a continuing relationship with leading apparel retailers. So retailers can use the threat of changing suppliers next season as their 'stick' to put price pressure on manufacturers. Alternatively, they can use the promise of a continuing relationship subject to good performance as a 'carrot' to encourage manufacturers to meet their needs.

Retailers can also *second-source* the garments. If they place firm orders with retailers to cover most but not all of their needs in season, they can then, even during the season, place additional volume with the manufacturer best meeting their needs.

Finally, they can *own more of the assets specific to the business*. Traditionally, manufacturers were responsible for buying cloth for garments. But to give themselves greater flexibility and bargaining power in season, retailers now often buy greige (cloth not yet dyed), stock it and, after dyeing in the desired colour, deliver it during the season to the manufacturer. This way the necessary cloth is bought early, in a competitive market, and retailers have to negotiate only the cost of manufacture. Not only are retailers less at risk to excessive pricing, but they have more leverage in the negotiations. If they were to take their orders elsewhere, manufacturers might find it difficult to find an alternative customer because they could offer only production without cloth.

Developing the ability to propose favourable terms

Fashion retailers face more of a problem in ensuring they have sufficient information to propose favourable terms. But they have options here as well, as shown in Figure 4.3.

Figure 4.3 Tactics for proposing favourable terms

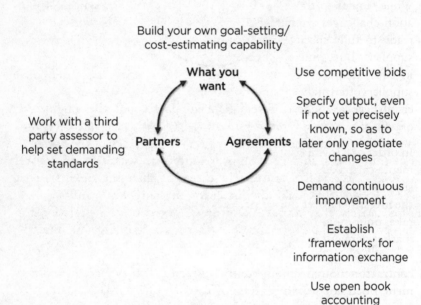

Build your own goal-setting/
cost-estimating capability

What you want

Use competitive bids

Work with a third party assessor to help set demanding standards

Partners   **Agreements**

Specify output, even if not yet precisely known, so as to later only negotiate changes

Demand continuous improvement

Establish 'frameworks' for information exchange

Use open book accounting

Most obviously they can invest in *building an in-house goal-setting/cost-estimating ability*. Even when they maintain their bargaining power, retailers will benefit from an independent check on the prices their manufacturer offers. Since they can't rely on the market to do this, they can assess the offer with in-house expertise. But this can be expensive.

Retailers can also do a lot to *specify the desired output even if not yet precisely known*. That's because retailers don't reserve manufacturing capacity in terms of machine and labour hours. Instead they choose a representative model of garment from each part of their range – for jeans, say, a five-pocket jean in a particular fit, size and colour. And they negotiate, in advance of the season, the price for a quantity of this model of jeans as if their demand for jeans were to consist entirely of this one model. Then, in season, they need negotiate only modifications in price to accommodate variations in manufacturing cost related to model, colour and size. These are small changes in relation to the price of a garment.

The automotive industry: a more difficult challenge

While similar to those in fashion, the automotive industry's collaboration challenges are harder to resolve. Car manufacturers often aren't ready to fully specify what they want done when they commit to a supplier. But unlike garment manufacturers, whose investments in equipment can be used for any of their customers, automotive suppliers often make specific investments on behalf of individual customers. A new car model, for example, might require an entirely new kind of part.

In order to convince suppliers to invest in this customer-specific equipment, carmakers need to offer much longer-term commitments to suppliers. Long-term agreements give the supplier a chance to amortize the investment over the life of the contract – but also mean the supplier takes on some of the risk of the new model. The two parties can't predict market demand for the model, so the contract may provide a windfall for either supplier or customer. A popular car model would give the contractor enough volume to generate a generous profit on the investment, but a flop would generate disappointing returns.

Maintaining bargaining power

What if, in response to this problem, the two parties leave prices on subsequent orders open? They may find it difficult to agree on those prices later on. If the cost of the supplier's investment were high relative to the subsequent orders for the part, which is likely, then the carmaker would find it difficult to switch to another supplier. As for the supplier, subsequent orders with this customer are the only way of generating additional revenues from the investment to make the part. A single potential buyer is negotiating with a single potential seller, which makes the outcomes unpredictable.

A carmaker can reduce the risks here by *owning more of the assets* or *doing more of the work in-house*.[3] If they can identify the expensive equipment in question and separate it from the other assets in the supplier's business, they could pay for the asset specific to their business while physically leaving it with the supplier to work with it. An investment in a mould or dye could be effectively handled in this way. If negotiations with the supplier over prices of follow-on orders for a part fall short, the customer can simply transfer the asset to a supplier with a better price for the parts.

But not all customer-specific investments are easily separable from other more general-purpose investments. The carmaker would then have to buy the contractor and vertically integrate (or develop its own internal capability for the part). But this is an extreme solution that can be quite costly, and bring some strategic disadvantages. (See 'Business Specific Investments and Vertical Integration'.)

Business specific investments and vertical integration

Vertical integration is a lively topic in the academic 'transactions cost' literature. Economists argue that customer-specific investments can make negotiations between contractor and customer so difficult that the customer will resort to vertical integration. Yet the real world of business shows less and less vertical integration of ownership and more deconstruction of the value chain. It is actually difficult to find good mainstream examples to support this hypothesis for vertical integration. Even the acquisition of Fisher Body by General Motors in 1926, a case often cited as evidence, turns out to have been driven by other motives.[4] As we see it, the argument for vertical integration depends on certain assumptions that rarely apply.[5]

The first assumption is that a contractor's investment is entirely specific to the one customer's business. In fact, few investments in practice are useless for other customers. For example, some aspects of a parts supplier's equipment may be specific to just one carmaker, but other aspects are likely to be of more general use, so the supplier can hope to recoup some of their investment. Who then should make the investment for this intermediate situation?

In particular, who is most capable of ensuring an alternative use for the investment if the initial customer turns out not to want the capacity over its full useful life? Typically the contractor is in a much better position than the customer. The component supplier has regular dealings with other car manufacturers, while the car manufacturer would have to sell to a competitor. So the component supplier has the advantage in finding alternative uses, and this advantage can overcome the car manufacturer's gains in reducing negotiation risk through vertical integration.[6]

The second assumption is that the efficiency of production is not affected by the choice of outsourcing versus vertical integration. But while suppliers make some investments that are largely specific to one customer, they also make many other investments that are usable by several or even many customers. Most suppliers also have a number of valuable skills that are transferable between customers. In asset investments and technical and management skills, suppliers will gain learning and scale effects that are shared across customers. But if the customer acquires the supplier through vertical integration, other customers (who compete with that manufacturer) may well shift their business to other suppliers. As a captive division, the supplier's volume and experience base will shrink, and so will their efficiency.

Both outsourcing and vertical integration have their downsides, so customers often seek a middle way with better trade-offs, one that involves sharing responsibilities for the activity. In reality, difficulties with business-specific investments mostly affect the details of what customers outsource and how they contract with suppliers, not the basic choice of producing in-house versus outsourcing. For example, a customer for moulded plastic parts may decide it wants to own the moulds for the parts produced by a contractor, but the customer is unlikely to produce the parts in-house. In the context of a service business, the brand owner may franchise out the brand and concept to store owners, rather than owning all the stores operating under the brand.

The interesting question here is therefore not about simple vertical integration, but instead, 'How can we devise a collaboration strategy to retain the benefits of working with a specialized supplier while avoiding the problems of that supplier gaining bargaining power?' We seek to answer this question throughout the book, and dividing and sharing entrepreneurial responsibilities and rewards – sharing business ownership – to get around collaboration problems is a major theme.[7]

Specifying favourable terms

Without vertical integration, carmakers with this problem can only work on showing suppliers that long-term relationships across multiple car models will depend on good performance. But then they must be able to assess performance, all the more difficult because customer-specific parts don't lend themselves to easy comparisons across suppliers.

As a car manufacturer you need a well-understood, transparent process for setting and monitoring performance standards. You also need to show contractors that you both want and are able to help them meet the standards you set.

This challenge is actually similar to that you face when producing in-house and managing your own employees. You make long-term employment commitments to your managers subject to their meeting demanding performance standards. You typically[8] use some process other than direct competition among managers to set standards. And, to get the best out of your managers, you need to convince them that you will support them in meeting the standards you set.[9]

Starting from an initial target cost, you can *demand continuous improvement* from your suppliers. Target costs for parts for any given model should go down year on year. Target costs for new models should be lower (and part performance standards be more demanding) than for previous models. Here it helps to know enough about your supplier's costs to estimate their profits given the targets you set. To meet suppliers' requirements for successful collaboration, target setting should allow your suppliers to achieve a reasonable profit given good performance. If suppliers exceed targets they will pocket the gain, but you will set more demanding targets in following years.[10]

Going further, you can *establish framework agreements*. These arrangements prompt the two parties to exchange a broad set of information that will support mutual learning, build trust and help drive the continuous improvement you want to achieve. The framework agreement will go beyond the mere exchange of information to describe, in broader terms, how you propose to collaborate with your supplier. What regular meetings are scheduled? Can your supplier have their staff working on your premises, and vice versa? It may include a commitment to work together with your supplier over the longer term subject to meeting specified performance goals.

If you and your supplier are locked in to working with each other, you need to break down organizational boundaries so that you can more effectively manage your supplier and your supplier can more effectively understand and respond to your needs. A framework agreement helps set the game rules for doing this.

Not ready to decide what you want: summary

Figure 4.4 summarizes your options with suppliers when you are not ready to specify what you want done at the time of contract. You can first reserve supplier capacity and then decide what outputs you want produced later, but then you may both jeopardize your bargaining power and leave yourself short of the information to specify favourable terms. Figures 4.4 effectively combines Figures 4.2 and 4.3 to bring the tactics to solve all these different problems together.

Figure 4.4 Tactics when you are not ready to decide what you want

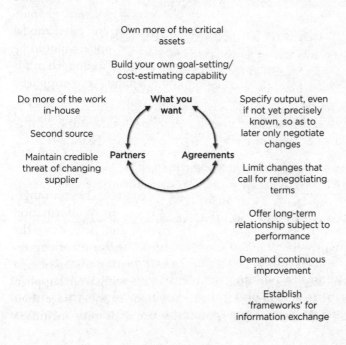

Own more of the critical assets

Build your own goal-setting/ cost-estimating capability

Do more of the work in-house

What you want

Specify output, even if not yet precisely known, so as to later only negotiate changes

Second source

Maintain credible threat of changing supplier

Partners   **Agreements**

Limit changes that call for renegotiating terms

Offer long-term relationship subject to performance

Demand continuous improvement

Establish 'frameworks' for information exchange

When you want help deciding what you want

When you work with a contractor, you commonly expect to define the output you want and then transfer the responsibility for production over to them. However, this is simply not possible when you need a contractor to help you define that output in the first place. As a film producer, for example, you need a film script, so you hire a scriptwriter. But you can't tell the scriptwriter the precise script you want, because then you wouldn't need the scriptwriter to begin with.

As a result, when you can't define the output you want, you can't set up a robust contract and you can't fully transfer responsibility for producing the output. This is a fundamental problem, and it's increasingly common in business. It happens not only with 'creative' contractors such as scriptwriters or advertising agencies, but also with other kinds of contractors that help you decide what to do – from the IT systems integrator to a business strategy consultant.

Figure 4.5 shows tactics you can use when you face a problem in setting output goals where you need help in deciding what to do.

The ability needed to get what you want

The challenge you face is to get the help in deciding on the output, while always retaining responsibility for the decision. So you need the self-awareness to assess if you have the personal ability to select and direct a contractor to get the result you want. If, after devoting more time and resources, you doubt your ability to come up with a clear brief for the work and then control the supplier's performance, then you have two radical alternatives.

First, perhaps you shouldn't be doing the work at all. For example, as discussed in Chapter 2, a CEO with little experience in supervising large IT projects may prefer to focus on other ways of creating value to avoid taking responsibility for designing and installing a new ERP system.

Second, perhaps outsourcing the complete process will make it easier for you to define the output you want. For example, if you are commissioning a new hospital building, you may be concerned that the design will be too expensive to maintain and clean. If you doubt that you can control the architect's building specifications to ensure that expenses

Figure 4.5 Tactics to address problems in setting output goals

Invest more time

Adapt your strategy

Outsource complete process

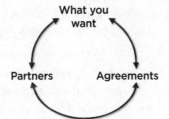

Direct and control
the work

Use 'briefing/
back-briefing'
process with
partner to define
and communicate
output goals

Take a partner
with a skill set that
plugs the gaps in
your own

Pay for combined
provision of output
and resource
capacity

Set-up income-
sharing agreement
to motivate partner
and limit your risk

are manageable, you can outsource the entire process of building, maintaining and cleaning the hospital. You can agree to lease a hospital building long term for a price that includes the cost of its cleaning and maintenance.

By doing that, you shift to the builder the responsibility for controlling the architect to ensure a manageable upkeep. Contracts for hospitals built under the Private Finance Initiative in the UK – which includes most new hospitals over the past two decades – have usually been set up on this basis. While this initiative is controversial, the design of buildings for lifecycle costing is frequently cited as one of its benefits.

Partners

The cost of deciding what to do is usually small in relation to the cost of going on to do the wrong thing. So if you are unsure of what to do, it is tempting to think that you can spend your way out of trouble in the design stage. But you don't necessarily add value by spending more or hiring a big name. Nelly Wenger, then the head of Nestlé Switzerland, hired the ateliers of star architect Jean Nouvel to redesign the packaging for the Cailler brand of chocolate. But Nouvel's innovative redesign flopped. Swiss consumers objected strongly to the unconventional use of PET plastic in the packaging design, as both ecologically wasteful and inappropriate for chocolate.[11]

You are better off to spend money on filling in the gaps in your own ability. Which contractor you want to work with depends on your own skill set, not merely on the job at hand. If you lack relevant experience, you need to pay for partners who bring relevant experience to limit your risk. In contrast, if you have a lot of experience, you need to check that your experience is not misleading. You may want to pay to get more diversity of experience and more creativity.[12]

Nelly Wenger clearly took too much risk in engaging Ateliers Jean Nouvel, a firm that had relatively little experience in designing packaging for fast-moving consumer goods. Nouvel might be expected to come up with some highly creative ideas, but it clearly needed to be closely guided and managed to ensure a good result in an unfamiliar area. Wenger's own background was in urban planning, having been appointed Nestlé country head after running the Swiss national exhibition, Expo.02.[13] She was in a weak position to take a risk working with a designer without a strong background in packaging design for fast moving consumer goods. She could not be expected to control the packaging design work.[14]

This problem is essentially the same as that faced by the CEO without experience of ERP projects we met in Chapter 2, but with a crucial difference: launching a new product is a core competence in branded goods. A CEO with more branded goods experience would have been less likely to trip up.

Agreements

When you need help defining what you want to do, it is particularly tricky to set up agreements to get the help you want, but there are some things you can do to improve your chances of success. If you do a good job of communicating your broader objectives, your partner will be more effective in helping you specify the output needed. And if you agree to share your business income from the work, that may help motivate your partner to do what you want.

Direct and control the work

In directing and controlling the work there are no miracle cures, but there are some good housekeeping rules that are often neglected.

A good briefing and back-briefing will encourage a closer fit between what you want and what the contractor delivers. Setting goals for the output of a contractor's work becomes an interactive process between you and your contractor. You must clearly describe the help you want (briefing) and then explicitly ask your partner to feedback to you his interpretation of your problem and how he plans to go about solving it (back-briefing[15]).

In the case of the chocolate packaging, because you can't precisely specify *what* you want – the output – you need to say more about *why* you want it, what is the output for, what it should do and what it should not do. What is the current position of that particular chocolate product in the market, and how do you want to change it? What role will the new packaging play in this repositioning? What constraints do you want to set on the design on cost, space requirements for transportation and display, and ease of recycling the material? In back-briefing, the designer plays back the brief in his own words to show that he has understood it, and further demonstrates his understanding by describing how he will go about fulfilling your brief. Often, this happens as part of the designer's proposal, which then becomes the basis for a contract to produce the design. The better the quality of this briefing and back-briefing process, the better the chance of a good result.

If you can't sufficiently define the output upfront, then your subsequent feedback on the progress of the work will be critical to complement the initial briefing. Controlling the work over time will let you provide more precise direction about the output you want or modify your description of what you want in the light of new information. This process will also help you motivate the contractor, especially for the long collaborations that are increasingly common in business. If you are making regular payments based on progress, you must be able to monitor the progress of the work. That way you can put pressure on the contractor by linking payment and progress.

Assuming you can't objectively measure whether you receive the output you wanted, you can at least ensure that your contractor puts enough effort into delivering it. Your contract will sensibly include a goal for the amount of resource capacity to be provided – such as days spent working on the new packaging design. You may also want 'key man' provisions to ensure your supplier does not offer his best team in the proposal and then have less qualified people actually do the work.

Set up an income-sharing agreement

As discussed in Chapter 3 for franchising, when you can't define the output you want, agreeing to share your business income may help ensure the contractor is motivated to do what you want. With ever more outsourcing to specialist 'creatives' and advisors, income-sharing contracts are increasingly common for many different types of external partners. Consumer goods companies no longer design most of their products in-house, while retailers buy design and manufacturing separately from different companies. Michael Graves, a well-known designer of household products, has worked for both upmarket consumer brands companies such as Alessi, who then sell to retailers, as well as directly for discount retailers such as Target.[16] Both Alessi and Target pay Graves and other external designers royalties on the corresponding products.[17]

In some particularly risky industries, you may want to share business rights with contractors as much to reduce the overall risk in the business as to motivate individual contractors. For example, film production is a highly risky business – only a few movies will be extraordinarily profitable and most of the rest actually lose money. Star actors will often expect largely fixed payment when working on a high budget studio movie, but will accept much of their compensation by way of a share of the gross or net profit when working with a lower budget 'indie' production. This is largely because independent producers often simply can't afford to pay stars their standard fixed fee, so they ask them to share the risk.[18]

Yet such income-sharing arrangements are limited by your ability to measure the value of what you're getting. A publisher can easily measure the impact of an author's work on publishing revenues, as the author is the dominant contributor. It is more difficult to measure the impact of a scriptwriter on the revenues or profits of a film, the impact of an advertising campaign on consumer goods performance, or the effect of many consulting projects on business results. We look at the issues in more detail in Chapter 9.

When you want help deciding what you want: summary

When you want help in deciding what to do, you can't solve the problem by waiting until you have more information. The options available to address the issue were shown in Figure 4.5. You need the self-awareness to clearly recognize the gaps in your own skills that your contractor must be able to fill. However, if the gaps are large, you may prefer to get around the problem by cancelling the work altogether, or outsourcing the complete process.

If you do proceed with the work as the owner, you need a contractor with a track record of experience whose back-briefing to you demonstrates his ability to understand your needs and do what you want. You can better motivate a contractor over the course of the project with regular check-ins on progress and increasingly greater detail on the desired output, just as you would do if you were working with employees. If appropriate, you can also set up an income-sharing contract, which not only motivates your contractor but also limits your risk. Usually, the most difficult challenge here is not only being able to give your contractor good direction initially but also over time. There is really no substitute for investing time and resources to build your skills in doing this.

When you want help deciding what you want, and then doing it

The most complex problems in setting up collaboration arise in two-stage projects that involve a fully realized design, and then execution on that design. Ideally, you want the same contractor to first help you specify what you want done, and second, to go on to do it for you. This was the case in Chapter 2 with IT consultants for a new ERP system. Here you face all the problems we have discussed so far in this chapter, with the addition that your contractor has an awkward conflict of interest. The more extensive the scope of work the contractor recommends be done, the more profit it stands to make from doing the work. So the contractor has a strong interest in proposing a project with an extensive scope.

To consider these challenges, we will focus on large engineering and construction projects. As mapped out in Figure 4.6, we lay out tactics available to solve problems more explicitly than we did in Chapter 2, and we will also introduce some new tactics.

Figure 4.6 Tactics to prevent awkward conflicts of interests with partners

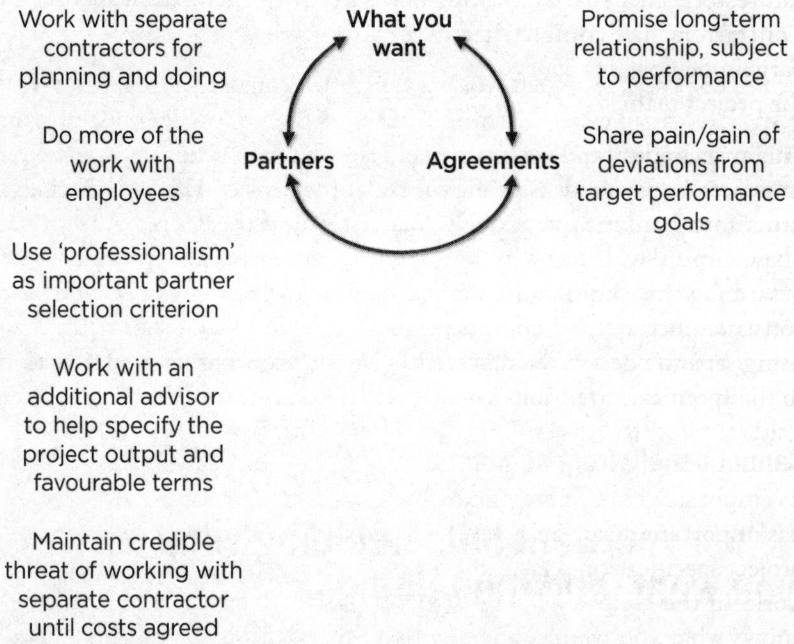

Work with separate contractors for planning and doing

Do more of the work with employees

Use 'professionalism' as important partner selection criterion

Work with an additional advisor to help specify the project output and favourable terms

Maintain credible threat of working with separate contractor until costs agreed

What you want

Partners

Agreements

Promise long-term relationship, subject to performance

Share pain/gain of deviations from target performance goals

Working with separate contractors for planning and doing the work

The traditional approach to collaboration for these projects focuses on a combination of the first two of the tactics listed for partners in Figure 4.6. Many clients take different partners for drawing up project specifications and for executing the work. They will hire an architect or an engineering firm or work with an in-house team to draw up building or project specifications. Then they will go out to competitive bid with construction contractors to get a fixed all-in price to build to the output specifications developed. The contractors that carry out the work on the project will not be involved in specifying it.

Adversarial relationship

Even with extensive design work, however, it is difficult to specify in advance all the desired details on these big projects. Contractors know this, so they bid low on the fixed price; once they've won the bid, they can restore their margins with high prices for the inevitable changes. Contractors hire project managers as much for their ability to use bargaining power to renegotiate contracts as for their ability to manage the project team.

This creates an adversarial relationship, and legal disputes over fixed-price contracts have driven Stone & Webster and other large contracting firms into bankruptcy. Stone & Webster was finally bought by The Shaw Group, whose CEO commented at the time, 'We have a way of describing that [kind of] business. We call it EPCL – engineer, procure, construct, litigate. We don't want to be in that business.'[19] Therefore, using separate design and construction contractors is no easy solution to the specification problem.

Cannot benefit from combined design and execution know-how

As emphasized in Chapter 2, taking separate contractors for each phase has important disadvantages. If you start to work with a partner in the project specification phase, it is expensive to go elsewhere to execute the work. In the context of a construction project, the designing partner knows what you want, understands your organization, has built relationships with your employees and may have proposed construction approaches that he can execute efficiently but other contractors cannot.

A new contractor taking over would require not just a new selection process, but also more formal and detailed documentation of specifications to make them as clear as possible to his 'fresh eyes'.

Additionally, a construction contractor has valuable know-how about the quickest, most reliable and lowest cost way to build things. They may be able to help you to specify an engineering design and construction approach that more effectively and efficiently meets your needs. There are design benefits in involving the construction contractor early in the process.

More costly coordination with subcontractors

Early contractor involvement on large construction projects also brings substantial secondary benefits, as the prime contractors typically subcontract most of the work. Selecting a prime contractor for a turnkey fixed-price contract creates a lot of bidding work for subcontractors, much of which will be wasted if the client chooses another lead firm.

Companies competing to become prime contractors put together their bids by requesting bids from subcontractors. They sum up the costs of subcontractor bids and then add their own costs. Competing prime contractors may each ask a different selection of potential subcontractors for bids and they may ask the same potential subcontractors for bids of different scope – so subcontractors can't just hand in the same bid to several different potential prime contractors.

When subcontractors put in their bids, they do not know how seriously to take the bidding process, whether any given prime contractor is a strong candidate. Even if they win the bidding process and their prime contractor lands the work, they may have to rebid to actually get the work. Months may elapse between bidding for the project and the start of construction, and market conditions may change. Demand for construction projects is highly cyclical and may have heated up or cooled down, affecting market prices for labour or materials. By contrast, when the client commits to work with a prime contractor ahead of time, prime contractors can work with subcontractors closer to the start of construction, with better information and less wasted effort.[20]

Using 'professionalism' as an important partner selection criterion

Given these disadvantages of taking separate contractors for design and construction, some clients for large projects decide to work with the same contractor for specifying the work and then carrying out the project. Often they pay time and expenses with a rough agreement on the target cost. They rely on the contractor's professional self-motivation to avoid problems with awkward conflicts of interest. Yet this can be a thin reed on which to rest.

Lack of discipline and performance pressure on both sides

Fixed-price contracts on big projects have their problems, but contracts for time and expenses are often worse. Both sides lack performance discipline and performance pressure. Indeed, contractors that take orders for both fixed-price turnkey projects and work charged by time and expenses sometimes have separate organizational units for each type of contract. One contractor we spoke with noted the substantial cultural difference between these units. Engineers working on fixed-price contracts often had lights on late at night, while the offices of their time-and-expense counterparts went dark at five o'clock.

With early contractor involvement and no competitive bid, and after an initial project specification phase, it is possible, in principle, to agree on a fixed budget and stick to it. But in practice, without competitive bids, work often starts before any firm budget is set. Some parts of the work move forward while others are still being defined. It is hard to discipline the contractor, and the client may also be tempted to allow the project scope to grow.

The Scottish Parliament building provides a painful example. The building's original estimate was for £40 million, but when it was completed in 2004, three years behind schedule, it had a total cost of £414 million. Design changes over time substantially increased the scope of the work and construction costs were not kept under control.[21] Even after it opened the building still wasn't entirely safe. MPs had to move into a makeshift debating chamber for some days after a '12ft by 1ft oak beam swung free – stopping inches from crashing into a glass screen and hanging 20ft above the Tory benches.'[22]

A growing interest in alliances as an alternative

Given how unsatisfactory these approaches have been, clients and contractors have been actively experimenting with new approaches. The goal is to permit early contractor involvement, but better align both parties' motivation and create performance discipline and pressure.

As previewed in Chapter 1, we can point to 'alliances' – a term used in the UK and Australia, the two countries where the approach is most common – as a promising solution. We can see this by looking at the results of an Australian survey that assessed 46 such alliance projects, each with a value greater than AUS$100 million, on a variety of non-price criteria such as quality of work, safety, team dynamics, flexibility of approach, and functionality. The survey found that clients generally rated performance on these criteria as either 'above expectations' or 'game breaking.'[23]

Alliances can be successful because they address the problems of retaining bargaining power and specifying favourable terms while working with a contractor with a potentially awkward conflict of interest. Alliances are not perfect, but in a wide range of situations they let the client get better results at lower cost than they would if working either with a simple output contract (turnkey fixed price) or a simple contract for resources (time and materials).

Alliance-minded clients use competitive bidding and non-price criteria to select the prime contractor. In a first phase of collaboration, client and contractor jointly define rough project specifications and an agreed target cost for the project. For this initial work the contractor is paid time and expenses using a capacity contract. For subsequent work to deliver the agreed project output at a target cost, client and contractor have joint decision-making responsibility for project decisions. They agree to share 'pain' or 'gain' as the project comes in above or below the target. This kind of 'pain-and-gain' sharing alliance contract, in effect, combines a contract to pay a fixed price for a specified output with an income-sharing contract. Instead of saying that client and contractor share decision-making and pain and gain around the target cost, you could say the client awards an output contract for a fixed price to an income-sharing 'joint venture' between client and contractor. This kind of approach is used in oil exploration and development, mining, complex building construction, regulated industries and government commerce. Recently we have seen that alliances are gradually extending their reach, sometimes under a different name, for example 'collaborative contracting' or 'integrated project delivery' to other countries and other industries beyond the UK and Australia.

Project Andrew

'Alliancing' first became popular after BP's highly successful use of the approach in the early 1990s to develop the Andrew oil field in the North Sea. For a start, circumstances were very favourable for the use of an alliance: the North Sea is a harsh environment, so developing its oil fields is expensive; oil prices were low at the time, and outside analysis showed the Andrew field was not economical. BP had an in-house team highly knowledgeable about oil platform design and costing, and they put the team to work on cutting the cost of design and construction for the oil field platform. The team made progress, but their cost estimate – £450 million – still fell short[24] and competitive pressures to induce contractors to offer low prices were unlikely to close the gap. BP needed contractors to come up with a radically different approach to design and construction.

Refusing to give up, BP looked around for any contractors willing to work on an oil platform project that would only go ahead if substantial improvements over current best practice could be achieved. Brown & Root was the first contractor to sign on, and they took responsibility for engineering design and project management. Once Brown & Root came in, a full team of contractors agreed to participate.

Together with BP, this expanded team came up with a revised cost estimate of £373 million. Yet the BP finance team was still skeptical of an adequate return on investment if BP had to carry the full risk of construction costs. Too many previous projects had come in over budget. To solve this problem, Brown & Root proposed that the contractors share pain and gain with BP and the other investors in the field. Eventually the contractors agreed to accept 54 per cent of the savings or overruns on the budget, with a cap on the downside for the contractors at £20 million.

Project Andrew was a resounding success. The project eventually came in £83 million below the £373 million target. This project was successful for a number of reasons: contractors had been involved early; through the pain-and-gain sharing, their interests were largely aligned with those of BP; members of the project team were all co-located in an office and they focused on talking problems out instead of dealing with them via negotiated contract changes and written agreements and they found a number of innovative solutions, such as doing a much higher percentage of construction onshore to limit expensive work in the North Sea.

Alliance collaboration problems and tactics to manage them

However, as we have previously stated, alliances are not perfect and setting sufficiently demanding target costs is their Achilles heel. Unlike Project Andrew, market conditions often do not ensure sufficient cost pressure. Even with pain-and-gain sharing, contractors have awkward conflicts of interest in determining the scope and target cost of the work. There are no competitive bids to execute the project work after its scope has been defined, so clients struggle to develop the information to win favourable terms for target costs.

Yet there are some tactics to mitigate these problems, most of them similar to tactics mentioned above, and an alliance approach does a particularly good job of aligning interests during the execution phase of the work. Figure 4.7 presents these tactics in full.

Awkward conflicts in determining scope and target costs

Alliance clients can start, as BP's did, by *doing more of the work with employees*. Your employees can build up a strong capability to scope and cost the work, and eventually can supervise the contractor. They can also *work with an additional advisor* to supplement this capability. This third party assessor[25] can help them develop an independent perspective on scope and costs and keep their alliance partners 'honest'. With the growing popularity of alliances, the supply of these assessors has grown.

Figure 4.7 Tactics used in project Alliances

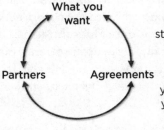

Build your own target-
setting/ cost-estimating
capability

What you want

Use 'professionalism'
as important partner
selection criterion

Use a capacity
contract when you
start working with the
contractor

Partners

Agreements

Work with an
additional advisor
to help specify the
project output and
favourable terms

Specify the results
you want even if not
yet precisely known
so as to later only
negotiate changes

Maintain credible
threat of working with
separate contractor
until costs agreed

Limit changes that
call for renegotiating
terms

Share pain/gain of
deviations from target
performance goals

Use open book
accounting

Clients can also *use 'professionalism' as a selection criterion.* Those with experience in alliances tend to become sophisticated in systematically evaluating and selecting contractors for their professionalism – and in particular for their track record of working in a collaborative, non-adversarial style for joint reward.[26] Selection on the basis of track record creates sanctions for contractors that follow their own interests at the expense of their clients and abuse their bargaining power. It helps align contractors' longer-term interests with those of clients.

Likewise, some clients can *promise a long-term relationship, subject to performance.* Large engineering and construction projects tend to be one of a kind for a client, so they can rarely offer the prospect of future work. But those clients that do have this possibility systematically use it to further align contractors' interests with theirs. They often set up 'Framework alliances', which are discussed in more detail in the textbox below.

Bargaining power and information problems in specifying favourable terms

While alliances presume that the client will work with the designing contractor to carry out the work, there is typically no formal obligation to do so until the target cost has been agreed. That enables the client to *maintain a credible threat of changing partners.* Such a threat, even if remote, restores some bargaining power to the client. With alliances the threat is more credible because once the contractor is selected, client and contractor move quite rapidly to define target costs for the execution of the work. This limits the wasted time and cost that would be involved in substituting the contractor if the client suddenly decided they were too far apart.

Alliances can define target costs rapidly because *pain-and-gain sharing* enables both sides to proceed despite lingering uncertainty around scope and cost. This limits the client's disadvantage from lacking the knowledge to propose a target cost at favourable terms.[27]

Prevent partner gaining bargaining power during project execution and align interests

Alliances shine in aligning clients and contractors after agreement on scope and target costs. Bargaining-power problems are minimal in the execution phase. Despite the lingering uncertainty, alliances *limit changes that justify renegotiating terms.* Alliance contracts are usually shorter and project specifications less precise than for a turnkey fixed-price contract. In setting the scope and target cost, client and contractor are taking risks.[28] Further detailing of or minor changes to project specifications are almost inevitable, and will affect costs. Such changes could cause serious problems with a turnkey fixed-price contract, since the contractor would exploit his leverage.

Alliances, by contrast, include upfront guidelines to limit renegotiation to substantial changes. Pain-and-gain sharing makes it easier for each side to accept these limits. And to make them stick, contracts incorporate the principle of 'no fault, no blame, no dispute' so that legal action by one party against another can be taken only for deliberate, damaging conduct. Contractors have a much smaller arena for renegotiating terms in their favour.

Sharing the pain and gain of minor adjustments to scope means that client and contractor have a mutual incentive to meet and beat cost targets – including an incentive to make minor changes that help reduce costs. This approach aligns interests much better than a time-and-expenses or a turn-key fixed-price contract. Time-and-expenses contractors see no benefit from cost savings, while fixed-price clients have no incentive to help the contractor keep costs down – by agreeing, say, to minor changes in scope or by rapidly taking decisions and providing information to expedite the work.

Use open book accounting

To make sure that pain and gain can be fairly calculated, contractors offer open book accounting for the project.[29] This openness itself further helps to reduce disputes.

Framework alliances

Alliancing has recently been extended to the management of a regular programme of major works. Most engineering and construction projects are 'one-offs' but some government agencies and most large utilities have a series of large works to manage.

Government authorities and regulated utilities frequently seek to push outsourcing to the limits and outsource a great deal of their business activities. Outsourcing enables them to introduce commercial skills and a degree of competitive pressure to their business activities. In this model they retain only a skeleton staff of their own and transfer day-to-day management to contractors with whom they set up long-term 'framework agreements' to run their business operations. These long-term agreements typically establish annual work programmes with targets for costs and other key performance indicators. Client and contractor then form an alliance to manage these works and share pain and gain around these annual targets.

As the UK water industry has shown, framework alliances can help meet the demands of both regulators and investors. The water industry regulator, OFWAT, focuses on driving continuous performance improvement. It uses current performance measures to set demanding future targets for water prices and other key indicators. It then sets target prices for each individual water company at levels that permit reasonable but not excessive profits subject to achieving stretch goals for these indicators.

A water company in turn tries to negotiate a set of prices and performance targets with OFWAT that are not too demanding. It then negotiates with its contractors to set their targets accordingly. Alliance contracts give contractors incentives to beat OFWAT targets, yet force them to share the risk if targets are not met.

Equity investors in regulated industries value this ability to transfer risk to contractors.

These investors aim to finance their companies with a high ratio of debt to equity, while maintaining a good credit rating to keep interest payments low. If they achieve these simultaneously, they can earn a good return on their equity investment with only a modest overall return on the assets employed in the company.[30]

To persuade banks or bondholders to finance a high level of debt at a low rate, they need to own companies with very stable long-term profits and cash flows. Companies in regulated utilities inherently meet these requirements, as their monopoly power gives them a secure market position and the market demand for the products is stable. But alliances meet these requirements even better, as contractors share more of the risk of volatility in construction costs. Contractors can even be asked to also share pain and gain on deviations from target levels of inventory, payables and receivables in the supply chain. Alliance incentives can thus be set to meet the specific performance demands of investors as well as regulators.

When you want help deciding what you want and then doing it: summary

When you want the same contractor to help you decide what to do and then go on to do it for you, you face problems in meeting many of the requirements for profitable collaboration. You face, all at once, problems with awkward conflicts of interests, problems in being able to set output goals, problems with preventing your partner gaining bargaining power, and problems in being sufficiently informed to specify favourable terms. Alliances, where client and contractor work jointly to develop project specifications and then share decision-making responsibility and cost risk, are an increasingly popular way to address all these problems.

Conclusions

We have looked at some of the most common and important problems faced in setting up to get what you want from contractors. If you are simply not ready to define what you want done, working with a capacity contract to pay for resources may give you enough flexibility to wait before defining the output. Without competitive bids, however, you will need to learn more about the process of producing what you want in order to get favourable terms. You will also need to set things up to avoid your contractor gaining too much bargaining power. Figures 4.2 and 4.3 are checklists of the tactics you can use to prevent your partner gaining bargaining power and to propose favourable terms.

If you need help in deciding what you want done, a capacity contract won't help. You must build a minimum set of skills to select a good contractor, to give your contractor sufficient direction, and to be able to assess the quality of what your contractor proposes you do. That sounds easy enough in theory but in practice can often be tricky. Figure 4.5 provides a checklist of the tactics for setting output goals for a supplier because you need help deciding what you want to get done.

It is particularly difficult to ensure your contractor does a good job in helping you decide what to do if the same contractor goes on to help you do it. To minimize the contractor's awkward conflict of interest, you need to work hard at setting up contractual mechanisms that align your contractor's interests with yours. The governance and income-sharing mechanisms of alliances are one way to do that. Figure 4.6 is a checklist of tactics you can use to avoid problems because your contractor faces an awkward conflict of interest.

Alliances are another example of the middle ground between performing work in-house and relying on the market for output. Companies that are willing to look beyond binary thinking, and consider creative ways to share responsibilities, can come up with collaboration strategies to overcome long-standing problems.

---

[1] There can be problems in meeting the other requirements for profitable collaboration when working with external partners, but our focus in this chapter is on what we have found to be the most common

and important problems. In the next chapter, Chapter 5, we address important but less common problems in working with monopoly suppliers who have too much bargaining power with a whole industry.

2 All of the tactics listed in Figure 4.2 are covered in this chapter except for the tactic point of insisting on good documentation. The idea is simply that if the information you need is in your fi les or in your computer and not in your partner's fi les or in your partner's head, then you are less dependent on your partner to get any work done that relies on having the information. We take the point up again in Chapter 6.

3 The difficulties of contracting when a supplier must make an investment in assets that are specific to its customer's business are very extensively discussed in the economic literature. The issue has been a particular focus in the work of Oliver E Williamson, see for example, *The Economic Institutions of Capitalism*, Chapter 2. The Free Press, 1986.

4 The case against the acquisition of Fisher Body being caused by negotiation difficulties due to business specific investments is convincingly made by Ronald Coase in 'The Acquisition of Fisher Body by General Motors', *The Journal of Law and Economics*, Volume 43, No. 1, (April 2000) pp. 15-31.

5 See Kentaro Nobeoka, Jeffrey H Dyer, and Anoop Madhok. 'The Influence of Customer Scope on Supplier Learning and Performance in the Japanese Automobile Industry'. *Journal of International Business Studies*, Vol. 33, No. 4 (4th Qtr., 2002), pp. 717-736. This article pursues an argument similar to that which we pursue in this section.

6 See, for example Benjamin Klein et al. 'Vertical Integration, Appropriable Rents and the Competitive Contracting Process'. *Journal of Law and Economics*, Vol. 21, 297-326 (1978), and Oliver E Williamson. *The Economic Institutions of Capitalism: Firms, Markets, Relational Contracting*. New York: Free Press, 1985.

7 We suggest there are comparatively few situations where it is so difficult to get around collaboration problems with external suppliers where vertical integration is the best alternative. However, collaboration problems are trickier in dealing with downstream business partners and there are some clear limitations to franchising as we discussed for Starbucks in Chapter 3.

8 Unless you have many employees acting relatively autonomously doing very similar jobs, as may be the case for example in a sales force.

9 If you will not be placing repeat orders for the same or a similar output, you will not so easily be able to ask for continuous improvement because you will have no historical benchmark to set targets. A different approach involving sharing pain and gain around a target – and as shown in Figure 4.3 – may then be a good way to motivate high performance. We discuss this option later in the chapter.

10 There are many articles describing the relationship between car manufacturers and their suppliers. We found the following practitioner-oriented articles highly useful and readable: Jeffrey K Liker and Thomas Y Choi. 'Building deep supplier relationships'. *Harvard Business Review*, December 2004; Horst-Henning Wolf. 'Making the Transition to Strategic Purchasing'. *MIT Sloan Management Review*, Summer 2005, Volume 46, Number 4. Also, covering a broader range of industries but essentially focusing on the same issue, Carlos Niezen, Wulf Weller and Heidi Deringer. 'Strategic Supply Management'. *MIT Sloan Management Review*, Winter 2007, Volume 48, Number 2.

11 'Nestlé reagiert auf die Kritik an Cailler'. ('Nestlé reacts to the criticism of Cailler') *Tagesanzeiger*, 3 July 2006 and Hugo Wyler Merki. 'Nestlé lanciert Cailler wieder neu; Produkte im Visier; Neue Cailler Anfang

2007; Pet-Verpackung bleibt' ('Nestlé relaunches Cailler; products in focus; new Cailler launch early in 2007'). *Berner Zeitung*, 20th October 2006.

[12] For tactics for dealing with misleading experiences, see Sydney Finkelstein, Andrew Campbell and Jo Whitehead. *Think Again: Why Good Leaders Make Bad Decisions and How to Keep it From Happening to You*. Harvard Business School Press, February 2009.

[13] 'Die neuen Frauen, Frauen ans Ruder'. ('The new women, women take the helm'). *Sonntagsblick*, 5th March 2006.

14 See, for example, Selina Mathis. 'Marketing professor Richard Kühn – 'Cailler-Verpackung ist nicht gut, ('Cailler packaging is not good'). *Berner Zeitung*, 1st July 2006.

[15] For an explanation of back-briefing and of how to set up an effective communication cascade down the company hierarchy, see Stephen Bungay, 'How to Make The Most of Your Company's Strategy'. *Harvard Business Review*, January–February 2011.

[16] Rosemary Feitelberg. 'Target product designer talks shop.' *Women's Wear Daily*, 21st March 2006. Not all of the value to Alessi and Target when working with big 'name' designers is in the quality of the designs; the recognition and image value of the designer's name is also important. However, other product designers, for example of children's toys, whose names are not well known to the public, are also often paid royalties on sales. See, for example, 'The One-Off fashions eco toys for Hape'. *Design Week*, 29th January 2009.

[17] See *Women's Wear Daily* article as above and Gary Pisano and Roberto Viganti. 'Which Kind Of Collaboration is Right For You?' *Harvard Business Review*, December 2008.

[18] On compensation in the film industry, see Paul A Baumgarten, Donald C Farber, and Mark Fleischer, *Producing, Financing and Distributing Film*. Limelight Editions, (Fifth edition 2004).

[19] Richard Korman with Tony Illia. 'The Shaw Group branches out. As his Stone & Webster deal pays off fast, James M. Bernhard Jr. wins a slew of contracts'. *Engineering News-Record*, 1st April 2002.

[20] See for example Charles Thomsen, 'Project Delivery Processes'. FAIA FCMAA 2006 <http://isites .harvard.edu/fs/docs/icb.topic1043613.files/72_Thomsen_Project%20Delivery%20Processes.pdf>. Downloaded 10th October 2012.

[21] Ian Swanson, 'Hard task of nailing down costs of building'. *Evening News – Scotland*, 30th June 2008.

[22] Russell Fallis, 'Scottish parliament beam drama: broken bolt blamed'. *Scottish Press Association*, 8th March 2006.

[23] Victoria Department of Treasury and Finance. 'In pursuit of additional value, a benchmarking study into Alliancing in the Australian public sector, an overview' <http://www.dtf.vic.gov.au/CA25713E0002EF43 /pages/alliance-contracting>. Downloaded 24th April 2013.

[24] For the full Project Andrew story see, for example, 'Risks well worth taking – BP oil field Alliance'. *The Engineer*, 27th June 1996.

[25] For example, in the UK, firms such as EC Harris or Davis Langdon.

[26] Contractors' hourly rates and overhead rates, including profit margins, are disclosed to the client and this may influence the decision. However, differences in hourly rates are typically modest and rates may be negotiated, so rates are usually not decisive in contractor selection.

[27] An alternative approach to avoid problems in setting scope and target costs might be to outsource the whole process (see tactics listed in Figure 4.3 for setting goals and constraints to measure performance). However, often outsourcing the entire process does not fit the client's business model. For example, the owner of an oil field facing difficulties in economically constructing an oil platform might decide to outsource responsibility for exploiting the oil field altogether and set up a contract to share income from the oil produced from the field. This would let the oil field owner avoid the problem of defining the specifications and target costs for the oil platform altogether. Government-owned oil companies wishing to exploit their reserves in some cases do just this, as we will discuss in Chapter 9. But for a multinational oil company, the ability to produce the oil in the oil fields they own is part of their core competence and it would not be part of the strategy to outsource to a single contractor the entire process of getting the oil out of the ground.

[28] There are some similarities and differences here to the situation of fashion retailers negotiating with garment manufacturers. When fashion retailers place an order for a quantity of a particular design, e.g. colour and size of jeans before the start of the season, they well know that in practice they will require a different mix of garments to meet demand. The critical difference between the fashion retailers and the client for a large engineering and construction project is that the fashion retailers continue to be in quite a strong bargaining position with garment contractors when they request contract changes: the garment contractors want fashion retailers' orders next season. Large engineering and construction projects are more typically one-off projects and there is no immediate follow-on order. It is expensive to change contractor mid-project and the client has no future business to offer the contractor as a bargaining card to ensure a good deal in negotiating the price of contract changes. This means that it is critical to choose the right contractor that ensures 'professionalism' and to set up intelligent governance mechanisms as part of the agreement to align interests. This is key to making early agreement on specifications and target cost a viable approach.

[29] A very helpful detailed description of how alliance contracts may be set up is provided in the *Project Alliancing Practitioner's Guide*. Department of Treasury and Finance, State of Victoria, Australia, 2006.

[30] Welsh Water carries this model to its logical conclusion. When originally acquired, the business was financed entirely with debt.

Chapter 5

Tactics for Managing Monopoly Platforms

In Chapter 4 we discussed the bargaining-power problem you face if your supplier acquires assets or know-how critical to your business, thus making it costly for you to substitute the supplier. Here we discuss a related problem: when there is too little competition to supply the industry as a whole – in which case the supplier is difficult for all participants to substitute.

Suppliers hold dominant market positions for many reasons. Some are of these are long-standing reasons. Many utilities in electricity, water and other public services are long-established monopolies. When privately owned, they are usually regulated so that they cannot abuse their market position. Sometimes, however, new contracts with a supplier may enable that supplier to establish a dominant position, and there is no guarantee that regulations will be put in place to prevent abuses.

IBM's contract with Microsoft to develop the operating system for its personal computer is a classic example of a contract that led to a supplier gaining long-term control of an important platform, and thus a very high share of industry profits. In 1981, IBM was hurrying to bring out its first personal computer and decided to speed things up by outsourcing its operating system development to Bill Gates at Microsoft. Instead of developing a new personal computer (PC) operating system for IBM, Gates simply bought another one and adapted it to meet IBM's needs. Gates then persuaded IBM to license that system from Microsoft instead of paying a flat fee for it, which had been IBM's original intention. Because the IBM PC achieved sales that exceeded expectations many times over, this licensing arrangement proved highly lucrative for Microsoft. Most importantly, Gates also persuaded IBM to let Microsoft license the operating system to other computer manufacturers. This particular operating system, called MS-DOS, became a computer industry standard for which Microsoft could charge high prices, and profits went largely to Microsoft because IBM and the other manufacturers had lost bargaining power. But IBM missed out in other ways too; Gates offered IBM the opportunity to buy a minority stake in his company but, for some unknown reason, IBM didn't take him up on the offer.[1]

Microsoft's use of a contract to control an industry platform is rare but not unique. The first steps towards establishing a monopoly may seem harmless enough to the companies later affected. In 1972, Bernie Ecclestone persuaded the Formula One racing teams to give him responsibility for transporting the racing cars to overseas Grand Prix locations. By taking this responsibility from the individual teams, Ecclestone was able to negotiate a package deal with a transportation company and substantially reduce costs. At the time the teams had very little money, so as payment they gave Ecclestone a small percentage of the racing prize fund.[2] This was Ecclestone's first move to becoming an exclusive supplier to Formula One racing. His second move was from transportation to managing the team's media rights for the races. As Formula One increased its popularity, Ecclestone profited handsomely because the service contract he set up gave his company exclusive control over media rights for over a hundred years.[3]

It's tempting to suppose that if you allow a supplier to set up a contract that gives them a monopoly, you have simply made a silly mistake. Surely Microsoft and Bernie Ecclestone should not have been able to secure such one-sided contracts? Yet PC operating systems and many services for sporting competitions such as Formula One are the natural homes for monopolies. A PC is much more valuable if many software applications can be run on it, and PC manufacturers that use such common operating systems, such as Windows, have had a substantial advantage over those with distinctive operating systems and few applications. Managing the Formula One media rights from a single source allows much better coordination and has done far more to promote the sport than the individual teams would have managed separately. If an industry platform has high value, it can be difficult to avoid a monopoly supplier.

These and other natural monopolies are quite widespread and play a major role in the economy. Traditionally, they arose from production and distribution economies in physical infrastructure. It is expensive to duplicate the network distribution investments, the pipes and cables, necessary to supply electricity, water or natural gas to homes and businesses. In the US, annual capital investment in utilities, for example, is expected to exceed $100 billion a year through 2020.[4] Similar problems abound in introducing competition to the transportation infrastructure for roads and railroads.

The most dynamic new area for natural monopoly is in intellectual property platforms. In addition to computer operating systems and media rights, many other types of platforms for communication and interaction are natural monopolies: think of Facebook for social networking, LinkedIn for business networking, Wikipedia for general knowledge, Google for general information, and even GS1 for data exchange between supermarkets and their suppliers.

Dealing with a monopoly supplier is never easy, and can often result in the supplier capturing most of the value despite the fact that you have jointly created that value by working together. There are, however, a variety of tactics that can be taken to mitigate the problem. These include government regulation or ownership, doing the work in-house, joint ownership of the platform by industry peers, and, for intellectual property platforms, relying on open source licensing. We will review the effectiveness of each of these tactics with a particular focus on newer approaches to managing monopolies in intellectual property platforms.

Government regulation or ownership

Monopolies based on scale economies in physical infrastructure are typically government regulated or sometimes, even in the most capitalist economies, government owned. For example, the Tennessee Valley Authority, one of the largest electric utilities in the US, is federally owned, so too is the United States Postal Service.

The regulation of natural monopolies based on physical infrastructure is comparatively simple because these monopolists usually supply products that are commodities or close to being such. There is limited debate, for example, about the goals that a water utility needs to meet.

It should reliably supply clean water.[5] Regulators work to ensure that a utility meets its goals on favourable terms for its customers, since market pressures will not force it to do so. Over time it has become clear that the traditional approach, to control the return on investment, does not ensure favourable terms. Limiting their return prevents utilities making excessive profit, but it does nothing to keep their costs or investments under control – in fact, rather the opposite. If you are limited in the rate of return – but the rate of return is sufficiently attractive – you will prefer to invest more and make your permitted rate of return on a higher investment. To get around this problem, utility regulators have in recent years adopted a new approach. They have started to set targets for the prices at which utilities can sell their products. In doing so, the regulators are in a similar position to the fashion retailers or automotive suppliers discussed in Chapter 4, who must place orders with their suppliers but cannot rely on competitive bidding.

To obtain favourable terms for customers, regulators need to become sufficiently expert in understanding the utilities' operations and know exactly what favourable terms are. This is relatively easy for a commodity such as electricity that is produced around the globe. Many benchmarks are available to assess prices, and, failing all else, the regulator can fall back on demanding some level of continuous productivity improvement from year to year. However, it is much harder to regulate something like an intellectual property platform. This involves far more than just directing and controlling monopolists to drive prices and costs down the experience curve, as these platforms are far from traditional commodities. The content of the platform, its scope and the requirements to interface with it are constantly evolving and shape competition in the industry, and governments are not well placed to take such highly complex decisions. You don't really want the government to decide on the next generation of Windows software or the construction rules for Formula One cars, and even if the government intervenes only to prevent abuse, remedies are likely to be slow and unreliable. Microsoft's decision to bundle a browser, the Internet Explorer, with its Windows operating system drew a lawsuit from Netscape, one of the largest and most successful early Internet companies. A court eventually ruled Microsoft's bundling illegal – but it was too late to save Netscape, which by then had lost its leadership position in the browser market. Government help is therefore best seen as your last resort in dealing with aggressive platforms.

Doing the work in-house

Alternatively, you could fight the development of a single supplier dominating the industry by owning the standard yourself. Apple has taken this approach, to date quite successfully, in mobile phones. The Apple iPhone has its own operating system exclusive to Apple hardware. Yet the same approach in personal computers was, for a long time, rather unsuccessful for Apple. If you want to go it alone against an emerging industry standard, you need to maintain a sufficiently high market share so that you achieve scale or network benefits. Apple's Macintosh computer failed to do that against Windows-based personal computers, and the company almost lost its independence before it moved into handheld devices.

It remains to be seen whether the iPhone will be able to maintain sufficient share to stay competitive against rivals, most of whom are using the Android operating system. Going it alone may prove in the end to be at odds with a realistic assessment of where you can effectively compete.

Joint ownership of the platform

If you don't want to go it alone, but still want an alternative to improve your bargaining power with suppliers, you can work with the other customers of your particular industry platform. A consortium of customers, all of whom have a strong interest in avoiding a monopolistic supplier, overcomes the scale problem in building a platform. Not only does the consortium ensure a sizeable share of customers adopt the platform, but it also brings the expertise and financial heft to invest in building a strong platform to begin with. For example, stock exchanges used to be owned by the banks and other financial services companies that trade shares on them. In the early 2000s, the main New York and London exchanges and others were IPOed. Independent investors took ownership of them, but banks agreed to the sale because they assumed the buying and selling of shares was becoming so global that no single exchange would have monopoly power. Soon after their IPOs, however, both the New York and London exchanges retained their strong national market positions and charged customers higher prices. In response, the banks launched a number of consortium joint ventures including BATS, Direct Edge, Chi-X and other alternative trading platforms. Building new electronic platforms, which had been difficult to construct at an earlier stage of technology development, had become relatively easy and the banks in the consortia offered a ready customer base. The move worked, as the new platforms gained substantial market shares and brought prices for trading services back down.[6] Banks prefer not to operate the platforms themselves, so they are spinning them off now that they have achieved their aim of establishing more competition. Should the market concentrate again and a monopoly supplier re-emerges, the banks can always establish new consortia.

If a market is a natural monopoly, a customer-owned alternative is a possible long-term option. Whether through a joint venture, cooperative or industry association, this approach can ensure that customers capture the value the business creates. Dairy cooperatives, for example, have featured prominently in processing farmers' milk and marketing dairy products. Dairy processing is scale intensive. As milk is a perishable product, traditionally it had to be processed quickly. Processing plants therefore were necessarily located close to the dairy farms, so it didn't make sense to have more than one processing facility in a local area. But this meant that farmers were dangerously dependent on a single processing facility owned by someone else. They would be better off if they came together to jointly-own the processing facility, even if their operation would be a bit less efficient. The economics of dairy processing has in many countries evolved, enabling much more competition among processors. Many cooperatives, such as Kerry Co-op in Ireland, have even become publicly traded companies. But, in 2011, four of the top 10 global dairy businesses – Fonterra, FrieslandCampina, Dairy Farmers of America, and Arla Foods – were still farmer-owned cooperatives, with dairy revenues over $10 billion.[7]

Some say that even with monopolistic suppliers, investing in a jointly-owned alternative platform will still not be attractive. Community-owned businesses, so the argument goes, simply aren't effective or efficient.

But these arguments mistake the goals of these kinds of platforms (see 'Measuring the performance of supplier- and customer-owned businesses').

Measuring the performance of supplier- and customer-owned businesses

The two most commonly used indicators of the performance of supplier- and customer-owned organizations, their profitability and their survival in community ownership, actually say little about their effectiveness, efficiency, or value to the suppliers or customers that own them.

Community-owned businesses don't need to make a profit to add value. A dairy cooperative, for example, can create value for farmers by making profits and paying out dividends or, alternatively, by paying farmers a higher price for their milk. If the cooperative pays higher milk prices, it may make little or no profit but still do a good job for farmers. Many customer-owned businesses are actually set up as non-profit organizations. They set their charges to cover their costs and give back any excess to members. Best Western, for example, with over 4000 hotels is the largest hotel chain in the world, and is incorporated as a non-profit in Arizona.

Survival in the customer-ownership form is also not a good measure of performance. No one would suggest that entrepreneur-owned businesses are ineffective and inefficient if they IPO; in fact quite the reverse. Similarly, the trading platforms BATS and Chi-X have been very successful regardless of whether they IPO and cease to be owned by their users.

What is more, community-owned organizations need not excel in order to be the best choice for members. All they need to do is enable members to capture a substantially higher share of the value created, after subtracting costs, than alternatives. That is not such a tough call when the alternative is a monopolist owned by a third party and demanding a high profit margin.

Supplier- and customer-owned businesses are certainly not a cure for all economic ills, but they tend to be judged by the wrong performance criteria, and hence are under-rated.

Many cooperatives or associations have done quite a good job in managing a natural monopoly platform. While Bernie Ecclestone has performed admirably in exploiting the media rights for Formula One, the racing teams receive only around half of the proceeds. In European soccer, by contrast, the media rights to the elite Champions League competition are controlled by the football association, UEFA, in which the clubs have a say.[9] The results were similar – UEFA has succeeded in giving the league worldwide prominence – but, as an industry association, it gives far more than half of the profits to the teams.

However, supplier- or customer-owned businesses are generally not good at innovation. For all their operational effectiveness, many of the jointly-owned platforms don't perform as well as organizations like UEFA in creating new value. In talking to managers in a range of customer-owned businesses, we heard that such businesses are usually quite cost efficient – customers don't like wasting money – but are seldom good at innovating or taking rapid decisions. This is for several reasons: members of the group that own the platform often want to compete with each other downstream; they take a long time to agree on what to do; and because their interests downstream differ, they often can come up with messy compromises in new product or process development, which, in the end, satisfy no one. In the early days of smartphones, Nokia tried to learn from IBM's difficulties with PCs. To avoid Microsoft Windows becoming the industry standard in smartphones, Nokia set up a consortium of handset manufacturers, Symbian, to develop operating systems. Symbian was highly successful for some years, but Nokia was not able to keep the consortium together, as taking account of each manufacturer's different requirements made it difficult to innovate. Nokia fell behind, initially to RIM's Blackberry and then to Apple's iPhone – both of which had in-house developed operating systems that were easier to control. Symbian failed, and ironically Nokia recently sold its handset business to Microsoft.

Cooperatives or consortium joint ventures can provide a solid platform in a relatively stable industry with a fairly simple product. So these are a good alternative to government regulation. But the slow pace of decision-making under collective governance puts these ownership forms at a disadvantage in developing new products.

Open source licensing

For intellectual property such as software, open source licensing is an intriguing further alternative to platforms controlled by a private company. Open source software is licensed to users for free not just to use themselves, but also to redistribute or further develop. (The textbox 'Open source, the many flavours of 'free'' explains the open source concept in more detail.)

Open source, the many flavours of 'free'

Software companies can offer products for 'free' while still restricting usage, further distribution or modification. At one extreme, software companies may offer their product free only for a limited test period, with no rights to distribute or modify it. The free distribution is simply a marketing ploy, and works to enhance, not to restrict, the owner's ability to capture value from the software. At the other extreme, software may be placed in the public domain with no restrictions on usage, further distribution or modification – effectively relinquishing ownership and giving everyone an equal chance of profiting from the asset. Between these extremes are approaches that provide varying degrees of freedom to licensees in their ability to use, modify and distribute the product, while restricting but not eliminating the owner's ability to profit.

'Open source' software means simply that the product is released with the source code and the binaries made available, so licensees can easily modify the product. Usually it carries a broader implication that the software is available without charge and users are free to modify the software as desired and then distribute either the original or the modified version under the same licensing terms as initially received.[10]

Open source licenses can be either copyleft or permissive. Under a copyleft license, if the software is modified, it can be redistributed under the same terms as originally received. Permissive licenses, in contrast, allow users to modify the software and then distribute this new version under a different license. This enables companies to incorporate open source software into proprietary software that can be sold. With a permissive license, the copyright owner has few advantages over licensees in exploiting the software. But under copyleft licenses, the copyright owner, in contrast to licensees, can charge for further developments of the software or require licensees looking to sell a modified version to purchase it under a different license.

Trademark provisions give owners some control over future development. Software products typically need refinement and go through a number of releases. When a software product is released open source, different licensees may further develop the product in a variety of directions. But the trademark owner can control which of these developments are entitled to use the software brand name. Other product developments, or 'forks', need to be distributed under a different name. When a product becomes an industry standard, it may be difficult for a fork to establish itself against the trademarked version because there will be concerns about connectivity.

Community-developed open source products

Organizations that license software on this basis cannot directly charge for and profit from their development work. In recent years, the main competitor to Microsoft's Windows in computer operating systems has been an open source development, Linux. While Linux has a tiny share of the market for PCs, it has a sizeable share, through the Android operating system, for smartphones and tablets and it has a large if not majority share in the market for server software.

Linux was originally developed by unpaid hackers who built on open source code initially developed by AT&T. Over time, however, major industry players such as IBM and Intel supported the work to make it robust and viable for commercial use. As hardware manufacturers, they were looking for alternatives to Windows that would give them bargaining power with Microsoft and other suppliers with particularly strong industry positions.[11] They were eager to help the hackers, often by directing certain employees to join the 'volunteer effort'. By helping out, they were also in a position to influence the software's development in ways that favoured their strengths. Open source software that has been developed with broad industry support shares much with a traditional cooperative company or consortium joint venture.

There is a tendency to suppose that community development of open source software requires no formal organization. But the most important open source communities are in fact highly organized, often by a foundation or other non-profit organization. This is further discussed below in the textbox 'Organizing open source communities'.

Organizing open source communities

Volunteer communities are often loosely organized, yet not necessarily chaotic. We can think of them as a looser form of cooperative or association. A member foundation or other kind of non-profit organization often governs the community, along with owning trademarks for products made available. Often a limited number of paid managers lead and direct the efforts of the volunteers.

Wikipedia has a management hierarchy not so dissimilar to a professional services partnership. Developing the online encyclopaedia requires comparatively little supervision. The risk of mistakes in an entry on, say, the Battle of Britain is small. Yet the organization has an elaborate system of supervision and control to ensure quality and build the scope of what is offered. Anyone can become an editor and edit Wikipedia pages, but Wikipedia Administrators, Bureaucrats and Stewards have special rights and duties over content, such as the ability to protect pages and block changes. All these contributors are ultimately responsible to trustees of the Wikimedia Foundation.

Approval to climb up the next step of the ladder in the Wikipedia hierarchy is a somewhat more consensus-driven process than in most professional services firms. With the exception of a quite small central staff, Wikipedia contributors are not paid by the foundation but are volunteers around the world offering their free time.

While there is no standard model, the more established, larger open source software projects tend to organize themselves quite a bit like Wikipedia. Apache, for example, is the leading software for web servers, the computers that store and then serve web pages.[12] The Apache Software Foundation owns the software and controls many other important open source projects. It has a hierarchy of participation from users, through Developers, Committers and Project Management Committee members all the way up to Members of the foundation. As at Wikipedia, Apache volunteers move up the hierarchy based on quality of contribution and a rather democratic process of gaining approval from peers.

Unlike Wikipedia, Apache is a commercially important product, so like Linux it draws heavily from customers in an indirect way. Many of its volunteers are sponsored by the larger customers of this platform, as some proprietary software needs to interact closely with web server software.

Open source initially raised high hopes for innovation as well as access. Yet community development suffers from the same challenges as any form of joint effort. How do you get agreement on which direction to take, and how do you get rapid decision-making? Many of the most notable open source software products actually emerged from proprietary products. For example, besides Linux, which emerged from AT&T's UNIX, the OpenOffice project came from the German company Star Division's attempt to compete with Microsoft Office. Open source software, when developed and controlled by communities of peers, is best suited for low-cost alternatives to a dominant proprietary software product in a large and well established market. It is less appropriate for rapidly growing markets with a high pace of innovation. For innovation, you likely need tighter control and ownership.

Open source development where one company takes charge

One way around these problems is to have a single for-profit company lead the development, but then release the final product as open source. But why would a company go to the trouble of developing a product and give it away for free? Consider Android, now the leading operating system for mobile phones. Google originally developed it and owns the trademark, but has released it under a permissive open source license. The company still makes money because Google search, maps, and e-mail services run easily on Android, enabling Google to sell more advertising. Google software works on iPhone as well, but because Apple controls the iPhone system, Apple can subtly encourage users to rely on alternative services.

Advertising revenues from global mobile users are so valuable that even a rather modest ability to shift the balance of usage to Google services can pay for a lot of operating system development work, and there are many other opportunities to make money on the Android. As Google's then CEO Eric Schmidt put it in 2010, 'You get a billion people doing something, there's lots of ways to make money. Absolutely, trust me.'[13]

Android has been a boon to mobile phone handset manufacturers, as they avoid sacrificing value to a monopoly supplier, but it may be the exception that proves the rule. Mobile phones are an enormous market offering intense user engagement – the perfect setting for advertising. Most open source platforms are too small to generate much in the way of side benefits to the developer.

Because of these difficulties of profiting from open source, companies tend not to release software on a fully open source basis. The software licence often comes with a catch. The free 'community' version may not be fully tested and suitable for heavy-duty commercial use[14] and you'll have to pay for the robust 'enterprise' edition. In certain cases these payments could extract sizeable fees, so an apparently open source platform could become something of a monopoly platform – at least until the customers fight back.[15]

Conclusions

Figure 5.1 below summarizes the tactics to prevent the emergence of a monopoly platform. Setting up collaboration to generate an alternative is likely to require radical solutions, especially for non-commodity platforms. You may need to backward integrate, team up with peers to establish the platform, or persuade an independent supplier to develop the platform and offer it to you under an open source license.

Each of these tactics can work well under certain circumstances, but all have their limitations. Choosing which tactic to adopt is not easy, and the stakes are high. If all players in the industry choose poorly and a monopolist controls the critical platform, the government may step in to limit the damage, but there is no guarantee that it will, and by the time it does, it may be too late for your company to recover.

Figure 5.1 Tactics when there is a lack of competition to serve market needs

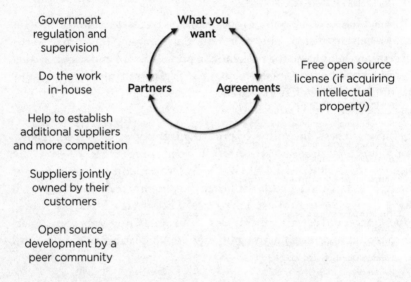

Government regulation and supervision

Do the work in-house

Help to establish additional suppliers and more competition

Suppliers jointly owned by their customers

Open source development by a peer community

What you want

Partners

Agreements

Free open source license (if acquiring intellectual property)

Joint ownership and open source licensing are complex solutions that require much more effort than a typical customer-supplier relationship. For joint ownership to work, customers need to reach consensus despite conflicting needs.

With community-developed open source software, customers should stand ready to help with development in informal ways. With open-source software from for-profit companies, by contrast, they need to leave the supplier enough rights to have an incentive to do a good development job, but not so many as to capture the lion's share of the industry's value.

---

[1] On the IBM/Microsoft story, see, for example, Paul Carroll, *Big Blues: The Unmaking of IBM*. New York: Crown Publishers, 1994 and Kathy Hornbach. 'Competing by Business Design – The Reshaping of the Computer Industry'. *Long Range Planning*, Vol. 29, No.5, pp. 616–628, 1996.

[2] Terry Lovell, *Bernie Ecclestone, King of Sport*, p. 59. London: John Blake Publishing Ltd, 2008.

[3] Elmar Brümmer, 'Das letzte Mysterium; Die Formel 1 stützt sich auf ein Concorde Agreement, um das regelmässig ein Machtkampf tobt'. ('The last mystery; Formula One depends on a Concorde Agreement

which is the subject of regular power struggles'). *Neue Zürcher Zeitung*, 18th October 2012. Ecclestone justified the extraordinarily long term of the contract on the grounds that he would have to invest heavily in television broadcasting. As it turned out, the technology and the TV market developed so much that he didn't have to make the investment after all.

[4] <http://www.booz.com/global/home/what-we-think/industry-perspectives/display/2013-utilities-industry-perspective?pg-all>. Downloaded 4th June 2013.

[5] There is of course substantial debate about the constraints to which utilities should be subject in achieving their goals. Is a water utility allowed to build a dam? Is an electric utility allowed to build a nuclear power plant? This debate about the constraints under which utilities should operate clearly has a strong political dimension to it as well as involving economic considerations.

[6] See, for example, Jeremy Grant, 'LSE to cut fees to regain market share'. *Financial Times*, 2nd July 2009.

[7] Rabobank International. *Global Dairy Top 20* <http://rabobank-food-agribusiness-research.pressdoc.com/32960-rabobank-global-dairy-top-20>. Downloaded 4th June 2013.

[8] <http://www.bestwestern.com/newsroom/factsheet_detail.asp?FactID=7>. Downloaded 22nd August 2011.

[9] The actual percentages vary somewhat from year to year both for Formula One and the Champions League. For Formula One, see for example, Elmar Brümmer, 'Das letzte Mysterium; Die Formel 1 stützt sich auf ein Concorde Agreement, um das regelmässig ein Machtkampf tobt'. ('The last mystery; Formula One depends on a Concorde Agreement which is the subject of regular power struggles'). *Neue Zürcher Zeitung*, 18th October 2012. For Champions League, see, for example, <http://sportsillustrated.cnn.com/2009/soccer/wires/08/21/2050.ap.soc.champs.league.revenue.1st.ld.writethru.0670/index.html>. Downloaded 8th September 2009.

[10] The Open Source Initiative, a non-profit corporation which is the recognized body for approving licences as Open Source Definition conformant, provides a more precise definition of open source. Although this definition is widely used, the term 'open source' is, in practice, commonly used with many slightly different meanings.

[11] At the time, this was particularly true with Sun Microsystems' Solaris version of Unix software for workstations and server computers.

[12] <http://www.webopedia.com/TERM/W/Web_server.html>. Downloaded 1st September 2009.

[13] Holman W Jenkins, 'The Weekend Interview with Eric Schmidt: Google and the Search for the Future', *Wall Street Journal*, 14th August 2010.

[14] The community edition of the software from a number of open source software companies was described to us as 'Crippleware'.

[15] This is generally easy enough to spot, so you know what you are getting into, but sometimes you need to read the fine print and understand the legal ramifications. Sun Microsystems, before being acquired in 2010 by Oracle, had committed heavily to open source software. They had open-sourced much of their Java software, but not quite all aspects of it. Google used Java in developing their Android software and was sued by Oracle for around $1 billion over the usage rights for Java in Android. Google won the initial court judgement but the case has been on appeal. See Ben Worthen, 'Judge Rules Google's Use Of Code Wasn't a Violation'. *Wall Street Journal*, 1st June 2012.

Chapter 6

Tactics for Collaboration with Employees

Having focused on suppliers and other external partners in the last two chapters, we now consider problems in working with employees. The same 10 requirements for success apply equally well here. But one simple difference between employees and external suppliers means that you face quite different concerns in developing a strategy to meet the requirements. In contrast to external suppliers, employees only provide you with their own labour; they may not provide business assets for use in your business.[1] Furthermore, employees have a contract with you to do a job of work and they cannot subcontract some of that work to other people – at least, not in such a way that they make a profit for themselves. If an employee financially benefits by subcontracting work, he or she has committed a criminal offense! This difference has far reaching implications for setting up collaboration.[2] Producing a substantial output, such as a house or a car, requires a team of people and some assets, not just the labour of one employee. You have to lay out the goals and constraints at a more granular level with employees than you do with suppliers. You must decide what you want each employee to do and how the work of all your employees will be integrated to produce what you want. You also have to make the investment in any assets needed to support employees' work.

Measuring employee performance is also more demanding. The measurable outputs of non-routine project work – a new product design, a consulting report – are usually produced over some time by a number of employees. It is difficult to measure the contribution of individual employees to the overall result. That makes it harder to appropriately motivate them by paying them for results. By offering powerful incentive rewards based on poor performance measures, you risk creating awkward conflicts of interest.

It may be harder to specify in advance the results you want from employees, or to devise a contract that pays them for results. But fortunately, in the absence of a robust contract to get what you want, employees face fewer conflicts of interest in helping you decide what to do, and they are less likely to gain bargaining power. Because employees may provide you only with their own labour, they have fewer external business interests – which means fewer interests that may awkwardly conflict with yours.[3] An employee helping you with the design of an IT system cannot directly benefit by over-engineering the scope of the design and therefore charging you more for a larger team to do the work, as a supplier can. Similarly, because employees do not control access to other critical resources that you may need in your business – for example, production equipment or other people – there are fewer ways for them to become difficult to substitute and gain bargaining power with you.[4]

Practically, this means you need be less concerned about agreeing upfront to what you want done before you take on employees. To meet the requirements in the framework, you can set goals and constraints and measure performance as the work proceeds. But in working with specialist employees carrying out non-routine tasks, setting goals and constraints and measuring performance as the work proceeds is tricky. Sometimes you find yourself squeezed between a rock and a hard place – unable either to do a good job of directing and controlling the work or to define the results you want in advance and pay to get them.

In this chapter, we look first at the types of jobs that will put you in a squeeze. We then take a detailed example to examine the different problems when setting up collaboration with employees and the tactics to solve them. As the squeeze is tight indeed with investment banking dealmakers and traders, we will address this at some length. Using this example lets us consider a broad set of problems and tactics to solve them. The same problems are present in other industries and types of jobs, just not in such sharp form. From there we can look at some different but equally difficult types of work to manage: R&D employees in Chapter 7, and CEOs and business general managers in Chapter 8.

Problems in directing and controlling employees

Managing employees in non-routine tasks is particularly difficult when you lack specialist know-how or, in a fast moving business, you lack time. You may struggle to provide sufficiently detailed goals for output and productivity (directing the work) or, when you can set adequate goals, you may have difficulty measuring performance against them (controlling it). These two dimensions generate a simple matrix, Figure 6.1, against which we can map a variety of jobs.

Figure 6.1 Different problems with different types of jobs

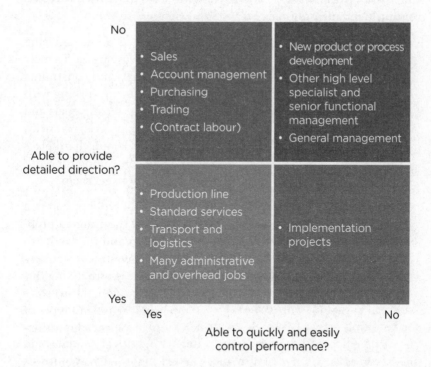

The bottom left quadrant covers the many production, service, transport and logistics jobs, particularly those strongly supported by machinery, where it is still practicable to provide detailed direction – set tight output and productivity goals – and to measure performance against these goals. With little variation in individual performance – perhaps an assembly line controls the pace – there are relatively few problems in setting up agreements to direct and control the work.[5]

There are also many administrative jobs in support processes, such as accounting or production planning, where you may not be able to precisely define the output you want, but you can clearly define the work itself – what you want an employee to do over a period – and measure if it has been done. Productivity differences should be modest, as you are unlikely to keep staff that can't complete these tasks.

A job's skill level is not what makes direction and control easy. A complex mission-critical job, such as piloting a jetliner, will still fit in the bottom left quadrant, because the desired result is straightforward to specify and measure against.

Problems in providing direction

The further away the job description gets from being driven by supporting machinery, the greater difficulties in setting tight output and productivity goals. A research chemist's work, for example, requires a good deal of experimentation and judgement, so her boss cannot tell her in detail the tasks to perform or the pace for performing them. But without detailed instructions, how can a boss then assess the employee's work? Companies can overcome this shortfall in direction by more broadly fostering employees' general motivation to do what the company wants.

Salary raises and promotions?

If the performance of a certain type of employee usually increases over time in a fairly predictable way, companies can simply raise these employees' annual salaries when they achieve higher performance. Different pay bands within the same basic job description are common for technical specialists such as chemists. With more experience, a chemist predictably becomes more productive in her job. At some point she becomes a senior chemist and receives higher pay accordingly. Promotions likewise reward superior performance by granting not just pay raises but also higher status and more power in the organization, and often more interesting work.

But there are many circumstances in which neither salary bands nor promotions align rewards with performance. Salary bands work well only when performance differences are modest and performance climbs slowly and steadily. If employees vary a great deal in performance, and some either improve quickly or actually get worse, then the bands will create more trouble than they're worth.

Promotions are most helpful when there are plentiful opportunities, as in a young and rapidly growing firm, and when job performance serves as a good basis for evaluation. Most companies do not have enough new spots to offer every strong performer. In the case of a sales manager supervising 15 sales people, the latter may differ widely in performance, yet the company has few openings at the manager level for the stars. And, in the case of sales or technical specialties, performance in the current job may not indicate one's potential as a manager. As for the top of the organization, the CEO cannot go any further up.

Problems in controlling performance

The performance of non-routine tasks can be hard to measure for several reasons. Much of the work involves projects, which can take a while to carry out and where the results may not appear for even longer. You may be able to define the desired output and productivity goals[6] – specify what you want done, how long it should take and what it should cost – but long timetables make it difficult to measure and control performance progress.

Staffing enough able people with enough of their time?

With non-routine tasks, you may not know until well into the project whether you have enough able people involved. If you can measure performance and it is satisfactory, then you know you have staffed to have the ability you need. But if you can't measure performance, it can be much more difficult to tell if you have the people you need. Staffing in-house project teams is a major problem – sometimes, as we discuss in Chapter 7 for product development, this is because the output is intrinsically difficult to measure. More often, companies staff teams poorly because they're in a hurry to get started with the project, most of the qualified people are elsewhere engaged, and nobody 'pulls teeth' to reallocate resources.[7]

Companies also get into trouble because they focus on securing resources for a small full-time project team and expect vital contributions from other employees to come out of what some organizations call 'magic time'. In projects to implement a new business process, the employees learning the new process often must keep up their regular workload as well. If the organization does not recognize or reward this extra effort, stressed and frustrated employees may refuse to cooperate.[8] You must make an effort to recognize and, in some way, reward the extra effort needed instead of assuming employees will just conjure up whatever time you need.

Defining early indicators of performance?

Lengthy projects benefit from early indicators of performance. Projects with clear milestones every two to three months demonstrably have a much better chance of meeting expectations than those with fewer or less well-defined progress points.[9] Frequent milestones step up the pressure on performance and can enable a company to correct problems earlier.

Harnessing employees' self-motivation?

A solid start is critical to project success, and it includes harnessing employees' self-motivation to do a good job.[10] For that to happen, employees must be clear about the project goals and their contribution and understand why the project will create value. Communicating both goals and constraints is a priority. Top management must be seen to be committed to the effort. Where team members have not worked together before, projects need strong leaders and early team-building events to develop personal bonds and loyalties.

Problems in both directing and controlling the work

You face the toughest challenge in setting up to work with employees when it is difficult to set output and productivity goals and constraints, and measuring performance is slow and hard. This is the situation, for example, when working with new product or process developers, marketing managers, strategy and planning managers, CEOs and other business general managers.[11] Here you encounter all the problems described above, and the combination compounds the difficulties in finding solutions.

Selecting top managers with the necessary specialist expertise?

When you can't easily set goals or measure performance, it is critical to have specialist expertise in the areas involved. A good general manager without the specialist qualifications to manage critical business activities may be at a loss, as we saw in the ERP example in Chapter 2. Companies do tend to insist that middle managers have strong functional qualifications, yet they often take on CEOs and board members lacking in deep experience in the most critical functions – and sometimes without industry expertise altogether. We explore the importance of specialist qualifications for CEOs further in Chapters 7 and 8.

Communicating strategic intent?

Another approach is to rely even more on employees' self-motivation by giving them a much stronger sense of purpose. When you can't set clear goals for the output you want from the work, you will need to communicate in more sophisticated ways. You must learn to clearly convey your strategic intent, while refraining from going into the details of the work.

If employees understand your high-level goals, they can think through for themselves what these mean in order to achieve what they need to do to help you achieve them. They can follow through despite limited instructions from you about what actions to take and also changing circumstances over time. But managers faced with the problem tend to do the opposite – they set many detailed goals. This leaves employees unable to meet conflicting demands on their time and confused about what really matters.[12]

Discretionary bonuses?

The sense of confusion is most often seen when bonus systems are put in place. For jobs in which employee performance varies widely but is hard to measure objectively in the short term, offering a substantial discretionary bonus can motivate employees to work productively. But managers are quite uncomfortable with retaining substantial discretion in setting bonuses. The more discretion used, the more adversarial their bonus discussions with employees, who suspect unfair treatment, will be. So managers tend to compensate with 'goal overload'. They set many different detailed goals in advance in a 'balanced scorecard' or similar process, and even give each goal a weight in order to reduce their own discretion. In this manner a discretionary bonus scheme quickly becomes a sophisticated control system – exactly the wrong way to motivate employees whose work cannot be directed or controlled.

Highly-qualified specialists and middle managers are most likely to suffer from this goal overload. They tend to receive modest bonuses based on complex plans in a zero-sum game – with bonus pools set at a fixed percentage of salaries regardless of actual value produced by the employees. Each employee has a target bonus, with a forced distribution of bonus percentages forming a bell curve around the target percentage.

As we see it, this sort of discretionary bonus motivates employees – if at all – largely by indicating where they stand in the company performance pecking order and their prospects for promotion or dismissal. Differences in discretionary bonuses among middle managers usually make only a modest difference to their overall compensation, perhaps 10 to 15 per cent. But the bonus discussion does prompt the boss to tell employees what they have done well and how they can improve. The income at stake helps to ensure the whole process is taken seriously. Bonuses can thereby motivate their performance in a general way in the absence of effective direction – if they don't undermine performance by sapping employees' self-motivation.

Long-term performance rewards?
If you can't measure short-term performance, offering longer term rewards may help get around the problem. But there is a catch here too. For long-term performance rewards to motivate, their value to employees should be contractually secured. And even over the longer term, you may find it difficult to measure performance well enough to set up a robust contract.

To compete with more focused smaller companies offering stock options, one large diversified high tech company we worked with offered substantial long-term rewards based on a set of internal performance metrics designed to simulate the market value of a number of small high-growth business units. But the company continued to have difficulties in hiring development engineers against these smaller rivals. 'Candidates don't trust our discretionary rewards. They largely discount them in evaluating the company's hiring offer', a senior HR manager told us. The next chapter goes into greater depth on this timing problem and its solutions.

Enhance the 'direct and control' model or move away from it?

Figure 6.2 summarizes the key problems in directing and controlling employees' work and basic approaches to solve these problems.[13] The approaches reflect two quite different broad strategies.

Figure 6.2 Key issues/possible approaches to solve problems

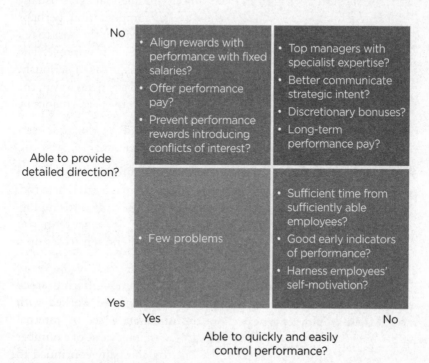

No

- Align rewards with performance with fixed salaries?
- Offer performance pay?
- Prevent performance rewards introducing conflicts of interest?

- Top managers with specialist expertise?
- Better communicate strategic intent?
- Discretionary bonuses?
- Long-term performance pay?

Able to provide detailed direction?

- Few problems

- Sufficient time from sufficiently able employees?
- Good early indicators of performance?
- Harness employees' self-motivation?

Yes

Yes

No

Able to quickly and easily control performance?

When it is hard to direct and control employees' work, one collaboration strategy is simply to adopt tactics that make it easier. We've just described a number of such tactics. When you can't specify the output you want from employees' work in sufficient detail, you become expert in communicating your strategic intent. When you can't establish objective measures of performance, you hire managers with a deep subject matter expertise who can form a well-founded subjective judgement. When it is hard and slow to measure actual performance, you develop early indicators of performance. When it will be a long time before employees can get satisfaction from achieving goals, you reinforce communication and team building to enhance employees' sense of purpose and ensure they share your aspiration to achieve company goals. And you complement all this by adjusting employees' pay rates and offering them interesting assignments. You do all of this to ensure a long-term match between employees' performance rewards and performance, sufficient to prevent them being tempted away by substantially better offers from rivals.

But, when these problems are acute, you may prefer to try a quite different strategy – one that removes the need to provide detailed direction and control in the first place. Instead you pay employees according to results tied directly to the business income they help to create, either revenue or profits. In effect you treat them a bit like external suppliers – you give them substantial autonomy and pay them according to hard results for the business, not for working as directed. Yet you still exercise some general direction and control over them, and still bear the entrepreneurial risks.

Performance-based pay

When performance varies substantially – which makes it hard to specify detailed productivity goals – but is quickly and easily measured, performance-based pay tends to account for a large part of total compensation. There are many jobs in sales, account management, trading and other functions where you can't precisely specify either what you want done or what income you expect it to generate for the business. But the business income these employees generate is readily measurable.[14]

Unfortunately, performance pay can also introduce awkward conflicts of interest between the company and its employees. Performance is often harder to measure than it looks. Employees may be tempted to manipulate an otherwise reliable early indicator of performance if their pay depends on it. In jobs where employees may destroy value from over-aggressive performance, performance incentives can induce them to take too much risk, cut corners or, in extreme cases, break the law. Companies need to either arrange for them to share in these losses or set constraints to prevent them.

Individual performance incentives, particularly in sales or account management, can also discourage employees from teaming up together to serve clients effectively. Here companies will need additional arrangements to promote cooperation.

Figure 6.3 offers a simple set of criteria to help think through whether performance pay will help to get around problems in aligning rewards with performance. We look at these issues in more detail below using investment banking as an example.

Figure 6.3 When is performance pay helpful?

Possible and worthwhile to pay for results instead of time spent?
- Hard to set precise goals for employee productivity?
- Employee performance (output or income created) is easily measurable?
- Wide spreads in performance between employees?

Salary bands not a better way to differentiate rewards?
- Relative performance of different employees not predictable?

Promotion not a better way to differentiate rewards?
- Few opportunities to reward superior performance with promotion?
- Good performance not a good indicator of suitability for promotion?

Performance pay does not set up awkward conflicts of interest?
- Employees' actions will not destroy value?
- Early indicators of performance cannot be manipulated to gain rewards?
- Able to set/enforce constraints to prevent employees destroying value?
- Incentives will not prevent 'teaming-up' where desirable?

Often, to make the approach of paying for results work, you need to change far more than simply the compensation structure. You may need to hire additional employees to set up and administer controls that prevent employees taking excessive risk to achieve performance rewards. You may need to create smaller performance units within the organization to be able to measure results within any given employee's control. To be able to get an objective performance measure as a basis for setting rewards, you may even need to outsource the work, or sell the asset or division in question to measure how much the work has increased its value.

Which solution you should choose – whether to adopt tactics for better direction and control, or whether to offer employees autonomy and pay for results – depends on both the type of activity you manage and your own personal abilities. The more specialist know-how you have, the better you will be able to employ tactics to direct and control the work.

The rest of this chapter – as well as the next two chapters in the book – look at situations where it is particularly difficult to direct and control the work, and the search for a collaboration design may take you a long way from working with employees in a conventional corporate hierarchy. We start by considering investment banking. It is a controversial example, but it is a good one to look at most of the problems involved in adopting a strategy of paying for results and describe tactics to solve them.

The challenge of investment banking

Many investment bankers are revenue-generating dealmakers and traders. They generate income for the bank by selling advice on mergers and acquisitions, underwriting new equity issues, or trading stocks, bonds and other financial instruments. Giving advice requires deep specialist knowledge of the subject matter, while successful trading requires acting with both knowledge and speed.

So, investment banks expect their revenue generators to work with considerable autonomy. In most cases, it is easy to quantify, fairly quickly, the value that revenue-generating investment bankers help to create by their work, as the profit or loss on the advice, deal or trade is soon measurable. And there are wide variations in these bankers' performance.

As expected, much of investment bankers' pay is closely tied to individual performance. The spreads in performance are too wide and hard to predict for pay bands to motivate. There are not enough promotion opportunities for this carrot to work either. And the best traders and dealmakers may also not make the best managers.

The danger with performance pay is that you swap a situation where employees have too little interest in doing what you want, for one where employees have a considerable interest in doing what you don't want. This may happen if the rewards are not in practice aligned with employees' individual performance, or not perceived to be so.

Problems in measuring individual performance

If generating business income for the bank is the basis for bankers' performance pay, the first problem you encounter is that it is not so easy to measure the income that *individual* bankers generate. These bankers often work in teams. You know how much revenue and perhaps even how much profit an M&A advisory assignment brought in, but you may not know which bankers contributed how much to landing the client and executing the work. Figure 6.4 shows tactics for solving problems in measuring individual performance.

Figure 6.4 Tactics to solve problems in measuring individual performance

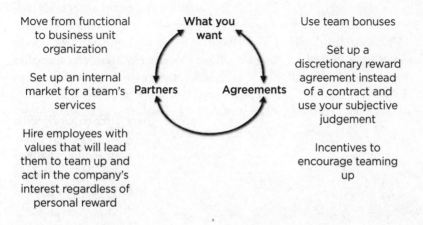

Move from functional to business unit organization

Set up an internal market for a team's services

Hire employees with values that will lead them to team up and act in the company's interest regardless of personal reward

What you want

Partners

Agreements

Use team bonuses

Set up a discretionary reward agreement instead of a contract and use your subjective judgement

Incentives to encourage teaming up

If bankers regularly work in the same small team, you can perhaps solve the problems by offering a team instead of an individual bonus. But, in practice, bankers often flexibly come together in different teams to work on different deals.

If you can't use team bonuses or satisfactorily solve the problem of how to allocate the bonus from deals to individual bankers, bonuses may be divisive and de-motivating. If bankers can't be sure they will receive a good share of the bonus, they may avoid teaming up to serve clients and go it alone to pursue deals. They may do this even if teaming up would increase the bank's chances of winning deals.

Banks use a number of tactics for dealing with problems in measuring personal performance. One approach is to get away from the bonus culture and rely more on the values and self-motivation of employees. In executive search, another industry that relies on powerful individual incentives to motivate, one major player has successfully broken ranks to do this (see the textbox 'Headhunters with values' below). But few banks take this approach. One that does, and advertises the fact, is Jyske Bank, the second largest bank in Denmark, but they are focused on retail banking.[15] In their small Swiss private banking business, Jyske has introduced bonuses on the order of 50 to 100 per cent of base salary.[16] And even private banking is a long-term relationship business. In investment banking, which focuses on deal-making more than relationships, powerful bonuses are generally accepted as a necessary tool to reward and motivate good performance.

Headhunters with values

Carefully selecting employees with values that closely fit your business needs may give you helpful flexibility in the way you set up collaboration. Egon Zehnder, a highly successful global executive search firm, has benefited from a strong focus on hiring consultants with a personality profile that makes them self-motivated to do what creates value for the firm. As one Zehnder partner put it to us, 'we are looking to hire people whose natural behaviour is to pull their weight for the team'. In contrast, the conventional approach to motivation in executive search is based on offering strong financial incentives for personally generating revenue from clients. Although this approach motivates sales powerfully, its disadvantage is that it tends to prevent effective collaboration between the partners of executive search firms. You 'eat only what you kill,' so you keep your clients and your knowledge of the candidate pool to yourself. However, Egon Zehnder lets all partners share in a single profit pool regardless of location and individual client performance. This sharing approach runs the risk of partners not working as hard as they could, but instead 'free riding' on the contributions of others. To get around this problem, Egon Zehnder's recruiting process and partner promotion processes specifically test for a particular type of personal motivation. Typically a prospective consultant is screened by dozens of Zehnder partners. Three of the four screening criteria are related to motivation and personality: building working relationships; getting things done; and personal fit – including having the qualities of a friend, colleague and partner as well as honesty and integrity. To avoid hiring consultants more aligned to other values, Egon Zehnder, uniquely, never hires from other executive search firms.[17]

Using discretion in assessing performance

The most common solution to address problems in measuring performance is for the manager of a team of investment bankers to use her subjective judgement to assess individual contributions to results. To make such evaluations efficiently, she must have the necessary information and expertise.

Banks usually make final assessments and decide on bonus allocations around Christmas time. But teams aren't stable – over the course of the year, employees may come together flexibly forming different teams to do different deals. The sums of money at stake don't make the task any easier. Before the financial crisis, the overall bonus pot in good years was typically half of the bank's net income before bonuses and taxes.

Even when the results are good, these discretionary allocations are time-consuming and potentially quite divisive. Senior managers from all parts of the bank discuss which parts of the bank and which individual bankers deserve how much of the bonus pot. In some cases, quite a large group of senior managers may spend a quarter to a third of their time for six to eight weeks deciding discretionary allocations. Any senior management team, even one that devotes a lot of time and prepares well, finds it hard to achieve consensus on this issue and this must be a consideration before you decide to use discretionary allocations.

Setting up a business unit organization or internal markets

Another approach involves organizational restructuring. You can give your business units greater independence and accountability. Or you can establish internal transfer prices to measure the value that one unit creates for others.

These tactics can work in various ways for an investment bank. You can eliminate the role of the broad-based client relationship manager responsible for talking to a client about a wide range of products. Instead, product specialists in M&A, loans, foreign exchange, etc. can be fully responsible for acquisition of any business in their product area. If they need help from other kinds of specialists, they must pay for it. At the end of the year, each specialist is fully responsible for the profit or loss in their area.

You can also let bankers that need to work together negotiate directly with each other over the bonus share from deals they all work on. On a cross border M&A deal for example, the US team might agree in advance to split the credit 50/50 with the UK team.

But there are downsides to these tactics. If there are potential advantages to a broadly based customer relationship, it is a pity to sacrifice them merely to better assess individual performance. And letting bankers negotiate directly for their share sets up a difficult negotiation between employees who are often at different levels in the bank hierarchy.

Setting up incentives to encourage 'teaming up'

To overcome resistance to teaming up because of concerns about bonus allocation, banks – or other organizations managing client relationships such as consulting companies – may want to create specific incentives. For example, they can explicitly allocate more bonus in relation to income to deals on which bankers team up successfully than to those where a single banker brings the business in alone. The Boston Consulting Group, where both authors used to work, has rewarded partners for teaming up in this way.

Problems in quickly measuring performance

In recent decades, investment banks have shifted their mix of business further from M&A and other advisory work to more deal-oriented endeavours such as trading and market-making in sophisticated financial instruments. It has therefore become harder for banks to rapidly measure the net income from what bankers do. M&A and advisory work involves only limited risk, while the risks from this market-making are substantial. The bank must acquire risky assets, and it can't measure the profitability of the deal until it definitively sells them – which can take months or longer. Banks often need to decide on someone's bonus allocations while many of the assets she acquired are still on the books. Figure 6.5 shows tactics for solving problems in quickly measuring performance.

Figure 6.5 Tactics to solve problems in quickly measuring performance

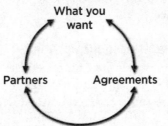

Develop early indicators of
performance

Sell assets/hedge, insure or
guarantee their values

Independent cadre of
managers to develop
and manage early
indicators

**What you
want**

Base rewards on
early indicators

Make partners wait
to receive rewards
until performance
can be measured

External partners to **Partners**
buy, hedge, insure, or
guarantee assets

Agreements

Involving independent partners to develop and manage early indicators of performance

If you can't easily measure performance in a sufficiently timely fashion to be able to control the work, you can develop and use early indicators of performance.

But relying on these early indicators of performance as a basis for setting performance rewards is dangerous. Managers whose performance is being assessed can manipulate early indicators to make their performance look better than it is. As a minimum precaution to avoid this problem, early indicators should be developed and managed by employees independent of those being assessed.

Investment banks often rely here on risk managers, who report through a chain of command separate from dealmakers, to assess the bank's risks from deals. The allowances they make for each deal amount to an early indicator of the deal's likelihood of success. If the bank's risk managers do a good job of evaluating risks, the bank can use these allowances to make timely bonus payments while risky assets are yet unsold.

Banks have invested considerable amounts of money in building up a separate cadre of highly-qualified risk managers with sophisticated systems. But it is still difficult to ensure that risk assessments are sufficiently independent of the dealmakers. Dealmakers are also the most powerful cadre in the bank because they bring in the income. Despite risk managers nominal independence and control of risk acceptance, dealmakers, because of their power, may in practice be able to influence decisions concerning risk assessment. And this very separation can raise problems of its own: dealmakers may have information suggesting a deal is too risky but not communicate it to the risk management group.

Making partners wait or insuring risks

Banks have started to use other, more reliable tactics: making your partner wait longer to be paid, and measuring business performance faster. Dealmakers are waiting longer for their bonuses, with the payout conditional on bank or business unit performance during the deferral period. And banks are also speeding up the process of selling the risky assets they take on in the process of doing deals. Even before the sale, they are protecting themselves by hedging or insuring against the risks involved in holding these assets. By transferring the risks to third parties they can sooner measure their own net business performance.

With a combination of measures, banks can do a good job of measuring their bankers' performance on the deals in question. The assets that investment banks take on, after all, rarely stay on their books for very long.[18]

Problems in aligning rewards with performance as measured

The biggest problem you face in setting up good income-sharing agreements in an investment bank is not that you can't measure performance. It is that you can't make the bankers share enough of the downside risk – in a highly risky business – to sufficiently align their rewards on the downside with their performance. There are direct and indirect approaches to solve the problem. These are shown in Figure 6.6 below.

Figure 6.6 Tactics to solve problems in aligning rewards with performance as measured

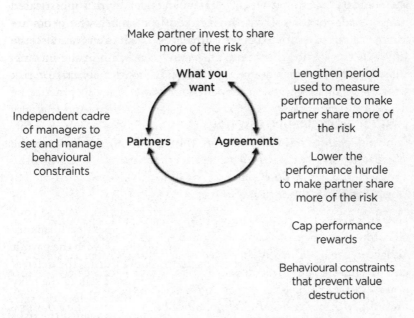

Make partner invest to share more of the risk

What you want

Lengthen period used to measure performance to make partner share more of the risk

Independent cadre of managers to set and manage behavioural constraints

Partners   Agreements

Lower the performance hurdle to make partner share more of the risk

Cap performance rewards

Behavioural constraints that prevent value destruction

Making employees share more of the risk

The direct way to reduce this misalignment is to make the bankers share some of the downside risk. Bankers can do this if they invest in the bank's equity, or if bonuses are deferred and can be clawed back if the bank makes a loss. But because there are many dealmakers in a large bank, the risks they take on from compensation deferred or made dependent on the bank's performance will not closely correlate to the risks from their own deals.

Making compensation payments depends on the performance of the banker's business unit offering better alignment. But because many deal-makers at middle levels in a bank can personally run up such considerable losses, it is still not possible to come up with a system that well aligns the payments to individual dealmakers with the outcome of the deals they do.

The high risks in the banking business make it very difficult to create full alignment of pay and performance. Yet deferring bonuses may in practice do a much better job of aligning the risk preferences of bankers and shareholders than might appear. Shareholders can diversify their risks by investing in a portfolio of companies. In contrast, bankers whose compensation is deferred or offered in the form of the bank's equity cannot diversify their risk with this income. They may therefore be expected to be substantially more risk averse, and measures taken may actually do a good job of aligning interests in many situations.

Limiting performance rewards

Limiting performance rewards on the upside is another possible approach to reduce bankers' temptation to take too much risk. But this approach too has its potential drawbacks, which are best illustrated by considering an extreme scenario.

Let's suppose competition for talent forces banks to keep bankers' overall compensation at the same absolute level, so they replace the bonus altogether with a much higher fixed salary. But then bankers actually end up sharing less of the downside risk. That's because performance bonuses have, in the past, helped to reduce the volatility of bank earnings. If performance bonuses were half of bank profits before bonuses and taxes, eliminating bonuses while keeping overall pay for bankers at the same long-term average level doubles the volatility of banks' annual net profits.[19]

If bonuses were eliminated altogether and it were not possible to find an alternative reward for performance, the creative energy and effort going into investment banks would likely decline. After all, performance varies enormously, and talented performers would move to boutique financial services companies, private equity or hedge funds that better reward individual performance. For those who consider that 'speculative' investment banking activities bring few benefits to the 'real' economy, this may not be a source of concern. But it will concern the publicly traded investment banks and their shareholders.

Banks are not about to replace all bonuses with fixed pay. The question is how to find the balance between providing incentives in a business with high variations in performance, and limiting the temptation to take too much risk.

Setting and measuring the observance of constraints as well as goals

Banks can also discourage excessive risk-taking with a variety of constraints on bankers' behaviour. Yet the banks face as many, perhaps more problems in setting and quickly measuring the observance of constraints as in measuring the achievement of goals.

Ensuring that employees who work autonomously observe constraints is a tricky business. A key intended advantage of paying for results is that you won't have to direct and control the work to motivate employees to do what you want. You should be able to rely instead on the incentive of performance pay. If you want to impose constraints, you have to control employees' work after all 'just' to make sure they observe constraints.

If you want employees to work largely independently but nevertheless to be subject to a few strict constraints on their behaviour, you must find a way to combine two different cultures: a culture of employees acting independently to get results, and a culture of rigorously controlling employees' work. And you need, in effect, two different management teams to drive these two different cultures. The revenue generators cannot be permitted to also control the observance of the constraints set on their behaviour. The investigation of 'rogue traders' suggests that banks often find it difficult to effectively combine these two cultures. Autonomy usually wins. When it comes to constraints on the volume and type of deals that traders are permitted to do, monitoring and enforcement are weak, and those responsible are often not sufficiently independent of the traders.

Jerome Kerviel, responsible for a $6 billion loss at French bank Société Générale, was operating in a 'general environment in which management failed to monitor traders', according to a PriceWaterhouseCoopers report.[20] One common practice to control traders' behaviour is to make them take holidays and have someone else step into their role while they are away. The substitute then has the chance to see if the trader on vacation has been following the rules. Kerviel managed to persuade Société Générale to allow him to skip his compulsory annual holiday.

To prevent rogue trading, it's important to watch for early indicators of misbehaviour and sanction these accordingly. Rogue traders don't break the rules just once. They usually have a history of small transgressions leading up to a big one that destroys an enormous amount of value. In a bull market,[21] exceeding risk limits tends to create additional profits for the bank, so managers are likely to ignore small transgressions. It is difficult to punish a trader who has just helped the bank make a lot of money. But if you don't take the constraints seriously in a bull market, traders may get used to lax controls and do the same thing in a bear market – where exceeding risk limits can result in heavy losses. A 'zero tolerance' approach, nipping misbehaviour in the bud, may have value in preventing rogue trading just as it does in preventing street crime.

It is critical to take employees' observance of constraints as seriously as their performance in achieving your goals. You may even want to be more stringent in your treatment of employees that don't observe the constraints than of those who fall short of performance goals (see the textbox 'GE's performance-values matrix' below).

GE's performance-values matrix

Companies conventionally evaluate employees on both current performance and future potential to improve performance, build capabilities and take on greater responsibility over time. But, at GE, Jack Welch introduced a different second dimension. That second dimension was 'values', and Welch placed great emphasis on it. Figure 6.7 lays out the four types he used[22] and shows them in a matrix.

Figure 6.7 The GE performance/values matrix

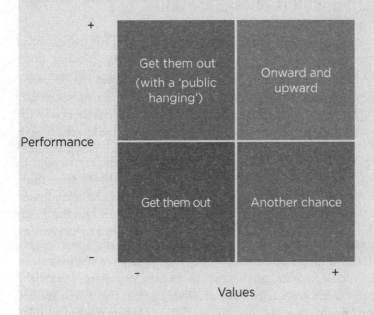

In two quadrants in the evaluation matrix, what you want to do is straightforward. An employee with strong performance and strong values is someone you want to keep, while someone with poor performance and poor values needs to leave. What drives the company culture is what you do in the other two quadrants.

The temptation is to give the strong performer with poor values another chance. Maybe with appropriate feedback his behaviour will improve. In contrast, you want to ask the poor performer with strong values to leave. But this gives precisely the wrong signal to the organization: that top management pays only lip service to values.

To ensure values are taken seriously, it is better to give those that have poor performance but strong values a second chance while asking those with the opposite tendencies to leave. Welch uses colourful language and suggests they be given a 'public hanging'.[23] A few prominent public hangings will soon change the behaviour of the organization and ensure it takes values seriously.

Awkward conflicts of interest and bargaining power

Companies generally face fewer 'awkward conflicts of interest' and 'bargaining power' problems when working with employees than when working with external suppliers. But these problems do arise with bankers managing important client relationships. For example, if a top M&A banker leaves a bank, key clients that she worked with may go with her. Banks need to pay relationship managers a high share of the value they help to create in order to keep them around.

The tactics to solve these problems with employees are essentially the same as when working with suppliers (see Figures 4.2 and 4.6 in Chapter 4), but with employees they may go under different names. From the bank's perspective, a good solution to prevent bankers from leaving would be a non-compete clause. Explicit, binding non-compete clauses for employees are not always legal. Yet deferred bonuses can amount to 'golden handcuffs' that discourage departures until the bonuses pay out. Investment banks have tended to pay new hires any deferred compensation lost as a result of changing employers, but the more compensation is deferred, the more of a barrier to hiring new people it becomes.

If you can't prevent bankers leaving to join the competition, you can at least seek to reduce the harm they do when they leave. The teaming up of relationship bankers to serve clients is akin to second sourcing with external suppliers; it creates competition and makes the bank less dependent on individual employees for important client relationships. When several bankers team up to serve a client, the relationship belongs to the bank, not to an individual banker, and it is more difficult for bankers that leave to take their clients with them.[24]

Persistent problems despite new tactics

Because investment bankers operate largely autonomously with wide and not easily predictable variations in performance, banks cannot properly align rewards with performance while paying a fixed salary. But the income that bankers generate is fairly easily measurable. So paying income-sharing bonuses is a promising option to solve the problem. Problems still arise in meeting the 10 requirements, but as shown in Figure 6.8, banks also have a variety of tactics to solve many of the problems and to mitigate them all. The biggest remaining concern involves the excessive 'risk appetite' in bankers who share in profits but not proportionately in losses, especially severe losses.[25]

If, after considering problems and using tactics to find the best response, you still find weak spots in the collaboration design you come up with, you have to use your judgement about whether these weak spots are so severe that you can't live with the proposed collaboration design.

For a publicly-quoted investment bank, it is hard to do better than Figure 6.8 for a good collaboration design. But investors and managers in a publicly quoted investment bank can go in quite a different direction by switching to a new ownership structure, as we discuss in the textbox 'Radical options'.

Figure 6.8 Tactics to set up collaboration with investment bankers

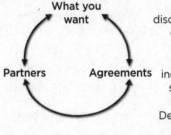

Develop internal early
indicators of performance
(for goals and constraints)

Sell assets/hedge, insure or
guarantee their values to
reduce risk

Powerful
independent in-
house risk managers

**What you
want**

Substantial
discretionary bonuses
(but with caps)

Profit centres to
reduce shared
accountabilities

Partners   **Agreements**

Use early
indicators of risk in
setting bonuses

Bankers negotiate
with each other to
share deal income
when teaming

Defer bonus payout
with ability to
claw back

'Golden handcuffs' on
deferred bonuses

Constraints on risk
taking with 'zero
tolerance'

Incentives to
team up

Radical options

Different ownership structures may be worth considering to provide a more attractive way of setting up collaboration in investment banking. Management partnerships could work well for most of the M&A advisory and underwriting activities of investment banks and something like a hedge fund or private equity structure could be used for much of their investment activities.

For M&A and underwriting, management partnerships can provide sufficient risk capital. Indeed, most investment banks used to focus on these activities and operate as management partnerships. For these activities, going public mainly works to put money in the pockets of then current senior managers – the bank's partners – at the expense of the earnings of future management generations. If management partnerships could again build up the capabilities and brand image needed to compete for the largest M&A and underwriting deals, their managers would be better off without paying a levy to shareholders who, for these activities, provide little risk capital. Smaller independent investment banks have indeed gained share in the M&A advisory market. They took close to 20 per cent of the market in 2013, up from 8 per cent in 2008.[26]

For market-making and for investment activities on the firm's own account, there is a need for more capital than a management partnership would be likely to provide. For market-making, it is difficult to find an ownership form superior to a publicly traded investment bank.[27] But investment activities can be carried out by an investment fund set up as a partnership, owned jointly by a fund management firm as general partner and by investors putting up risk capital as limited partners.

This is the solution adopted by hedge funds and private equity funds. A publicly traded investment bank can, in principle, stay in the game both as a fund management firm and a limited partner investor, as Goldman Sachs has done. But for fund investment, a publicly traded investment bank is an unnecessary intermediary. Investors can invest in the fund directly instead of making an indirect investment as shareholders of a publicly traded investment bank that invests some of its equity in the fund.

Changing ownership structure is clearly a radical option that should not be undertaken lightly. But radical options are worth considering if more conventional tactics for dealing with a collaboration problem are not felt to be sufficiently powerful.

New regulations such as the Volcker Rule in the US will help to drive investment activities out of publicly traded investment banks and into private funds. But the trend for these activities to be managed by private funds was well established before this legislation, which, at the time of writing in early 2014, has still not kicked in. Assets under management in hedge funds amounted to around $2 trillion in 2011.[28] Wharton MBAs, traditionally focused on Wall Street investment banks, have increasingly been taking jobs in private equity and hedge funds instead.[29]

Conclusions

Most of the requirements for profitable collaboration are easier to meet with employees than suppliers. But with non-routine work, you'll still find it hard to provide detailed direction to employees or assess their performance. You then have a strategic choice between boosting your ability to direct and control their work, or giving them autonomy and relying on performance rewards to properly motivate them. Figure 6.3 shows the circumstances in which performance-based pay can be most helpful.

Whichever strategy you use, meeting the critical requirements of 'setting goals and constraints to measure performance' and 'aligning rewards with performance' will likely be the main challenges. Companies face problems in measuring personal performance and in aligning rewards with performance as measured. Figures 6.4–6.6 lay out a number of tactics to address these problems.

The conventional tactic to measure an individual's contribution to team performance is to rely on the team manager's judgement. For this, a manager requires both sufficient information and expertise. In difficult situations, companies can instead set up more focused performance units or internal markets, focus on hiring exceptionally professional employees, or use specific incentives and constraints to correct behavioural biases – such as reluctance to 'team up' – that uncertainty about the fairness of personal performance assessment may cause.

The conventional tactic to address problems in measuring performance in a timely fashion is to establish early indicators of performance. But if companies use them as a basis for rewarding performance, employees may manipulate them to increase their rewards. An independent cadre of managers set up to manage the indicators can help prevent this. In difficult situations, companies can alternatively ask employees to wait longer to obtain rewards, or take steps to measure this performance sooner than is now possible. Trading out of risky assets is an important way to make performance more rapidly measurable for investment banks, and we will discuss in the next chapters how buying and selling assets and companies plays a major role in measuring the performance of pharmaceutical R&D managers and of CEOs and general managers.

There is no dominant tactic to address problems of misalignment because employees cannot carry sufficient risk to be expected to pay for any losses they cause. One tactic is to avoid powerful performance rewards, but this will put you at a competitive disadvantage if competitors find a way to more powerfully reward employee performance without introducing too much risk. The direct approach to improve alignment is to ask employees to share in more company risk by investing or by deferring compensation. Employees don't need to share fully proportionately in the downside with investors for interests to be aligned, as they are more risk averse because their risks are less diversified. But just how much skin in the game employees need to align interests is inevitably a matter of judgement.

The indirect approach is to set up effective constraints on employees' behaviour. This requires a separate cadre of managers to establish and monitor constraints. But two cadres of managers with different objectives – one to promote performance and the other to minimize risk – creates considerable cultural tensions. Top management may need to be overzealous in ensuring constraints are observed.

There are no 'silver bullets' to solve these tough problems. A number of tactics can work well, but then create new problems such as awkward conflicts of interest. The trick is to put together a package of tactics with appropriate checks and balances to try and ensure you have met all 10 requirements for setting up profitable collaboration.

If you can't find a package of tactics that satisfies you, you can consider outsourcing or a change in ownership. These two options play an important role in setting up pharmaceutical R&D and in addressing the governance issues in public companies, the subjects of the next two chapters.

---

[1] There are some exceptions, such as uniforms or private cars used on business.

[2] This difference in fact has implications for the problems in meeting all the 10 requirements except for the requirement to create customer value. In this chapter we focus just on those implications that are most critical in defining the problems you face when working with employees.

[3] Unless you set up agreements which themselves cause awkward conflicts of interest for employees.

[4] Additionally, employees, and particularly specialists and managers, generally have an expectation of long-term employment. They are not usually, in contrast to many external suppliers, hired on a

project-by-project or order-by-order basis. If partners are committed to working together longer term – but subject to performance – that helps to align their interests. Poor performance on a project is harmful to an employee's career. Poor performance by an external contractor hired for a one-off project and paid time and expenses, may be harmful to the contractor's reputation in the market but, if there is a substantial cost of changing the contractor mid-project, the customer has few direct and effective powers of sanction.

5 There may be problems of collective bargaining, not the subject of this book, but few problems in setting up to work with individual employees.

6 As we discussed with ERP systems and construction projects, a large part of the problem with many long implementation projects is that, in fact, it is very difficult to sufficiently clearly define what you are trying to achieve.

7 Staffing a project poses a more difficult problem if the skills needed are simply not available within the organization. In that case there will be advantages to working with an external contractor. That raises its own special problems, which we discussed in Chapter 2, in the context of working with a systems integrator on an ERP project.

8 For a very convincing and highly entertaining demonstration of this point see the video of the fourth part of the series of *Jamie's School Dinners*, a British Channel 4 documentary from 2004, in which Jamie Oliver, the celebrity chef, runs into trouble with the dinner ladies in converting 20,000 children in Greenwich primary schools to eating healthy food in the attempt to create a 'cooler, cleverer, healthier nation'.

9 See Harold L Sirkin, Perry Keenan and Alan Jackson, 'The Hard Side of Change Management'. *Harvard Business Review*. October 2005.

10 It is one thing to appeal to employees' self-motivation to persuade them to perform as well as they can even when you can't easily measure their performance in the short term and so can't impose sanctions for non-performance. It is quite another to appeal to employees' self-motivation to persuade them to perform as well as they can when it is transparent that they are creating much more value than other employees but receiving the same pay. Appealing to self-motivation to get employees to perform is more likely to help address the first problem (which we are discussing here) than the second problem which we will discuss shortly.

11 This may sometimes also be the situation when working with employees in other functions, for example, in support functions. Many employees in support functions are engaged in carrying out standard activities which have a production or service character, for example, in the IT function, ensuring desktop and mobile support. But employees in support functions may also be engaged in complex design, development and planning tasks such as those involved in setting up an ERP project.

12 For a thorough discussion of this problem and the solution to it, see Stephen Bungay, *The Art Of Action*. London: Nicholas Brealey Publishing, 2011.

13 Note that if you face problems both in setting goals and in measuring performance – the top right quadrant in Figure 6.2 – then you also face all the problems in the top left and bottom right quadrants and the solutions and issues listed there are also relevant to your situation.

14 For many routine tasks not supported by machinery, such as sewing or picking fruit, there are also substantial measurable differences in output productivity. One agricultural worker works faster and

picks more fruit in a day than another. For these sorts of tasks, which used to be much more common before widespread automation, employees are often paid, like external suppliers, for the quantity of the output they produce.

[15] Jyske Bank is, in a rather isolated market, the second largest bank.

[16] See Daniel Imwinkelried, 'Sanfte Andersartigkeit' ('A modest difference'). *Neue Zürcher Zeitung*, 5th September 2013. Bonuses at Jyske bank in Switzerland are deferred, not paid annually, but this is now standard practice for the industry.

[17] Egon Zehnder's practices have been extensively documented in numerous Harvard Business Review articles, and also in Daniel Goleman, *Working with Emotional Intelligence*. New York: Bantam 1998, and in Susan Lowe, *Marketplace Masters: How Professional Service Firms Compete to Win*. Praeger Publishers. 2004. For more information see the Egon Zehnder website: <http://www.egonzehnder.com/global/ourfirm/aboutus>.

[18] In contrast, commercial banks making long-term loans, such as mortgages, have a much greater problem if they want to measure actual deal profitability before paying any bonuses they offer. Although much of the discussion post financial crisis has been about the risk of investment banking, there were more failures among ordinary commercial banks such as Washington Mutual, or RBS and HBOS in the UK.

[19] This of course assumes that the volatility of bank profits is not affected by whether you pay bankers fixed salaries or offer substantial performance bonuses. If paying fixed salaries reduces bankers' risk appetite, profits might be less volatile – but perhaps also on average lower. How this all plays out is hard to say. The point of the example is to show that while it is often suggested that bankers paid performance bonuses have an upside but no downside and carry no risk, they actually share quite a substantial amount of bank risk.

[20] Scheherazade Daneshkhu, Peggy Hollinger and Ben Hall, 'SocGen flouted rules, says report'. *Financial Times*, 24th May 2008.

[21] A 'bull market' is a rising market and a 'bear market' a falling market.

[22] Jack Welch letter to GE Shareholders accompanying GE 2000 Annual Report.

[23] <http://www.forbes.com/sites/stevedenning/2012/04/26/jack-welch-ge-the-corporate-practice-of-public-hangings/>. Downloaded 13th May 2013.

[24] Good management succession planning is another tactic to minimize the damage from employee departures. It also ensures there is competition to do the job. This is, however, not so helpful in getting round problems of client relationship managers leaving a bank. The problem there is the loss of a client relationship, not a lack of skills. Good formal documentation is likewise another tactic to prevent employees becoming difficult to substitute. For example, long-serving software engineers with knowledge of your legacy software systems are in a strong negotiating position when the knowledge about legacy systems exists only in their heads. The better you document knowledge assets such as software, the less you depend on specific individuals. Making sure the knowledge belongs to your company and not to your employees is also helpful in preventing conflicts of interest. For example, in luxury department stores, salespeople have valuable personal relationships with their regular customers with large wardrobes. To protect the department store's interests, information about these customers should be in the department store's computer system, not just in a pocket book the salesperson can take when she leaves.

[25] For example, recently in 2012, three traders in the chief investment office of JPMorgan were, without apparent criminal intent, responsible for losses of $5.8 billion. JPMorgan announced that their bonuses would be clawed back but it is safe to assume that this did very little to cover the losses. See Tom Braithwaite and Kara Scannell, 'JPMorgan roiled by wake of the "whale"'. *Financial Times*, 13th July 2012.

[26] See Ed Hammond and Daniel Schäfer, 'Small proves beautiful at boutique banks'. *Financial Times*, 17th March 2014.

[27] Neither the hedge fund nor the private equity fund approaches described below are well suited to market-making activities. To make the hedge fund approach work, the fund should focus on investing in financial instruments which are themselves market traded, such as currencies or stocks. The fund should also not need to trade in these instruments in such high volumes that the fund's own trades affect the market price of its investments. So the hedge fund approach can't be used for market making. It is conceivable that market-makers could be owned by private equity funds but the idea is not at all promising. For example, in the time required for a private equity fund to evaluate the asset portfolio of a market-making company and complete a deal to buy the company, the market-maker's portfolio and its value might change beyond recognition.

[28] Estimates of hedge fund market size vary but are all very substantial. This one is from *Forbes* <http://www.forbes.com/sites/halahtouryalai/2012/03/01/hedge-funds-a-2-trillion-industry/>. Downloaded 17th December 2012.

[29] See Dan McCrum and Michael Mackenzie, 'Rule changes trigger flight to asset managers; the new Wall Street'. *Financial Times*, 3rd October 2012.

Chapter 7

Tactics for Innovation

So far we've talked about getting partners to do work for you along well-established lines. You may not know exactly what you want, and you may need a lot of customization, but at least you and your partner can point to existing models of the product or service in question to help you achieve your goals. But what about when you need to develop an entirely new product for customers? In this case, the uncertainty behind many of the struggles we've discussed is magnified, whether you are working with employees or suppliers.

Setting up collaboration for new product development involves many of the difficulties we have already discussed – specifying goals and constraints, measuring performance, and managing risks. However, when it comes to major innovation – not incremental improvements – the challenges are qualitatively greater. Reliably measuring performance in a timely fashion is almost impossible. Developing new products and bringing them to market often takes many years, with few objective indicators of the value being created. So it's exceedingly hard to provide good direction, offer motivating rewards, or even to know if you have the right people working for you.

Perhaps the clearest example of these challenges, and the one we'll focus on here, is the pharmaceutical industry. While arguably an extreme case, it illustrates both the problems and challenges so effectively that it can be a model for other industries relying increasingly on innovation. (To see why some industries rely heavily on innovation and others do not, see the textbox 'Why innovation matters less in some industries' below.)

Because innovation can be a powerful source of competitive advantage, drug companies have typically built a strong in-house capability to develop new medical formulations. But the challenge of selecting, directing and motivating employees here is so great that many of these companies have lately retreated and now rely more on acquisitions to fill their pipeline and sustain growth. Indeed, investors have had so little confidence in big pharmaceutical companies' ability to research and develop new drugs that, over the past decade, stock markets have placed almost no value on the drugs in the R&D pipeline. Share prices have simply reflected the future earnings of their current products.[1]

As in other chapters, we focus on the collaboration requirements that you are most likely to have problems in meeting. For new problems we develop new tactics. We'll pay particular attention to an intermediate approach that mixes in-house and external partners. To overcome the challenges of innovation, companies need to move past either/or approaches to getting the work done.

Why innovation matters less in some industries

Some industries depend on innovation more than others. One way to assess the importance of innovation is to consider both the sales life of new products in relation to the time it takes to develop them, and the importance of other business functions in relation to new product development (see Figure 7.1).

Figure 7.1 Importance of innovation in sustaining success varies by industry

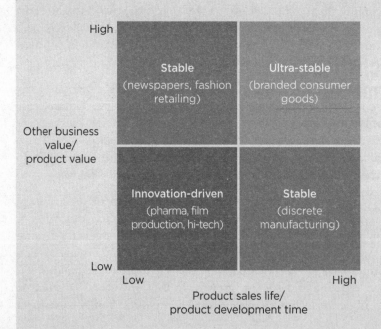

The longer the product sales life in relation to the time it takes to develop a new product (the horizontal axis in Figure 7.1), and the greater the importance in the buying decision of sales, marketing and other factors in relation to product characteristics (the vertical axis in Figure 7.1), the less the pressure to innovate. For many industries, innovation is an opportunity but not a necessity. Some large consumer brands companies do struggle to develop new products, but long product lives, and the importance of marketing and distribution strength, means that this is less of a concern than it is in pharmaceuticals. For example, Coca Cola was introduced on the market in 1886 and the Mars bar in 1932 and both are still strong brands today. Rather than innovating, the food and drinks industry can rely instead on acquiring other companies with popular products to strengthen their product portfolios. But if consumer goods companies could more successfully innovate, they would do even better.

In pharmaceuticals, the on-patent sales life of a pharmaceutical drug may be shorter than the time it takes to research and develop it. So although marketing and distribution strength are important in driving overall business success in the pharmaceutical industry, they cannot begin to compensate for a lack of strong patented drugs. When a drug goes off-patent, revenues drop sharply and profits may disappear altogether. A steady stream of new drugs coming out of development to replace old ones is essential.[2]

The challenges of collaboration in pharmaceutical R&D

CEOs of big pharmaceutical companies face acute problems in managing R&D to get the results they want. Drug development involves large financial investments and risks. Pfizer's experience with Torcetrapib, a 'good cholesterol'-enhancing drug,[3] illustrates the issues. In 2006, Pfizer expected Torcetrapib to help sustain its leading position in cardiovascular drugs. At the time, its top selling cardiovascular drug was Lipitor, with high margins on annual sales of $10 billion. Lipitor was due to go off-patent in 2011 but the new drug Torcetrapib offered the promise of working in combination with Lipitor to reduce the risk of heart trouble. After the company spent nearly $1 billion in developing the drug and preparing for production, clinical trials indicated that patients taking Torcetrapib and Lipitor together were substantially more likely to die than those taking Lipitor alone.[4] When Pfizer decided to stop further trials of Torcetrapib in December 2006, its stock price fell 11 per cent, wiping $21 billion off their market value.

And yet Torcetrapib is not so far from the norm. Research and development for a new drug can easily take 15 years. The work starts by understanding the mechanism of the disease to be treated and identifying a target molecule in the body that influences the development of the disease. The company then needs to discover a chemical compound,[5] i.e. a drug, to alter the behaviour of the target and hence prevent the development of the disease. After screening 10,000 compounds that affect the target, a pharmaceutical company can expect a yield of roughly five new candidate formulations and then three phases of clinical trials commence. After the second phase of trials, which demonstrates safety and efficacy for a small number of volunteer patients, the investigational drug is said to achieve 'proof of concept'. But not all of these drugs make it past phase three. Typically, of the five potential formulations only one is finally registered and approved for sale. The total cost for that one drug , including the expense of investigating the dead-ends, is, on average, $800 million.[6]

This complex, bureaucratic process is important to ensure that drugs are safe and efficacious. But the drawn-out schedule works against companies eager to recoup their investment through years of sales under patent protection. Pfizer's losses from Torcetrapib were especially stark, but other big companies have also struggled to manage their R&D pipelines. A 2007 report from PriceWaterhouseCoopers concluded that:

Even allowing for inflation, the [pharma] industry is investing twice as much in R&D as it was a decade ago to produce two-fifths of the new medicines it then produced. Moreover, only nine of the [twenty-two] new treatments launched in the US in 2006 came from the labs of the thirteen companies that comprise the Big Pharma universe, a pattern that has changed very little over the past few years.[7]

It is hard to pinpoint a reason for this poor performance in recent decades. The industry may have become mature with fewer rich research niches to mine in discovering new drugs. The companies may have got worse at R&D as mergers have made them bigger and more complex organizations. Regulatory authorities have, in some cases, set tougher criteria to approve new drugs for sale. Whatever the reason for the decline in productivity, to make good returns in the current environment, Big Pharma needs to find a way to set up R&D activities to be more productive.[8] We will see that big changes in collaboration strategy have been made in response to difficulties. Some appear misguided, but there are also some encouraging signs that recent moves are paying off.

What you want from innovation

Let's tackle this innovation challenge with our framework for collaboration. First we will look at the three requirements for getting what you want and we will continue to use the pharma industry as our example. When setting up to innovate, you are pursuing *customer value* and *competitive advantage*. And, as you do so, it is critical that you carefully *take account of your abilities*.

To *create customer value*, the top management teams at Big Pharma companies have sought to focus their new product development effort on meeting market needs. They have been coordinating R&D and marketing more strongly and focusing R&D on areas of clear commercial potential. But this has not been so successful. In pharmaceutical R&D, even if you can identify the market need, you may not be able to meet it. In focusing pharmaceutical R&D, you need to balance considerations of the revenue potential from success – *customer value* – with the actual probability of success – *taking account of your abilities*.

A similar pitfall comes in seeking *competitive advantage*. Torcetrapib was a perfect fit with Pfizer's business strategy, providing a patented combination with Lipitor just as it was going off-patent. Pfizer was carrying out clinical trials and initially intending to seek registration for Torcetrapib only in combination with Lipitor.[9] Doctors wishing to prescribe Torcetrapib on its own or in combination with other statins competitive to Lipitor would be unable to do so. By showing Torcetrapib's efficacy only with Lipitor, in a tied-sale strategy, Pfizer could, in effect, gain renewed patent protection for Lipitor. The enormous leverage that Torcetrapib offered may have unduly influenced Pfizer to press ahead with and invest aggressively in the candidate drug, despite what appeared to be mixed support for Torcetrapib from initial clinical trials.[10]

Finally, as we have discussed, *taking account of your abilities* requires thinking not just about your company but also your own personal abilities. Here is one clear area of concern for Big Pharma CEOs. Research and development is the most difficult set of tasks for pharmaceutical companies, but in recent years CEOs have seldom had a background in any of the specialist disciplines relevant in R&D. The former CEO of Pfizer, Hank McKinnell, made his career in the marketing side of Pfizer, not in R&D. His successor, Jeffrey Kindler, was a lawyer hired from McDonald's as general counsel. Less than one in five CEOs of the large companies have, over the past 15 years, had a scientific education and career background attuned for pharmaceutical R&D.[11]

If it is difficult to delegate and control results in R&D, and R&D is critical to overall company performance, then a CEO should have a background in R&D. That would enable him or her to get directly involved in decision-making there, while delegating more decisions in other functions, such as marketing and manufacturing, where performance is more easily measurable and control is more easily possible. Without some level of expertise in R&D, it will be difficult for the CEO to implement a strategy that depends on innovation – and most Big Pharma companies depend on just such a strategy. By contrast, close to half of all CEOs of high-tech companies have a technical education and substantial hands-on experience in product development. Many of the most successful CEOs have had this, such as Steve Jobs at Apple, Larry Ellison at Oracle, and both Eric Schmidt and Larry Page at Google.

Some say that pharmaceutical R&D is such a specialized capability that it is impossible to find someone with both the skills and experience needed in pharma R&D, and the leadership, finance, customer relations and general management skills needed by a CEO of a large company. But if there are few managers with this valuable combination of capabilities, surely that is a challenge for HR and career development rather than an excuse to give up?[12]

We discussed this hypothesis in conversations with top managers in several big pharmaceutical companies.[13] They suggested focusing instead on the senior executive team as a whole. A CEO with a professional background in R&D may be helpful, but then the team runs the risk that there will be too little debate on R&D. A better alternative may be to rely on a strong head of R&D in the top team, but ensure that the CEO and other members have enough industry knowledge to challenge the head of R&D and create a good discussion of R&D issues.[14]

These minimal game rules seem logical, but in 2005 not one of Pfizer's four-person top management team had a professional background in medicine or pharmaceutical R&D. After the spectacular failure of Torcetrapib, by 2011 Pfizer had established a much larger, thirteen-person leadership team, four of whom had a medical/pharmaceutical R&D background.[15]

But let's suppose your CEO and top team lack a strong background in R&D. As a result, they are unlikely to create value by investing heavily in R&D, and they would do better to focus on activities such as M&A and post-merger integration – activities where general business management skills and not specific skills in R&D may determine the outcome. Within R&D they would do better to buy more drugs that have passed through early stage research, where results are especially difficult to predict, and they should concentrate in-house work on later stage development. However, if the core value driver in the business is successful new drug development, there are limits to simply searching elsewhere for sources of value.

Sometimes there is another way around the problem. The film industry, for example, faces difficulties similar to pharma in predicting the success of new films. But for animated films, you can more easily test and learn at low cost before you place any big bets (see the textbox 'How the film industry manages innovation'). In pharmaceuticals it is difficult to find such drug development segments where you can easily test and learn. If the CEO and the top team lack sufficient background in the hard-to-manage new product development function, they can't be expected to effectively direct employees to develop new drugs.

How the film industry manages innovation

Box office films, like pharmaceutical drugs, have high costs and short revenue-generating lives at the box office in relation to the time it takes to make them. And film studios, like big pharmaceutical companies, find it difficult to control the results of development. So film production is a risky business and few films make money. But we will see that animated films are breaking the mould.

To ensure successful results and manage the risks of development, film studios' main solution has been to offer their development partners autonomy and entrepreneurial rewards. Not so different, as we will discuss, to the recent approach of many big pharmaceutical companies. Film studios work with a number of producers with whom they often have a relationship across a number of films and share the film profits with them. Not only the producer but all 'creatives' working on a film – director, actors, script writers and others – receive a share of film net profits as part of their compensation. These creatives follow an ad-hoc model where groups of people come together to make a movie and then disperse. This motivational approach may help improve the chances of success, and it shares the risk between studios and development partners. But the film industry remains highly risky, with a few winners and an enormous number of flops. Sequels are one of the few tricks studios have up their sleeve to increase the chances of success. For example at the time of writing in 2014, Pirates of the Caribbean 5 is in the works, and the next instalment of the countless James Bond films is due for release in 2015.

The most successful studio in recent years, Pixar, makes animated films where the development process is quite different from live-action movies and is more easily controllable. Because of the importance of the technology base for animation, animated film studios work differently. Over time, they gain organizational and technical learning to control results both long and short term. The workforce stays together as in a normal company (rather than dispersing at the end of the film) and workforce capability can be improved by experience and selection.

The process of making individual animated films is also more controllable. In live-action films, once a scene has been shot and the cutting takes place, there is little opportunity to control the output by iterating around the loop of shooting and cutting again. But, as Peter Schneider, who worked for Pixar for 10 years, put it in an interview with Fortune:[16]

'Animation is a recursive process, not a linear process. That allows the story to have more time in development, so you know exactly what you're going to get, and then you can re-animate and re-animate it if you don't like what you see. That's why the success rate for animated films is so high.'

Choosing partners

Even when you know what strategy you want to pursue in pharmaceutical R&D, it may not be easy to find *able* partners to help you implement it. When what you are trying to do is so difficult that you can't be certain of success, you need to reach out as widely as you can for ideas, often beyond the confines of your own organization. Selecting able partners can involve more than merely hiring able employees.

In recent years the high-tech and consumer products industries have experimented with a more 'open' approach to innovation. As scholar Henry Chesbrough explains:

Useful knowledge these days is widely diffused. No one has a monopoly on knowledge the way that, say, IBM had in the 1960s in computing, or that Bell Labs had through the 1970s in communications. When useful knowledge exists in companies of all sizes and also in universities, non-profits and individual minds, it makes sense to orient your innovation efforts to accessing, building upon and integrating that external knowledge into useful products and services.[17]

To innovate most effectively, companies should set themselves up to connect with those most able to help them do what they want, whether inside or outside the company. In consumer goods, P&G[18] established an internal network of 'technology entrepreneurs' worldwide to make connections with university and supplier researchers, and to scan the shelves of stores for new product ideas or technologies that could support P&G's own new product ideas. P&G also makes active use of ideas marketplaces, such as NineSigma, which offer prizes for solving published problems. Speed of new product development is valuable in the market place and if you have to get things done fast, you are more likely to look outside for ideas and make sure you aren't wasting time reinventing the wheel. So P&G explicitly rewards the speed of innovation as well as project success.

Open innovation can be taken a stage further than this. Book publishers, for example, have few if any employees in product development and rely on external partners for their new products. They must publish new books to generate continued revenue, but unlike newspapers that employ their writers as journalists, book publishers do not hire writers. Instead they provide a platform through which authors can sell the books they write. With this loose association and providing little direction, publishers share the income from the books written with their authors.

Big Pharma companies have certainly made efforts toward open innovation. Innocentive, a market for ideas similar to NineSigma, was founded by the Big Pharma company Eli Lilly. But in a number of respects these efforts have become more difficult for them. Traditionally, knowledge flowed quite freely between universities and pharma companies. But today academic researchers are under more pressure to obtain commercial funding, and are more likely to keep their new ideas to themselves or sell them to a single pharma company that funds their research.

To make it easy to find external partners for collaboration, you need to set up a platform with an open interface that partners can easily plug in to. Large pharmaceutical companies already provide a sales platform for drugs registered by independent companies, but they could consider extending this to provide a research and development platform as well. As we discuss later in the chapter, a company could offer external development teams a standardized package of laboratory, regulatory affairs, clinical trials, manufacturing and other development services in return for a share of the revenues of the drugs developed. If large companies were to offer these services on the market, it would force them to organize these R&D 'support' functions for efficiency and effectiveness. If they don't do this, contract research organizations such as Quintiles are likely to play this role and offer platforms that go well beyond their current core offer of carrying out clinical trials.

Similarly, at one time all doctors involved in clinical trials would participate with the pharma company to draft the 'protocol' – the precise definition of what is to be tested in clinical trials and what information will
be gathered to evaluate trial results. Today, companies work with only
quite a small number of opinion-leading doctors for the protocol. They
also outsource much of the interaction with doctors during clinical
trials to the contract research organizations that manage the trials.
This streamlines the process and reduces costs, but insights that could
have come from broader discussions with practising doctors may be
missed. As many as a third of new prescription drugs arise from projects
originally targeted at other medical problems. The active component in
Pfizer's blockbuster Viagra was originally intended for hypertension
and angina pectoris. Its effects on erectile dysfunction emerged incidentally in clinical trials.[19]

Even internally, pharma companies are less able to connect researchers than they were in the past. Earlier companies often had 'father
figures' with a history of successful research, who would go around
pointing out to researchers help and ideas they might usefully
get from counterparts elsewhere in the organization working on
different issues. Paul Janssen of Janssen Pharmaceuticals in Belgium,
for example, would, so we heard, walk around the labs, smoking and
making connections between researchers. Advances in medicine and
technology and the structure of education mean that both scientists
and pharmaceutical companies' organizations have become increasingly specialized. Specialization makes it more difficult to see across
different areas.

Accordingly, pharma companies need to make specific investments to
find the unexpected connections that can contribute to successful
drugs. Novartis has begun involving practising clinicians in early stage
research to generate additional ideas,[20] and GSK has created an
Academic Discovery performance unit to work with academic researchers on a portfolio of novel target drugs.[21]

Figure 7.2 sums up the special tactics for finding able partners for innovation.

Figure 7.2 Tactics to find partners able to help you innovate

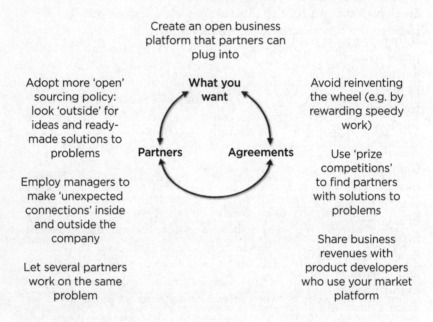

Create an open business platform that partners can plug into

Adopt more 'open' sourcing policy: look 'outside' for ideas and ready-made solutions to problems

Employ managers to make 'unexpected connections' inside and outside the company

Let several partners work on the same problem

What you want

Partners

Agreements

Avoid reinventing the wheel (e.g. by rewarding speedy work)

Use 'prize competitions' to find partners with solutions to problems

Share business revenues with product developers who use your market platform

As for *self-motivation*, conventional wisdom has long assumed this wasn't an issue for pharmaceutical researchers. Scientists, the thinking went, are naturally motivated by the fascination of discovery and the search for new knowledge. They are also excited by the opportunity to treat important diseases and save lives, and they are not especially interested in money. Hire the right people, provide an attractive work environment, fund the investments to support their discoveries and experiments and they will be self-motivated to innovate.

Unfortunately, while scientists may be fascinated by the potential of new discovery and wish to develop new drugs that treat diseases and save lives, it isn't so simple to ensure they are, in their daily work, actually motivated to do what companies want. Researchers have ample reason to become distracted from the main task. Pharmaceutical research can be immensely frustrating because the chances of success are so low. It is possible to devote a lifetime to research and not come up with any effective new drug. To make things worse, big pharmaceutical companies have large, complex R&D organizations. Many people need to work together successfully to get a result. If the process isn't well organized, you may feel that the organizational barriers to your success are so high that you, personally, cannot make a difference.

If their project is not well directed, led and managed, researchers may prefer to use their time to write interesting papers for leading scientific journals. Publishing a paper in a scientific journal may not contribute to the development of a new drug, but it will at least give researchers a feeling of personal success and boost self-esteem. Alternatively, R&D employees may leave altogether to join a smaller, entrepreneurial venture that offers more freedom of action and greater financial upside.

Companies need to harness employees' self-motivation. When your own personal work may not create value or the value of your personal work is hard to measure, it is particularly important that you feel part of a larger team whose work will measurably create value. There are many simple things that managers at all levels can do to help people see how what they do fits into the bigger picture, and to create team spirit and a sense of purpose. One manager told us, for example, that he found it helpful to get all the people working for him together to discuss the results of experiments, regardless of each individual's direct 'need to know' about the specific outcomes.

Taking specific measures to create team spirit is important, but harnessing employee self-motivation does not, for the most part, rely on a separate specific set of tactics. To harness employees' self-motivation, it is most critical to meet the requirements for setting up profitable collaboration from employees' perspective. Employees will believe that their company will succeed if they see that their company has set up research to create customer value, that top executives making the decisions can carry out this strategy, and that other employees are able and motivated. Employees will only be convinced that they can make a personal contribution if their managers clearly communicate to them the goals that they want them to achieve, and provide them with the resources and support they need to do it. Conversely, employees will not be convinced they can make a personal contribution if they are asked to meet a multiplicity of different goals and constraints by different managers and left without clear priorities.

Figure 7.3 shows a set of tactics for harnessing employees' self-motivation. Meeting the requirements for setting up profitable collaboration from employees' perspective takes pride of place and is fundamental.

Figure 7.3 Basic tactics to harness self-motivation of employees

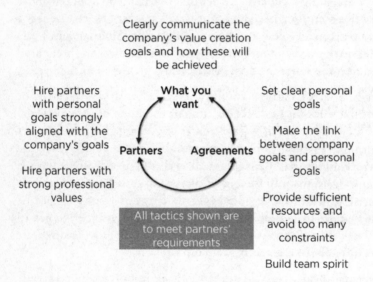

Establishing agreements

While meeting the requirements to get what you want and to select the right partners can be challenging, perhaps the biggest hurdle in setting up for innovation lies in putting in place agreements with partners. In order to harness employees' self-motivation, and reinforce this motivation with appropriate performance rewards, companies need agreements that create clarity and alignment around the goals and constraints to be met.

Because pharma R&D involves high uncertainties, long time horizons, heavy investment, and serious dangers to human life, it is exceptionally difficult to set goals and constraints for employees, measure their performance in meeting these goals and constraints, and align their rewards with their performance.

Drug development requires participation from a wide variety of specialist disciplines (biologists, chemists, pharmacologists, medical doctors, regulatory affairs specialists and others). So pharmaceutical companies have traditionally organized in a matrix of projects and functions representing the different specialist disciplines needed on projects. A great deal of information is gathered and evaluated by specialists from all these different functional disciplines before key decisions are taken. Often several committees must give their approval before trials can proceed. Early stage research and later stage development functions may report separately to the CEO. Both functions then play a role in deciding how drugs move down the development pipeline. The marketing function also has input into the focus of R&D investment.

The intention in taking decisions in committees and involving a range of different functions is that all perspectives should be taken into account and decisions well prepared and thoroughly vetted. But as a result, decision-making is a slow process. By the time decisions are made there is often new information that calls them into question. Decisions are then frequently overturned, leaving an impression of confusion rather than clarity.

The project agenda may also clash with the agendas of different special and support functions. Pharmaceutical R&D depends on rapidly developing science, and success requires meeting changing regulatory requirements. So training and learning activities of one form or another take up a significant amount of management and specialist employee time. In theory these should support meeting R&D project objectives. But there may, in practice, be conflicts. For example, to meet changing regulatory requirements companies frequently set up new standard operating procedures for clinical trials and other aspects of R&D. There is a constant need for retraining in new procedures. Regulatory affairs staff working on a project may be pulled off project work for training at critical moments for the project agenda. To battle against these problems, which create confusion and conflict and reduce companies' ability to create value, Big Pharma companies have tried a variety of different tactics with varying success.

Develop and use early indicators of performance

At the heart of effective agreements are clear *measures of performance*. Because actual success won't be seen until far into the future, companies have invested in developing early indicators of performance and using these to reward managers. There are some simple and useful early indicators of pharmaceutical R&D performance. Unfortunately, as we saw in investment banking, it is dangerous to explicitly base powerful incentives on early indicators.

The most common early indicator is the number of candidate drugs that move forward each year from phase one to phase two to phase three of clinical trials. This is a useful measure of the number of drugs that you may eventually be able to register for sale. But it is not reliable. On this measure of performance, pressing ahead with Torcetrapib development contributed to Pfizer's performance progress until the moment that high mortalities forced the company to stop trials.

More important, rewarding managers for the number of candidate drugs moving forward can undermine performance. R&D managers have a significant influence on decisions made about which candidate drugs move to the next stage of clinical trials. Offering rewards for progress here has encouraged R&D managers to commence with the next stage of clinical trials before there is sufficient evidence to do so – and even when the balance of the evidence is against proceeding. More drugs have moved down through the pipeline, but late-stage failures have increased – at much higher cost to the company.[22]

Move to autonomous 'performance units' judged on medium-term performance

Along with better measures of performance, companies are working on ways to set common *goals and constraints* for project teams. As we saw, the multitude of functional organizations involved in R&D have their own needs and objectives that can conflict with the project itself. Since 2000, a number of major pharmaceutical companies have moved away from functional organization structures within R&D in an attempt to more easily measure the performance of small organizational units and make them more accountable in the medium term. They have created internal performance units focused on a specific area of therapy, with control over all the different functional expertise needed for drug discovery and early clinical trials.

The managers of these therapy areas hold considerable autonomy and are judged by their medium-term results in identifying candidate drugs and managing them – at low cost – through the different stages of clinical trials forward towards regulatory approval. These units also avoid the awkward conflicts of interest that arise from bringing together functional organizations. Team members put the needs of the project ahead of training or learning activities.

GlaxoSmithKline (GSK) is one company that has carried the approach of setting up independent performance units a long way.[23] Senior executives no longer focus on supervising and controlling decisions of R&D managers and employees, but instead on allocating funds for investment to the units – which are then accountable for achieving agreed medium-term goals. GSK has about 40 Discovery Performance Units (DPUs), each comprising 30–60 people. They are focused on particular therapy areas such as heart failure, or on the therapy potential of particular new scientific developments, such as pattern recognition receptors in the treatment of autoimmune diseases.[24] Functions not integrated into the DPUs have become internal service units, with performance benchmarked against market, or simply outsourced. When we spoke to GSK in early 2011, they were optimistic but cautious about the progress they had made. Now (at the time of writing) they are more confident of their restructuring of R&D. Their rate of return for R&D has increased by 30 per cent over the past four years[25] and is now up to 12 per cent,[26] well above the industry benchmark of 7 per cent.[27]

Involve a broader range of partners in assessing performance

DPUs have three years to show results; at that point they must apply for new funding from an investment board. With such a large number of small performance units, performance units are not 'too big to fail'. After the performance review in 2011, three DPUs were closed and five had their funding cut by more than 20 per cent.[28] By stopping funding for poorly-performing units, GSK creates clear performance pressure.

The investment board that evaluates GSK development projects has had a number of members external to GSK, from venture capital to biotech companies and other sources. Including external members on the investment board is perceived as particularly valuable in ensuring that decisions to continue funding are not excessively influenced by personal loyalties to particular DPU managers. The broad membership of the investment board helps to avoid bias.

This approach looks rather more promising as a basis for directing and motivating R&D employees. The investment board has early indicators of performance available, but has the freedom to form a subjective judgement around them. The three-year rhythm allows enough time to elapse and evidence to accumulate to be able to form a judgement even with imperfect information. Reorganization into independent perform-ance units helps create the personal accountability necessary to use control of performance to motivate.

Tactics that big pharmaceutical companies have used to make perform-ance more measurable and to create more accountability are shown in Figure 7.4.

Figure 7.4 Relevant tactics for making performance more measurable

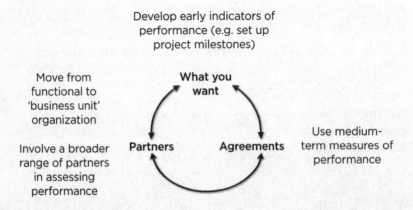

Develop early indicators of performance (e.g. set up project milestones)

Move from functional to 'business unit' organization

Involve a broader range of partners in assessing performance

What you want

Partners   Agreements

Use medium-term measures of performance

Outsourcing to better motivate researchers

GSK and other big companies have worked hard at breaking up internal R&D into more accountable performance units to motivate R&D managers to perform. But much of the motivation to perform is from fear of the downside of not performing. Managers lose funding for further research or development in a performance unit that is not achieving goals. The companies have not gone the next step from setting up performance measures to strongly differentiating employees' financial rewards based on differences in performance as measured. And they may be right not to do so. We have suggested that rewarding the early indicators of performance, which are the best measures of performance that Big Pharma companies have available, can create just the wrong incentives.

Outsourcing R&D makes it easier to create an entrepreneurial culture with independent decision-making and strong rewards for performance. And that's what many big pharmaceutical companies have been doing. Outsourcing also makes it easier to find the intellectual property and people with the specific capabilities you need, as well as to set measurable medium-term goals for R&D managers.

Throughout this book we have emphasized that companies have options in between controlling the work with employees and buying from the marketplace. Pharmaceutical R&D is no different; a wide spectrum of options is available between the extremes of doing all the work in-house and acquiring major companies for their portfolios and pipelines. Big Pharma have been outsourcing some of the work to research and develop new products but also retaining some of the work to do in-house.

Venture capital

Research and development in small biotech companies funded by venture-capital investors, who exit their investment via sale to a big pharmaceutical company, is a well-established alternative to in-house research and development. Biotech venture capital funds buy and then, after a few years, sell small drug development companies.[29] You can measure how much the market thinks the biotech company was worth when the VC fund bought it; and then you can measure how much the fund invests and how much the fund sells the biotech company for. The profit on the fund's investment is the value that the fund managers and the teams running the companies in the fund's portfolio have created for investors.

This profit is measurable sooner than any eventual revenues from sale of the drugs in development, and it takes account of the research and development costs incurred. A similar process happens with small companies with publicly-traded stock, where the R&D managers hold stock options.[30]

The venture capital business model thus makes it easy to offer aligned and motivating entrepreneurial rewards to R&D managers. Rights to drugs in development, and to drug development businesses, are being bought and sold, and the market prices at which these transactions take place can be used as the basis for triggering managers' payouts.[31]

Research and development alliances

A small company is better placed to offer entrepreneurial freedom and rewards to managers in R&D, but for Big Pharma, leaving research and early stage development to these companies has a considerable disadvantage. Big companies buy these small firms in a competitive market, bidding against other big companies. Any benefits in research and development efficiency go to the venture-capital funds or share-holders in the entrepreneurial firms. Additionally, big companies acquire commercial rights to the drugs at a late stage in development and their access until then is less secure than if the drugs came from their own research.

Big Pharma would prefer to capture more of the value of the research and development work and secure the rights at an earlier stage, and they have found a way to do this. Ownership-sharing alliances are a new trend in organizing pharmaceutical development. In such an alliance, drug development is carried out by small external entrepreneurial research and development companies, while big companies obtain or retain exclusive marketing rights to the drugs developed. Big Pharma may structure the deals they make to obtain drug marketing rights so that they take most of the drug development risk for those drugs and receive most of the rewards related to carrying the risks of their development. That way, a big company can secure its pipeline from an early stage, but also let candidate drugs to which they own the rights be developed by an entrepreneurial organization.

One way of looking at ownership-sharing alliances is as a further evolution of internal performance units, such as the DPUs at GSK, to place the responsibility for development in a more truly autonomous and entrepreneurial organization. In addition to the internal DPUs, the GSK investment board invests in cooperative agreements with external partners to gain rights over an almost equal number of external development ventures. GSK has also set up a more traditional VC fund to take capital stakes in start-up ventures.

The ownership-sharing alliances that Big Pharma and entrepreneurial drug development companies have entered into work generally as follows. First, the development company takes responsibility for developing one or more candidate drugs, the commercial rights to which are owned by a Big Pharma company. Then, in return for these services, the development company may receive an equity investment from the big company and milestone payments for achieving milestones on the road to registering the drugs. In combination, these payments finance the costs of developing candidate drugs. The development company also receives royalties on the sales of drugs successfully developed and registered. Roche, for example, linked up with Molecular Partners in 2013 to fund its development of improved anti-cancer therapies using biotechnology. Roche paid the small firm an upfront payment with the promise of more as development and sales milestones are met, culminating in tiered royalties on the actual sales of products that emerge.[32]

As a tactic to address timing problems in measuring performance, this use of outsourcing combines four elements, shown in Figure 7.5.

Ownership-sharing alliances are a promising drug development business model. But it is unfortunately not possible for a big company to adapt this model in a way which lets it not only retain the rights to market drugs but also own and control a majority of the drug development company.

Figure 7.5 How outsourcing helps measure and reward performance: four elements

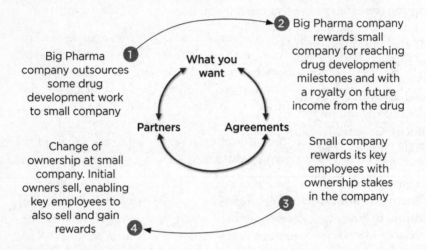

Roche/Genentech

For a while the collaboration between Roche, a Swiss Big Pharma company, and Genentech, a leading San Francisco-based bio-technology company, allowed Roche to 'have it all': drugs were developed by an entrepreneurial development organization, and Roche had the exclusive rights to market the drugs as well as a majority interest in the organization developing the drugs. The arrangement was highly successful.

In 1990, Roche acquired a majority of Genentech, with an option to acquire full ownership of the company. In 1999, Roche exercised their option to buy the remaining shares in Genentech but, shortly after acquiring full ownership, again floated a minority of Genentech on the stock market. Over the next 10 years Roche's arrangement with Genentech provided an interesting balance of autonomy, control and motivational incentives.

Despite owning a majority of Genentech, Roche gave the Genentech board substantial autonomy over decision-making. However, Roche controlled some crucial special rights of high value. In return for paying a substantial proportion of Genentech drug development costs and a royalty on sales to Genentech, Roche had an option on the rights to marketing and distribution of Genentech drugs outside the US. This option could be exercised at the end of phase two trials for each drug or, in return for paying a higher share of development and a higher royalty, at the end of phase three trials. To help motivate them, Genentech managers received options in Genentech, a smaller, more focused company than Roche. This more closely aligned the rewards Genentech managers received with the value they created than would have been possible by offering them options in the parent company, Roche. The Roche/Genentech collaboration on this basis was very successful. In 2008, five of Roche's top-10 selling drugs had been developed by Genentech, and three of those five achieved registration after the Genentech floatation.[33] Given Genentech's success, option awards to Genentech employees represented a considerable part of their compensation. In 2007, for example, the value of the annual option grant was roughly $36,000 per Genentech employee.

Despite this success and rewards for all parties, Roche decided, towards the end of 2008, to once again acquire full ownership of Genentech and continue Genentech research and development within the context of a more traditional Big Pharma R&D organization. Given the success of the relationship while it lasted in that particular form until full acquisition in 2009, what prompted this decision? In communicating their acquisition offer, Roche argued plausibly that Genentech had become a very different, much larger company than at the time of the floatation. By 2008, Roche saw considerable duplication of effort and cost at Roche and Genentech in functions such as production and late-stage development, which could be eliminated after full acquisition. Moreover, although not mentioned by Roche, Roche's 'commercialization agreement', giving them exclusive rights to market Genentech products outside the US, was due to run out in 2015. This was surely an important consideration in doing the deal. Had Roche negotiated for an extension of their rights, reaching a satisfactory new agreement would have been difficult. Other big capable pharmaceutical companies would most probably have been interested in competing with Roche for the rights. Genentech could also have decided to go it alone in marketing abroad. Roche might have lost the marketing rights or been forced to pay a very steep price for them.

Roche's commercialization agreement with Genentech secured access for Roche to the output of a highly productive R&D organization with powerful performance incentives for its R&D employees, but only for a limited period of time. To secure this benefit for the long term for Roche, by setting up an evergreen 'commercialization agreement' with Genentech, would probably not have been possible. For Roche to obtain a permanent right would have required Roche and Genentech to permanently fix the percentages of the income of Genentech drugs marketed by Roche that each would receive. Should the economics of pharmaceutical development, marketing and distribution have changed, this would have left either Roche shareholders or Genentech independent shareholders with a legacy agreement putting them in a disadvantaged position. Permanent contracts are difficult to set up in a satisfactory way. In the long term, there is simply too much that may change.

Breaking the trade-offs in creating vs. capturing value

Both ownership-sharing alliances and the majority-owned arrangements such as between Roche and Genentech are attractive solutions in setting up a motivating environment for pharmaceutical R&D. Yet both have drawbacks from the perspective of Big Pharma shareholders. Alliances are able to offer entrepreneurial rewards to employees, but venture capital investors and R&D employees themselves can be expected to capture much of the benefits. The arrangement between Roche and Genentech allowed Roche shareholders, for a while, as majority shareholders in Genentech, to have their cake and eat it. But this arrangement was not sustainable. Big Pharma companies face a difficult trade-off between creating value by collaborating with an entrepreneurial R&D organization able to set up motivating incentives and capturing a good share of the value created.

The tactics listed in Figure 7.5 hint at an interesting possibility to get around this problem. When R&D managers receive shares in a company, they receive rights whose value reflects the value of their work. But R&D managers could be given rights whose value more directly reflects the value of the work they do: namely, rights to the income from the drugs that they research and develop. R&D managers in the pharmaceutical industry are usually not rewarded in this way. But, as mentioned above, creative workers in the film and other industries are frequently rewarded with rights to the income from the products they develop.

If Big Pharma companies want to motivate R&D employees by letting them share in the business income they help to generate, it is attractive to do so directly by offering employees rights to a share of the income from the drugs they develop. That way, pharma company shareholders and employees can capture more of any gains in productivity. No additional investors are needed to set up an arms-length transaction to value the product rights granted to R&D managers. Once candidate drugs are successfully registered for prescription sale, they are then marketed and sold by the pharmaceutical company and R&D managers get their share of the revenues or profits.

However, from the perspective of R&D managers, there is a disadvantage to receiving rights to income from drugs developed rather than rights to the shares of a drug development company. Shares in a drug development company are more attractive because the shares are traded. This allows the managers to sell their shares to get timely rewards, and the price at which they sell their shares reflects the market's estimate of the value of their work when they complete it. In contrast, there is no established market in rights to the potential future income of drugs in development. In the absence of such a market, R&D managers would have to wait to cash in their rights until their company actually received revenues from sale of the drugs they have researched and developed. They might receive their share of the revenues only 10–20 years after carrying out the work – not timely rewards. And the rewards they get would also relate to the success of subsequent work outside their control but necessary to further develop, register and commercialize the candidate drug rather than to the success of their own work.

These disadvantages could be removed if there were a market in royalties on the potential future revenues of drugs in development, as there is a market in company shares. Because investments in pharmaceutical R&D are so large, Big Pharma could probably create such a market if they chose to do so, and would then be able to offer rewards to R&D

employees with characteristics much more similar to those available to them from small drug development companies.

A Big Pharma R&D organization could be set up to resemble a portfolio of venture capital funds, financed entirely by the company – with the critical difference that, at the end of a defined period, instead of selling a portfolio of small R&D companies and rewarding fund managers and company managers with a share of the profits, Big Pharma companies would sell shares of the rights to the future revenues of drugs under development in the portfolio of projects. Individual R&D project managers could then be rewarded with a share of the proceeds. The big company would continue to own the majority of the rights to the revenues and would have the assured right to further develop, manufacture, market and sell the drugs. It could thus become a platform for a number of independent new product development teams in much the same way as a publisher provides a platform for a number of independent authors who develop the new products, the books that the publishing house needs.

There are plenty of difficulties with putting this specific idea into practice. For example, there is a need to set up a mechanism to ensure R&D managers have an incentive to keep R&D costs down as well as to generate revenues. But the radical idea of setting up an active market in minority rights to the development assets of pharmaceutical companies – their candidate drugs – is not an entirely fanciful idea. There are already substantial companies in this area. Royalty Pharma has 'royalty interests in 39 approved and marketed products and two products in clinical trials and/or under review with the United States Food and Drug Administration (FDA) and/or the European Medicines Agency (EMA).'[34] There appears to be an appetite among investors for this type of investment.

Conclusions

While Chapters 4 and 5 focused on problems with suppliers, and Chapter 6 looked at employees, this chapter focused on an activity, innovation and, in particular pharmaceutical R&D, which occupies a middle ground. As we say in Chapter 2 with ERP installations, it may be so difficult to set up collaboration with suppliers that it is worth doing more of the work in-house. But here we have seen that the converse is also true: it may be so difficult to set up collaboration for in-house work that it is worth outsourcing – even for activities in which you do intend to build competitive advantage. That is the case for new product development. Outsourcing makes it easier to find people who have the capabilities you need and easier to measure their performance by putting a market value on the work they do. Being able to more rapidly and objectively measure the value of the work done makes it easier to create a sense of purpose in the R&D team as well as making it easier to offer timely financial rewards for good performance. Unfortunately, the more responsibility you transfer to partners, the more difficult it is to capture the value created by doing the work for yourself. Outsourcing may create more value as a whole, but your outsourcing partners will likely capture most of it.

If you can effectively direct and control R&D in-house, that is still likely to be the best route to capture value for your company and its shareholders. But to do this the CEO and top management team need to have specialist expertise to effectively direct employees in new product development. Using their expertise, they need to create organizational alignment around clear goals – which can be facilitated by setting up accountable performance units evaluated on medium-term rather than short-term performance goals. Top management also need good early indicators of performance – but they should avoid explicitly basing powerful performance rewards on these early indicators. And they may want to involve external partners to further enhance the quality of their evaluations of people and performance.

If you choose to outsource, there are two tricks to pull off to be successful. The first is to make it as easy as possible for the people with the capabilities you need to find you and offer to collaborate with you, so that you don't have to heavily invest in finding and integrating them as partners. You can do this by means of a platform with an open interface, offering standardized research capabilities that external development teams could plug into.

The second is to outsource in a way that minimizes what you need to pay to third-party financial investors. To do this, you can take ownership stakes in the small companies that you work with, in order to share in the value they create. And you will want to set up agreements with the companies under which you retain responsibility for work and assets where you have distinctive advantages, so that you preserve as much bargaining power as possible.

If you still fear that outsourcing will give away too much value to your external partners, you can consider more radical alternatives for how to set up R&D in-house and to reward those who are key to its success. In order to establish highly autonomous internal R&D units, with wide responsibilities, and rewards linked to their performance, you could even seek to establish an active market in royalty rights to new drugs in development. What you will be looking for is a set up that provides most of the benefits of outsourcing, while retaining as much control and value in-house as possible.

In introducing new products into the portfolio, there is no clear path to finding the 'sweet spot'. You have to work out what collaboration strategy best lets you meet the success requirements based on who you are and your specific situation. For pharmaceuticals and other innovation-reliant industries, a good collaboration design itself becomes a key source of competitive advantage.

---

[1] Andrew Jack, 'Back to the lab: Pharmaceuticals'. *Financial Times*, 13th August 2013.

[2] So how have the big pharmaceutical companies been able to maintain their market positions even while struggling to innovate? Pharma R&D is much more expensive and time-consuming than in other innovation-dependent industries such as high-tech R&D, and as a result only the larger pharma companies (referred to as 'Big Pharma') have been able to put up the table stakes necessary to finance all the work necessary to bring a new drug to market. In addition, many Big Pharma companies such as Sanofi-Aventis and Pfizer have pursued very active acquisition policies, buying other pharma companies for the drugs in their portfolio and integrating the sales and marketing organizations of the acquired companies into their own. The companies have been able to maintain revenues, but at the cost of investor skepticism mentioned above. And because drugs have such a short patent life, companies reliant on acquisitions have to 'run to stand still'.

[3] High levels of cholesterol are generally associated with an increased risk of heart disease. However, cholesterol can be carried in the blood by two different types of lipids, low density lipoproteins (LDL) and high density lipoproteins (HDL). People with a naturally higher percentage of cholesterol occurring in high density lipoproteins, 'good cholesterol', have a lower risk of heart disease. Unfortunately, using drugs to increase the percentage of cholesterol carried in high density lipoproteins does not, it turns out, necessarily reduce the occurrence of heart disease.

4   See Carl Bialik, 'Relatively Small Number of Deaths Have Big Impact in Pfizer Drug Trial'. *The Wall Street Journal*, 6th December 2006, which also covers a number of other points made in the paragraph.

5   Or a device or an immune response modulator (e.g. vaccine) or bioequivalent.

6   For details on the funnel in the pharmaceutical drug pipeline see, for example, <www.pharma.org/inno­vation>. There is a fairly wide range of figures for the costs of developing a new drug. $800 million is definitely at the low end; you will find values up to $2 billion quoted in various sources but $800 million is quite high enough to make the point that developing a new drug is very expensive.

7   'Pharma 2020: The Vision. Which Path Will You Take?' PriceWaterhouseCoopers 2007.

8   For 2011, 2012, there are signs of a modest uptick in performance based on the number of US FDA approvals of new drugs. Some of the efforts to improve productivity we describe in the chapter may perhaps be paying off.

9   See, for example, Gordon Schnell, 'Outside Counsel; Pfizer's Cholesterol Gambit: Dodging the Antitrust Laws; The Law of Tying; FDA Immunity; Dealing With Abuse; Conclusion'. *New York Law Journal*, p. 4, col. 4, Volume 234, 12th October 2005.

10 'Trial Data May Delay Lipitor Follow-On', Analyst Says. *Washington Drug Letter*, 21st November 2005.

11 Based on research by the authors together with CE Asset Management AG, a Swiss asset management company focused on corporate excellence. What constitutes a 'background in pharmaceutical R&D' includes some element of judgement but the directional conclusion stands.

12 There is also an alternative organizational solution: the 'Co CEO'. Among the top hi-tech companies both Motorola and RIM in 2011 had two Co CEOs, one with a more technical background and one with a more general management background. This solution may work well in specific circumstances, particularly if the Co CEOs develop a very close working relationship. (In fashion businesses where there is a similar problem of blending the creative and innovative with the commercial, the creative partner and the commercial partner are sometimes husband and wife!) But divided responsibilities may create a problem. Philips, the Dutch electronics company, for example, historically had Co CEOs in all business units but accountability problems led to this double-headed structure being abandoned.

13 We also attempted to test the hypothesis empirically with the generous help of and a database from CE Asset Management AG. There is unfortunately a very small sample of Big Pharma companies, 12 for the purpose of our analysis, and we can observe no strong consistent differences in company performance based on CEO qualifications. We did, however, also look at the evidence on the performance of CEOs with different educational backgrounds and work experience in high-tech and fashion retail, two industries where, as in pharma, new product development plays a critical role. We tested the hypothesis that CEOs with strong job experience in this development function (product development in high-tech, product range development in fashion retail) would perform better than those without such job experience. In high-tech and fashion retail, where the sample of companies is in both cases large, we found that, on average, CEOs with a strong background in development perform better than those with industry experience in other line functions and they in turn perform better than CEOs from outside the industry or with a background in a support function, such as legal or finance. On the basis tested, the difference between CEOs with a background in development and those from outside the industry or from support functions appears statistically significant at the five per cent level. The performance difference between CEOs with a background in development and other line functions does not

appear statistically significant. This is consistent with what top pharma managers were telling us about appropriate qualifications in the pharma industry.

[14] A number of big pharmaceutical companies have at different times split the responsibility for R&D. There were varying opinions on the advisability of so doing. If done, it may make it more difficult to ensure that R&D is properly represented in a small top executive team.

[15] There is an element of judgement in deciding who counts as having a relevant educational and professional background. Others might perhaps count slightly differently but the basic message remains.

[16] Brent Schlender, 'Incredible: The Man Who Built Pixar's Innovation Machine'. *Fortune*, 15th November 2004.

[17] Henry Chesbrough in an interview with Peter Andrews, *Open Innovation: using research from everywhere for new product and service development*, May 2003 from IBM Consulting Services, see <http://www-935.ibm.com/services/in/igs/pdf/g510-3300-00-etr-research-from-everywhere.pdf>. Downloaded 12th March 2011.

[18] See Larry Huston and Nabil Sakkab, 'Connect and Develop: Inside Procter and Gamble's New Model for Innovation'. *Harvard Business Review*, March 2006.

[19] Sildenafil is indeed also, under another brand name, Revatio, used to treat hypertension.

[20] Robert Weisman, 'At Novartis, a winning formula; Fishman's research tack, Cambridge ties pay off'. *The Boston Globe*, 4th January 2011.

[21] <http://www.gsk.com/collaborations/academic.htm>. Downloaded 3rd June 2011.

[22] Peter Tollman, Yves Morieux, Jeanine Kelly Murphy, and Ulrik Schulze independently make this observation in the report 'Can R&D Be Fixed? Lessons from Biopharma Outliers'. The Boston Consulting Group, September 2011.

[23] Reorganization of R&D into independent performance units at GSK began under Jean-Pierre Garnier, see 'Rebuilding the R&D Engine in Big Pharma'. *Harvard Business Review*, May 2008. It has continued under Sir Andrew Witty's leadership and was discussed in Q4 2008 GlaxoSmithKline Earnings conference call.

[24] <http://www.gsk.com/content/dam/gsk/globals/documents/pdf/GSK-RandD-Seminar-March-2012.pdf>.

[25] Ben Hirschler, 'GlaxoSmithKline boss says new drugs can be cheaper'. Reuters Health E-Line, 14th March 2013.

[26] Patrick Vallance, President of pharmaceutical R&D, GlaxoSmithKline plc at JPMorgan Global Healthcare Conference, January 2013.

[27] 'Measuring the return from pharmaceutical innovation 2012' – a report from Deloitte and Thomson Reuters, December 2012.

[28] <http://www.gsk.com/content/dam/gsk/globals/documents/pdf/GSK-RandD-Seminar-March-2012.pdf>.

[29] Biotech venture capital funds are a form of private equity fund. We will discuss how private equity funds work in some detail in Chapter 8, but we focus there on buyout funds and not on venture capital. Two key differences between venture capital funds and the buyout funds are that venture capital funds do

not leverage their investments with debt and, while buyout fund managers are usually generalists, venture capital fund managers typically have a specialist background in the field that they invest in, biotech, hi-tech or clean-tech, for example.

[30] Big companies can offer stock options too, but one R&D team manager would have far less effect on this stock than on the stock of a small R&D focused company.

[31] These market-driven estimates of the likely value of candidate drugs are still quite rough, but at a minimum the VC process provides a more objective basis for managerial rewards than the equivalent effort within a Big Pharma company.

[32] 'Roche and Molecular Partners Enter Into Alliance'. Roche press release. 4th December 2013 <http://www.roche.com/research_and_development/partnering/partnering-media/partnering_news-2013-12-04.htm>.

[33] 'Basel will Aufholen' ('Basle wants to catch up'). *NZZ am Sonntag*, 13th September 2009. Drugs registered since floatation: Avastin 2004, Tarceva 2004 and Lucentis 2006 (marketed by Novartis).

[34] <www.royaltypharma.com>. Downloaded 29th January 2013.

Chapter 8

Collaboration between Investors and Managers

Now we tackle another tough collaboration challenge, one that arises from the separation between ownership and management in business enterprises. How can owners ensure that the managers they hire are able and motivated to pursue the owners' interests? This is difficult even for entrepreneurs who devote substantial amounts of time to the business. But most large Western companies are now owned instead by financially-oriented investors, such as pension funds, mutual funds, endowments, sovereign wealth funds and wealthy private individuals.

Working from our framework, we can see that financial investors face major collaboration issues (see Figure 8.1 below). With little time available to devote to individual investments, and with the need to take collective decisions about joint investments, they are severely limited in their ability to select or direct managers. In order for these owners to select able managers and set up effective agreements to get what they want, everything needs to be made easy for them. Here again is the framework, emphasizing this special challenge for investors.

Without the ability to select and provide good direction to managers, investors may see subpar or even negative returns. Designing effective collaboration between investors and managers is important not just to investors but also to managers, as it influences the demands put on them, their pay, and the strategies they can pursue to create value. This is an old problem with no perfect solution, but investors and managers now have more options at their disposal. Besides the mainstay of the publicly held company, they can work with varying kinds of privately-held structures through private equity.

Private equity over the years has occasioned heated debate on its social and economic merits. But now that it has matured, we need a more balanced perspective. A popular view is that private equity is good for investors but bad for the economy – private equity funds make money

Figure 8.1 'What you want takes account of your abilities': a problem for investors

by short-term asset stripping. In this chapter we argue the reverse: private equity is good for the economy yet not particularly good, on average, for investors – who receive little of the additional value created to compensate for the investments' higher risk and lesser liquidity.

The different tactics used to keep things simple for investors also make private equity relatively more attractive for some types of business investment and business strategy than others. We illustrate this by describing some examples of private equity buyouts. Finally, we argue that publicly held companies with diversified portfolios, though able to pursue some of the strategies adopted by private equity owners, have some basic disadvantages in competing with private equity.

Publicly held companies

The most common vehicle for collaboration between financial investors and managers is the public company.[1] To make governance simple for investors, boards of directors act as special partners to investors, helping them overcome their governance difficulties. Investors, as shareholders, retain 'ultimate control' via their appointment of directors, most of whom are non-executive overseers of the actual executives. But the board takes away from investors almost all of their responsibility for selecting managers, setting up agreements with them and making these agreements work.

While public, 'joint-stock' companies have prospered, observers have long recognized that, as a result of lack of time, expertise or motivation, their boards may not do a good job in representing investors' interests.[2] As far back as 1776, Adam Smith commented that these directors:

Being the managers rather of other people's money than their own, it cannot well be expected, that they should watch over it with the same anxious vigilance with which the partners in a private co-partnery frequently watch over their own . . . Negligence and profusion, therefore, must always prevail, more or less, in the management of such a company.[3]

While Smith's language is colourful and his conclusions extreme, he nevertheless put his finger on what has remained a perennial problem for the investors in public companies.

Figure 8.2 shows the tactics that public company investors typically use to simplify their responsibilities for collaboration. Essentially, these types of investors meet all the requirements by transferring decision-making to non-executive directors.

Non-executive directors as intermediary partners for investors

Because a public company has an unlimited life, it will eventually need a new CEO and other top managers. Investors can be involved in the selection, but they need help to collectively decide if and when a new leader is required and to come up with a specific proposal as to who it should be. They get this help from non-executive directors who typically chair the governance (or nomination) committee of the board.

Figure 8.2 Public company investors' tactics to be able to get what they want

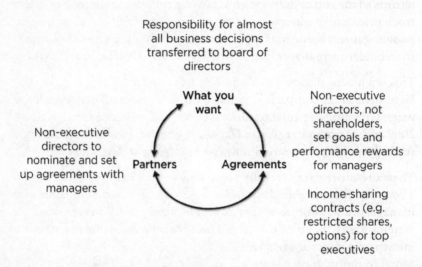

Responsibility for almost all business decisions transferred to board of directors

What you want

Non-executive directors, not shareholders, set goals and performance rewards for managers

Non-executive directors to nominate and set up agreements with managers

Partners   Agreements

Income-sharing contracts (e.g. restricted shares, options) for top executives

Investors also need help from non-executive directors to set up agreements that will motivate managers to do what investors want.[4] This is difficult because investors lack reliable objective measures of managers' performance on their behalf. But even non-executive directors are not particularly well placed to exercise their subjective judgement about how well managers are performing.

No reliable objective measure of performance for all shareholders

As a financial investor in a public company, you can specify in general terms the result you would like managers to achieve by their decisions and actions. Of course, you would like them to boost the returns from your investment by creating 'shareholder value'. But connecting that goal to an agreement that motivates managers is harder than it looks.

The best measure of the value that managers create for shareholders is *total shareholder return* (essentially the increase in the market value of the company plus the dividends paid out) over a certain period. This accurately measures the actual value created for shareholders that buy and sell shares on specific dates. But shareholders don't all buy and don't all sell at the same time. If the CEO is paid on the basis of shareholder returns to the end of one year and, at the beginning of the next year, the stock price and market value of the company fall sharply, there may be poor alignment between the CEO's compensation and the returns most shareholders actually receive.

This is a practical as well as a theoretical problem. Stock prices, even of large diversified companies, may be quite volatile over a number of years. GE's stock price, for example, reached $40 in 2007, fell to $7 in 2009 and, at time of writing in 2014, is at $26. So value created depends strongly on when you buy and when you cash in your shares.

There are other dangers to basing managers' rewards on stock prices. The stock price is a leading indicator of business performance, but managers can manipulate this indicator at least in the short term. In extreme cases, as at Enron, executives may break the law to distort information for stock markets and thereby boost their compensation. More commonly, managers may simply favour short-term financial results – which are readily visible to markets – over long-term opportunities that would better serve the company.

To limit these problems, investors can tie executive compensation to a broader and more sophisticated set of performance measures. If they use stock options, they can require that the company perform better than peers – so executives don't benefit from cyclical factors. Performance rewards may be linked to non-stock-price measures such as profits, or to non-financial measures such as market share.

But with no fully reliable measure (this side of eternity) of the true returns for investors, it is impossible to say if adding sophistication and complexity to goals will better align the interests of managers and shareholders. And most compensation systems suffer from the added problem, discussed in a general way in Chapter 6 on employees, that executives share in gains when the company prospers, but do not share proportionately when the company falters.

Limits on the help non-executive directors can provide

Since there are no reliable metrics, investors need their boards to use subjective judgement to set goals and measure performance. But there is a limit to what non-executive directors can be expected to do on shareholders' behalf.

Ability of non-executive directors

Directors have limited ability to oversee businesses because they serve on a part-time basis.[5] A survey carried out for the 2003 Higgs report on the role and effectiveness of non-executive directors in the UK[6] – where these directors spend more time on the role than in many others – suggested that they spend about 15–30 days a year in the role.

Serving part-time is helpful in many ways. It differentiates their roles from company managers and gives them a more impartial view of executive selection and compensation. Without strong personal ties to the full-time managers, and without the dependence that a full-time position would entail, they can take a dispassionate view of company performance measures and risk. Their compensation can be modest, so investors need not be concerned with it; they can have other jobs and so bring a diversity of perspectives to company decisions. Top executives from other companies who may be well qualified can find the time to take on this role.

But not surprisingly, when asked about their ability to add value in the Higgs survey, non-executive directors' greatest concern was the limited number of days they were able to devote to the role. Part-time non-executives can't go deeply into the issues.[7] This basic difficulty has not changed since the Higgs report, as it is inherent in public company governance.

Motivation

Besides their limited ability to represent investors, non-executive directors may not be motivated in the same way as investors.[8] A large group of financial investors cannot be expected to motivate non-executive directors to act in their interests by directing and controlling their actions. It is, after all, shareholders' inability to direct and control executives that makes it valuable to have non-executive directors. At most large public companies, investors have little to do with selecting these directors in the first place – they simply ratify lists chosen by the management or the existing board. And there are, if anything, more problems in setting up financial incentives to appropriately motivate non-executive directors than to motivate executives. Offering powerful performance incentives to non-executive directors tends to compromise the role of the board in controlling executives.[9] These directors play a key role on audit and risk committees, ensuring that executives are not artificially inflating company performance or taking excessive risks. Directors with powerful performance incentives will be inclined toward exactly these behaviours. Likewise, the compensation committee is responsible for setting not just executive compensation but also their own. This works because board compensation is fairly small and simple. If directors start to have strong incentives, investors will need to get directly involved in setting their compensation – which will be difficult.

Figure 8.3 shows all these challenges for investors in public companies. It is these difficulties that make the public company such an imperfect vehicle for collaboration between investors and managers, as Adam Smith observed over 200 years ago. But it has not been easy to come up with an alternative.

Figure 8.3 Difficulties with the public company approach

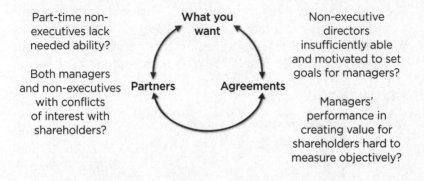

Part-time non-executives lack needed ability?

Both managers and non-executives with conflicts of interest with shareholders?

What you want

Partners

Agreements

Non-executive directors insufficiently able and motivated to set goals for managers?

Managers' performance in creating value for shareholders hard to measure objectively?

Private equity

Smith's 'private co-partnery' has, in recent decades, made a comeback and become just such an alternative. Advocates of private equity, such as Michael Jensen in his seminal work 'Eclipse of the Public Corporation' in 1989,[10] argue that private equity solves many of the collaboration problems in the public company – such as executives' tendency to horde or unproductively use their cash flow. Private equity has grown enormously and is now the ownership form for a large number of US and European companies.

But there are also prominent critics who argue that private equity firms take excessive risks for investors and damage the businesses they acquire to create short-term returns. In 2005, for example, Franz Müntefering, then Chairman of the ruling German Social Democratic Party,[11] started a prominent 'Heuschreckendebatte'[12] in the German media, comparing private equity firms to a plague of locusts who feed on businesses and suck them dry. The 2012 US presidential election, featuring a candidate who had become wealthy as a private equity fund manager, included similar concerns.[13] (Readers not familiar with private equity may wish to read the textbox, 'How private equity funds work' before continuing.)

How private equity funds work

Private equity funds are generally set up as partnerships. A private equity firm – typically itself a partnership – combines the roles of 'general partner' and 'fund manager' in the private equity fund. A number of outside investors each commit to putting a certain amount of money in the fund as 'limited partners'. As such they have rights to most of the fund profits but not to any management control. Although funds typically have an investor advisory council, it has few powers, and the general partner cannot easily be removed during the life of the fund.

Once the fund has reached an investment commitment of a target amount of money, the private equity firm closes it to additional investment. The private equity firm then identifies suitable business opportunities and invests the fund accordingly. Each fund is liquidated, selling all its business investments within a pre-set time frame, usually about 10 years.

Fund profits come mostly from capital gains on the sale of portfolio businesses.

General partners often expand the reach – and profitability – of their funds by using debt leverage. They buy a company for a certain amount of money, but much of the cash comes from debt added to the company's balance sheet. When it's time to sell, if the company has done well, then the fund pockets all of the gains and merely pays the debt off at face value.

In return for managing the fund, financial investors pay the private equity firm in two main ways. First, the firm receives a fee as a percentage of the value of assets under management. Then, frequently at the end of the life of the fund, it also receives a share of the profits from the fund – a so-called carried interest in the profits – often subject to achieving a minimum rate of return. For a fund investing in large buyouts, for example, firms typically charge investors 1.5 per cent to 2 per cent of assets under management in the fund, plus 20 per cent of all fund profits.

The partners in a private equity firm do not directly manage the companies invested in or acquired by the fund. Instead they exercise control over portfolio companies by serving on the corresponding boards of directors, which in turn hire and oversee the CEOs in question.

A different collaboration strategy

Compared with public companies, investors in private equity funds find it easier to set up collaboration. Figure 8.4 shows their tactics. They go much further than public company shareholders in transferring responsibility for decisions to partners. They allow the private equity firm to decide not just on management but also which companies they will invest in. They also adopt a second, less obvious but very powerful, tactic that simplifies their involvement. They make their investments of strictly limited duration. These tactics make it much easier for private equity investors to choose partners and set up agreements with them.

Figure 8.4 Private equity investors' tactics to be able to get what they want

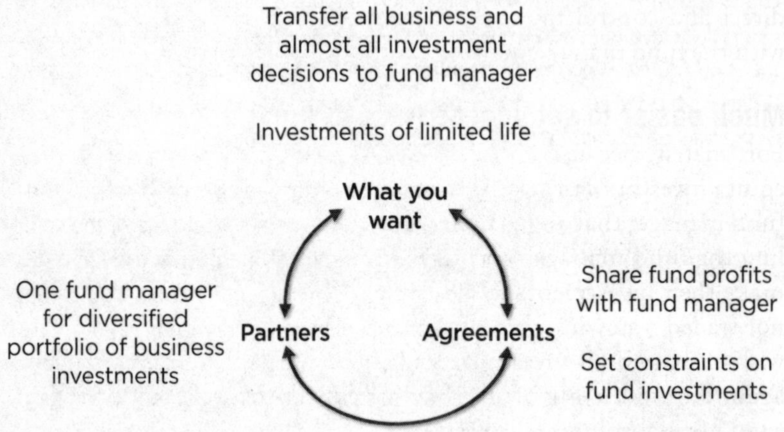

Transfer all business and
almost all investment
decisions to fund manager

Investments of limited life

**What you
want**

One fund manager
for diversified
portfolio of business
investments

Partners   **Agreements**

Share fund profits
with fund manager

Set constraints on
fund investments

Full-time intermediary partners

Investors in a private equity fund of limited life are easily able to directly choose the management team.[14] A fund management team presents itself to potential financial investors, and their track record with previous funds simplifies the investors' decision.[15] If enough investors individually agree to invest, the team can establish and run the fund. For a fund with a limited and fairly short life, it should not be necessary to appoint a new fund management team during the life of the fund[16] – a choice that would require a difficult collective decision on the part of investors.[17]

In contrast to non-executive directors in public companies, the partners in private equity firms that manage funds on behalf of investors are full timers and, as we will discuss, powerfully motivated to do what investors want. They serve among the directors of the companies the fund invests in, and the fund's investment gives them far more power than the non-executive directors of most large publicly-owned enterprises. While they manage multiple companies at a time, they generally have more time to put into each one than these public-company directors. And they have support from their firm in exercising their duties as directors. Private equity firms frequently appoint two directors to each company in which they invest, one senior partner and one more junior manager.

Reliant on simple effective agreements to motivate managers

Private equity investors don't have non-executive directors to help them direct and control the fund manager. So the agreements they set up with the fund manager have to do all the work of aligning interests.

Much easier to set goals to measure performance

Fortunately, because a private equity fund has a limited life, private equity investors can relatively easily set up a simple agreement with a fund manager that aligns their interests, without directing and controlling the fund manager during the life of the fund. All fund investors make their investments at the same time and – as funds are generally not traded – stay invested in the fund over its full life. The fund starts with cash, and all investments must be made and liquidated or sold again during the life of the fund. So the return to investors over the fund life is absolutely clear.

In contrast to the total shareholder return to shareholders of a public company, the return to private equity investors over the life of the fund is not a potentially misleading early indicator of the cash value they will eventually receive from their investment. It is the cash value they actually receive. Agreements that share a fund's profits with its manager should therefore motivate the manager to do what investors want. Likewise, the limited lifespan makes it easier for the directors of fund companies to set strong performance incentives for their executives. They can measure exactly what the individual company will be worth at the end of the fund, because they will sell or liquidate it.

Because investors can measure their return so accurately, they can establish a powerful profit-sharing agreement with fund managers. With such an effective agreement, investors are able to transfer extensive responsibility to the fund managers, relinquishing almost all control over what gets done with their money for the life of the fund. The different elements of private equity work closely together to promote effective collaboration.[18]

Similar difficulties in aligning rewards when performance is poor

In contrast to public company shareholders, private equity investors can easily set goals for managers and accurately measure their performance in achieving them. This is a big advantage. But private equity investors do face problems in meeting the other requirements for setting up good agreements.

Private equity fund managers share the fund profits with investors, but do not share proportionately in fund losses. This means that rewards are not fully aligned if the fund makes a loss – which could lead the managers to take more risks to make a profit than investors would want. Public company shareholders face a similar problem when they offer a CEO stock options, but they have the benefit of support from non-executive directors to manage any conflicts that may arise. Private equity investors have to manage the problem without this support.

Private equity investors do have a number of tactics to limit the problem (see Figure 8.5), similar to those we discussed for investment banking in Chapter 6.

Figure 8.5 Tactics for aligning rewards with performance measured

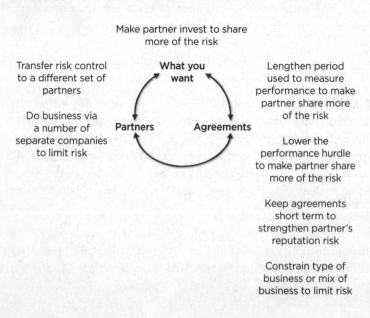

Make partner invest to share more of the risk

Transfer risk control to a different set of partners

What you want

Lengthen period used to measure performance to make partner share more of the risk

Do business via a number of separate companies to limit risk

Partners

Agreements

Lower the performance hurdle to make partner share more of the risk

Keep agreements short term to strengthen partner's reputation risk

Constrain type of business or mix of business to limit risk

All the tactics draw on one of two broad strategies: make your partner share more risk, or set constraints on your partner's behaviour to limit the risk or the magnitude of loss. We can expect these tactics to be quite effective in private equity, which involves less risk than investment bank trading. And while private equity investors have fewer tactics available than public company shareholders, they make more extensive use of those they have.

Private equity funds take measures to ensure that managers share in the business risk. Top managers are expected to invest in the businesses they manage, to have 'skin in the game'. Much of the rewards for private equity partners are long term. This helps to prevent them capturing value in a good business year – or on a single good deal – and then not sharing in later losses. Private equity firms are also in the public eye and suffer major reputation risks if they don't produce good results – the partners may find it difficult to raise the next fund.

The funds do struggle to set the height of the hurdle for managers to receive performance rewards. It should be high enough so that the fund manager receives rewards only if the fund meets demanding targets, but low enough so that the manager isn't tempted to take excessive risk to meet the targets. Finding the right balance involves some difficult trade-offs. But the hurdle rate is in practice probably not a major issue for private equity. The business model is based on highly leveraged investments with a wide spread in returns: these investments tend either to make a high positive return or a negative return, with comparatively few investments yielding positive returns which are below a modest performance hurdle.[19]

Setting constraints to limit the risk of poor performance

Any constraints that private equity investors set on fund managers' behaviour to limit risk must be quite simple, as investors themselves have to enforce them. Fund management contracts commonly include two powerful and simple constraints to reduce risks.

Most helpfully, the fund contract can oblige managers to invest in a diversified portfolio of businesses. The probability of a large, widely diversified buyout fund making a loss over its full 10-year life is quite low.[20] One of the main causes of low returns, particularly for previously successful fund managers, has been individual investments that were large relative to the size of the fund. For example, such an investment in XO Communications contributed to Forstmann Little's near demise.[21] More recently, an unsuccessful investment in the music company EMI, representing 30 per cent of the investment in two of their funds, has caused problems for private equity firm Terra Firma. Its response has been to state that no more than 10 per cent of future funds will be committed to a single investment.[22]

The fund management contract will also prevent the fund from taking on debt or guaranteeing debt taken on by the portfolio companies in which it invests. If this is done, all debt will be taken on by the individual portfolio companies and the fund's liability for problems in individual portfolio companies will be limited to the level of the equity investment in the individual company concerned. This is quite helpful in reducing the fund losses if one of the businesses in which a fund invests goes bankrupt. Diversified public companies often guarantee the debt of their subsidiaries and their liability is not limited in this way.

Greater difficulties in specifying favourable terms

The great advantage of private equity for investors is also its Achilles heel. Investors, who have little expertise or resources to manage investments, benefit from delegating nearly all of these responsibilities to the fund manager – who can now act more aggressively with portfolio companies than their counterparts directing public companies. But fund managers, in return, have so much authority that they gain substantial bargaining power over these investors – so that they collect the lion's share of the returns from the funds.

Private equity funds certainly make high gross returns. But these are necessary to make net returns for fund investors comparable to what these investors would receive as shareholders in public companies. After subtracting the fund managers' 'two and twenty,' not to mention the rewards to company executives who also do quite well under private equity, there is not so much left for investors.

Some fund managers are able to achieve persistently strong returns for their investors. Yet many studies suggest that average returns to investors in private equity buyouts are pretty similar to shareholder returns in public companies.[23] Any additional value created by buyout invest-ments appears on average to go to the fund managers and, to a lesser extent, the company executives. (You might say, 'Who's worried about the average? Let's identify fund managers with persistently high returns and focus on them.' But, as explained in the textbox 'Making use of persistence?', that is not quite so easy to do.)

Making use of persistence?

It should be easy, in principle, to find a really good fund management team with a supernormal return. There is some persistence in the returns that fund managers achieve. A fund run by a particular manager is more likely to make an above-average return if the manager's previous fund did similarly well.

If a public company has excellent executives, there will be more demand for its shares and, with a fixed number of shares, the share price will go up. But private equity funds all tend to have similar terms regardless of their success. Only a few buyout fund managers, such as Bain Capital, demand a higher share of the profits to reflect their strong management track record.[24]

At first, this seems like a bonanza for fund investors. Identify managers with the best fund returns and invest the next time they raise a fund! Making money, unfortunately, is never quite that simple. There are two main prob-lems. First, fund managers seek to raise a specific amount of money for a fund. They don't just take any money they are offered. So, the funds of top-performing fund managers are often oversubscribed. It is a bit like an IPO of a popular stock: you have to be friends or family to get the allocation you want. You can't invest as much as you would like.[25]

Second, you often don't know the return of the previous fund when the fund manager goes out to raise the next one.[26] Fund managers raise new funds after they have invested the last fund but before they have harvested it. While there is persistence of returns between one fund and the next from the same fund manager, there is much less persistence between the returns of the current fund and the fund after next.[27] It doesn't help that private equity returns are not entirely transparent. If you ask the fund manager, their returns are always first quartile!

This is what you would expect if the market for risk capital does a good job. After all, public company shareholders own and control the access to distinctive assets, such as brands or manufacturing facilities, and they ask managers to exploit these assets on their behalf. Private equity investors in funds of limited life have nothing more to offer managers than their own cash, which is an undifferentiated commodity. The only distinctive asset that a fund has before it starts investing is the talent and track record of the management team. If the private equity firm managing the fund is a traditional partnership, owned by its managers, then any reputational value that this talent and track record creates belongs to the managers.

Additionally, investors in a private equity fund of limited life relinquish all control over managers and rely on financial rewards to motivate them to do what they want. With this approach, you must expect to pay managers more than if you direct and control them. Managers take more responsibility for decisions and, because their compensation depends on performance, carry some of the business risk.

Finally, because it is easier to align rewards of investors and managers in a fund of limited life than in a public company, it makes sense for you as an investor to pay managers more – you know there will be no wasted expenditure, no high payments to managers without high value creation for you personally.

Private equity funds may, for many businesses, be able to create more value than public companies, but on average this doesn't help investors much, because private equity managers[28] capture such a high share of any value created.[29]

The pros and cons of the different approaches

We can now summarize the difficulties with and limitations of private equity funds (Figure 8.6) and contrast them with those of public companies. Public companies, as we have discussed, offer investors much more flexibility. They can choose which businesses to invest in, and these investments are liquid. But the price of this flexibility is high.

Setting up collaboration is inherently complex, and investors' partners – the non-executive directors and the company executives – likely to lack the time or the motivation to maximize value for investors.

Figure 8.6 Difficulties with and limitations of the private equity approach

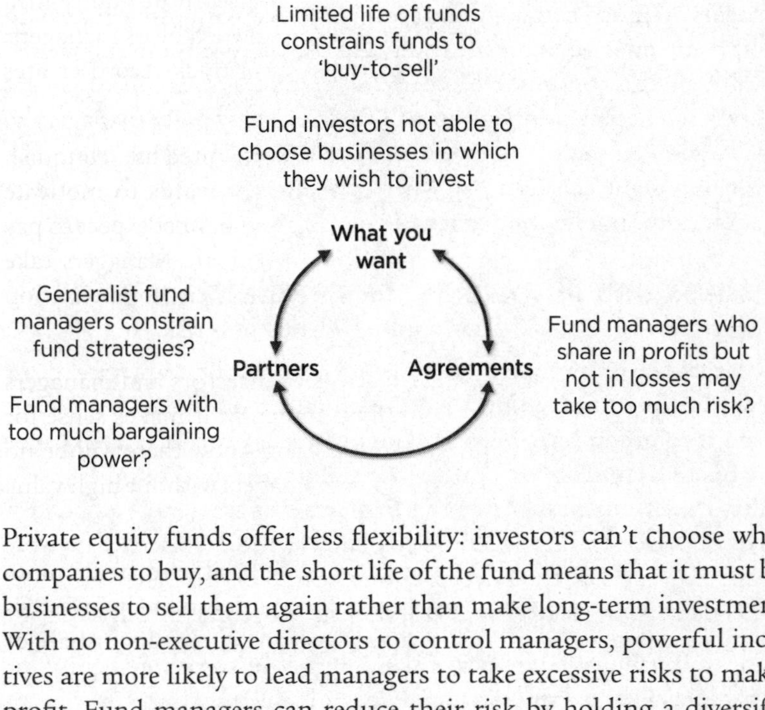

Limited life of funds
constrains funds to
'buy-to-sell'

Fund investors not able to
choose businesses in which
they wish to invest

**What you
want**

Generalist fund
managers constrain
fund strategies?

Partners   **Agreements**

Fund managers who
share in profits but
not in losses may
take too much risk?

Fund managers with
too much bargaining
power?

Private equity funds offer less flexibility: investors can't choose which companies to buy, and the short life of the fund means that it must buy businesses to sell them again rather than make long-term investments. With no non-executive directors to control managers, powerful incentives are more likely to lead managers to take excessive risks to make a profit. Fund managers can reduce their risk by holding a diversified portfolio of companies and industries. But that approach leads fund managers to be generalists rather than possess deep industry-specific skills. That includes adapting the mix of industries to the market opportunities. Funds managed by generalists should shy away from investment targets requiring much specialist industry know-how, such as high-tech businesses.

Accepting all these constraints makes it easier for investors to motivate managers to act in their interests and create more business value. But this comes at a high cost. Investors transfer so much responsibility to managers that the managers gain bargaining power and capture much of any extra value they create.

Where private equity has the advantage over public companies

Managers do much better and investors no worse with funds than with public companies – and private equity has become a substantial market. How far will this continue? While overall predictions are difficult – and depend on whether competition will force private equity managers to sacrifice some of their high rewards in order to entice more investors – we can highlight the territory where private equity has the greatest advantage over public companies.

Business unit buyouts as the heartland for private equity

The largest private equity buyouts involve public-to-private deals where multiple funds jointly acquire an entire public company. But far more common have been buyouts where a fund acquires one or more business units from a diversified public company or takes over a family-owned business. After the first wave of very large public-to-private transactions in the late 1980s, such as RJR Nabisco, there were few such deals until the buyout boom from 2005 to 2007. Since the financial crisis, from 2009 to 2013, they have become rare again.

Business unit buyouts are particularly attractive to private equity for two reasons. First, compared to public company investors, the managers of private equity funds are more skilled at assessing the potential of unquoted business units. Multi-business companies could spin off their unwanted business units with an IPO. But these units have no recent track record as independent businesses, so public company investors would find them hard to value. Companies rarely want to take the time and do the work necessary to get the businesses they divest ready for sale on the public market. In the absence of a 'strategic buyer' – a company with similar operations willing to pay a high price because of synergies with a company business unit – that makes a private equity buyout attractive. Likewise, family-owned companies are also often not ready for an IPO.

Second, their previous owners have often neglected these businesses buried deep in the hierarchy, leaving them with plenty of potential for simple performance improvement via better asset utilization or cost reduction. As one partner in a leading private equity firm told us 'I dream of buying a subsidiary of a subsidiary'. If not neglected, business units may often be managed with a view to meeting broader group objectives, rather than to maximising their own freestanding profit potential. For example, if you are a car company, like Ford, and you own a rental car business, like Hertz, you may be tempted to use it to help sell Ford cars. When Clayton, Dubilier and Rice, together with Carlyle and Merrill Lynch, bought Hertz car rental from Ford, they were later able to float the business on the public market with very attractive returns to investors.[30] Business unit buyouts often have the potential for performance improvement of a kind that is just not available when buying an independent public company. For an example of a successful business unit buyout, see the textbox 'Wincor Nixdorf'.

Wincor Nixdorf

The retail and banking segment of Siemens Nixdorf Information Systems, renamed Wincor Nixdorf and acquired by KKR and Goldman Sachs from Siemens in September 1999, was a subsidiary of a subsidiary. It illustrates the opportunities in business units buried in the hierarchy of large public companies.

When Siemens sold Wincor Nixdorf, the unit's prospects were unclear. Its hardware revenues were expected to come under pressure in their home market, Germany, after the pre Y2K information technology boom. Profit growth would likely depend on substantially increasing revenues and margins in their solutions and services businesses, and in markets outside Germany. And now they would no longer benefit from assistance from Siemens units that were more geographically and operationally diversified.

Wincor Nixdorf's own managers did have a plan for growth, and KKR and Goldman Sachs were able to evaluate its potential as well as its risks. They saw an opportunity, and gave the managers greater entrepreneurial freedom as well as strong performance incentives. They also offered a broad range of employees an opportunity to participate in the IPO on preferential terms. The new private equity owners paid close attention to the business and made top-level decisions rapidly when Wincor Nixdorf management needed them. They also strengthened the unit's cash flow discipline, which had previously been weak.

Under private equity ownership, Wincor Nixdorf successfully made the difficult transition from supplying hardware for the German market to supplying hardware, software solutions and related services globally. Share of international sales grew from 49 per cent just after the private equity buyout[31] to 67 per cent in 2004. The revenue share of solutions and services grew from 33 per cent to 40 per cent over the same period, with a substantial increase in profit margins.

From the year before the buyout in 1999 to the IPO in 2004, a five year period, operating profit increased from €63 million to €116 million, or 13 per cent per year.[32] KKR and Goldman Sachs sold out for almost four times the value of their initial investment.[33] In the four years following the IPO, Wincor Nixdorf continued to perform well but since 2008 there have not been further gains. The sharp increase in profits following the buyout was a one-time performance improvement opportunity. No such opportunity lasts forever, making it sensible for private equity firms to sell when they did to ensure strong returns for their fund investors.[34]

Public-to-private transactions as a tougher challenge

While private equity funds can also make good money on a public-to-private transaction, private equity fund managers are less able to add value here. Public companies are easier for investors to assess as the market values them daily. Funds also face more competition in correcting the underperformance of a public company as opposed to a business unit. Activist investors, such as hedge funds, may perceive the management opportunity and pressure the board to take action. And once a fund bids to take a public company private, the existing shareholders and board of directors may wake up to the opportunity and decide they can themselves take measures to enhance company value.

This competition will drive the acquisition price up relative to business unit buyouts. This is particularly true for large public companies where there is a more liquid and efficient market.

Even here, though, fund managers have two important advantages. Public company boards are simply not as able to spot and correct under-management of strong businesses. Funds also benefit from using debt to leverage the value of profit improvements for investors.

Public company directors not able to set stretch goals

Private equity funds focus on taking companies private where setting stretch goals may be difficult, but measuring progress and keeping management on track is relatively easy. These are 'under-managed' companies with performance upside, but also little performance downside, so the business is suitable for acquiring with high financial leverage.

Under-management is most likely in companies with businesses that have valuable intangible assets – consumer brands, high market share or intellectual property. These businesses may be making, by normal standards, good rates of return. If a business is already making these good returns, it can be hard for the non-executive directors to spot the potential to do better, or to decide how much better. The relative success also makes it hard for directors to push the executives to improve.

Accordingly, funds look for companies whose goals have not been suffi-ciently demanding, but which nevertheless have stable cash flows. These companies require few big risky investments, and performance progress towards meeting goals is easy to measure, permitting rapid corrective action if performance is off track. Once acquired, fund managers are better able to motivate executives to realize the improvement. However, they don't need to direct and control their work to do this. Instead they can rely on offering managers powerful incentives. These are easy for them to set up because the value that business executives create will be accurately measurable when the fund sells the business.

Public company less willing to accept high debt leverage

If companies have stable cash flows and there is little performance downside, they can carry high debt at modest risk. Investors benefit from debt greatly in this case because it leverages the value of any performance improvements at acceptable cost. Investors reap the full profits from gains at the operation while fronting only a small proportion of the capital needed to acquire it. As a result funds have usually acquired companies with high levels of debt.[35]

Unless a focused public company needs debt to finance critical investments or make major acquisitions, shareholders find it hard to make these companies take on a high level of debt.[36] Their executives shy away from debt because their personal risks are much less diversified than the risks of a fund manager investing in a broad portfolio of businesses. Additionally, as Michael Jensen forcefully argued in 'Eclipse of the Public Corporation', public company executives see low debt and a positive cash balance as valuable resources that give them greater freedom of business action.[37]

The high debt makes bankruptcy somewhat more likely, and nearly one in 10 public-to-private buyout transactions[38] ends that way with the fund writing off the investment. But with a portfolio of 10 or more such investments, funds can lose one investment completely and still make a good overall return. Each portfolio business investment is separately financed. For an example of the successful use of debt leverage for a business that was already performing well, see the textbox 'HCA Holdings'.

HCA Holdings

HCA Holdings Inc., which owns a large chain of for-profit US hospitals, shows how private equity funds can prosper with public-to-private transactions. Bain Capital and KKR led a consortium of funds that took HCA private in 2006, and the acquisition was successful for these two key reasons: fund managers' greater ability to set stretch goals, and their greater use of debt leveraging. The HCA buyout had an enterprise value[39] of $33 billion[40] and was, at the time, the largest buyout ever, exceeding even that of RJR Nabisco in 1989.[41]

HCA had been achieving good returns before the buyout.[42] In 2005, it had a return on equity after tax of 32 per cent and a return on net assets before tax and interest of about 16 per cent. But it was the leading hospital chain in the country, and the industry offered significant economies of scale both in purchasing supplies and in jointly developing superior processes. The HCA board demanded a review of opportunities from management and from consultants in 2006, but neither saw potential for substantial growth in profit. Management projected EBITDA growth to continue at the same 3 per cent annual rate, while the consultants expected only 1.4 per cent.

The fund consortium, by contrast, saw much greater potential and was able to make it happen.[43] It set up powerful incentives for HCA managers to grow profits by giving them an ownership stake in the company four times greater than they had before. With a combination of existing restricted stock and stock options with a strike price at the buyout price, plus extra options if the company did especially well, executives had their attention focused on medium-term performance as never before. Short-term performance compensation for top executives was also set up, linked to EBITDA growth. Partly as a result, HCA's EBITDA grew more than twice as fast as these executives had projected: over 7 per cent annually from 2006 to 2010.

While HCA stepped up its performance substantially, debt leverage was essential to making the deal attractive for investors. HCA returned to the public market in 2011, after five years with the funds (and after paying out about $4.5 billion in dividends), at an enterprise value of $41 billion. If HCA had stayed with its existing level of debt, of about $10 billion prior to the buyout, investors would have had to invest, roughly, $23 billion of equity to acquire the company and to achieve, we estimate, a money-multiple, before paying charges to fund managers, of about 1.7 times their initial investment, or an annual rate of return on their investment of about 14 per cent, unremarkable given the risks of a buyout. But the fund consortium had HCA take on an additional $18 billion of debt and invested only $5 billion in equity. With the benefits of this leverage, buyout investors were able to receive a considerably more exciting 3.6 times money-multiple and 35 per cent annual rate of return on their investment. [44]

Advantages of private equity over public conglomerates

At this point readers may wonder why investors can't achieve many of the same advantages of private equity with diversified public companies. These conglomerates compete with private equity funds and add value in similar ways. With their portfolio of unrelated or only loosely related investments, they can do most of the things that a private equity fund can do, including taking controlling ownership of a company and stepping up the management, or taking on more debt at the portfolio level. And they have more flexibility; they can keep investments for the long term instead of selling them.

From the 1960s through the 1980s, acquisitive conglomerates, such as ITT in the US and Hanson in the UK, were a force in the market. Like private equity funds, they focused on buying companies and enhancing their performance. But private equity has largely replaced them since.[45] Most remaining conglomerates, at least in the US and Europe, are family-owned or -controlled.

Conglomerates compete with private equity funds and add value in similar ways. But in private equity it is easier to measure performance and set up appropriate incentives. Being forced to sell the businesses they buy helps private equity funds maximize their returns and maintain sustained performance pressure.

Easier to measure performance and set up appropriate incentives

Conglomerate investors try to set up powerful performance incentives for conglomerate managers, just as private equity investors do with fund managers. But the value created by conglomerate managers is not as clear. Shareholders face the same problems in calculating the true performance for shareholders of a conglomerate as they do in any other public company. So they aren't so comfortable offering powerful incentives. They can't ensure they are well aligned with their own cash returns.

In some respects, the problems of performance measurement are worse for a diversified conglomerate than for a focused company. The value of a conglomerate can be calculated in two different ways: its own market value or the sum of the values of the portfolio companies it owns. Directors need to decide whether to reward managers for increases in the market value of the conglomerate as a holding company or for increases in the asset values of the underlying investments. These values are often quite different. Conglomerates may trade at a substantial premium or a substantial discount to the sum of the values of the companies in their portfolio.

The supposed benefit of greater flexibility to keep portfolio investments for the long term makes the performance measurement problem worse still. If portfolio companies are not systematically sold, it is harder to say how much value the subsidiary company managers have created in these businesses. That makes it more difficult to assess the performance of the business managers as well as the holding company managers in a conglomerate. Performance measurement, and consequently performance management, is a great deal easier in a private equity fund.

Buying-to-sell maximizes returns and creates sustained performance pressure

More importantly, the forced requirement to sell is probably the best strategy for creating value when you acquire a diversified portfolio of unrelated businesses. To maximize returns, you should sell business investments soon after you have corrected underperformance. The market value of the business grows rapidly while you demonstrate its higher return potential. But the longer you hold on to a business with performance on track and that the market is able to correctly value, the more you dilute the return on your initial investment.

Buying-to-sell offers other significant benefits.[46] It maintains performance pressure on operating executives – portfolio businesses are always under the spotlight, as they have either just been acquired or they are just about to be sold. What's more, keeping up the pace of buying and selling investments ensures buyout firms reinforce core skills in business acquisition, performance improvement and disposal. Forced sales also keep fund managers from unproductively investing to create synergies between businesses owned. They maintain their sense of purpose and hold companies only for as long as they can add value. Far from benefiting from the flexibility on selling, many conglomerates suffer from it.[47]

Conclusions

Both private equity and public companies are prominent examples of a phenomenon we have observed throughout the book and will examine explicitly in the next chapter: sharing the different responsibilities and rewards of business ownership among multiple parties.

The underlying problem for financial investors as business owners is that they have little ability, particularly when acting collectively, to take business decisions. Their difficulty in directing and controlling their employees, a focus of our discussion in Chapter 6, is evident. Like the hapless CEO in Chapter 2 who needed a new ERP system but knew nothing about such systems, financial investors must nevertheless find ways to delegate decisions, select managers and set up agreements with them that will align managers' interests with their own.

Managers are equally helpless without the support of investors; they don't have the personal wealth to carry the business risks. Public companies and private equity funds seek to solve the problems of collaboration between investors and managers in very different ways. Private equity investors and managers simply accept their different strengths; investors transfer all decision-making responsibility to the private equity firm that acts as general partner in the fund. Shareholders in public companies try to fudge the issue. Although they are not good at taking decisions, with the help of part-time non-executive directors, they hope to become good enough to somehow retain control.

Private equity's heartland has been in acquiring subsidiary business units and, to a lesser extent, family-owned companies – solid operations with a likely upside once taken over by professional management and managed as independent businesses. Private equity can set up powerful performance incentives for business managers to make sure this is captured quickly and effectively, and can use debt to leverage their efforts. Unless there is a 'strategic buyer' willing to pay a premium price to gain synergies, private equity is hard to beat in this market segment.

Private equity has also made some inroads with acquiring public companies, because fund managers can be more aggressive than non-executive directors in pressuring operating managers. They can also offer strong performance incentives. Moreover, it is difficult to motivate either executive or non-executive directors in a strong, focused public company to take on as much debt as investors might find valuable.

On the other hand, there are still many businesses where a public company works better. Companies that are already publicly quoted and have a good track record, that are performing well, that are engaged in more volatile industries with limited possibilities for debt leverage, or that require specialist management to achieve their full potential, will draw little interest from private equity. Private equity acquisitions are highly disruptive, and fund managers are very well rewarded, so there has to be considerable upside to pay their costs. It's hard to get sufficient upside if you can't leverage the performance gains with a considerable amount of debt.

Private equity is a simple and elegant strategy for setting up collaboration between investors and managers, but it is able to compete against public companies only in a restricted market segment. So private equity and public companies are horses for courses, not direct competitors. After all, the goal of most large private equity buyouts is to sell out to a public company, either directly or via IPO. Understanding the different ways in which public companies and private equity meet the 10 requirements for successful collaboration helps to see which of these very different collaboration designs works best for which type of business, and who profits most from adopting which design.

---

[1]   We make the simplifying assumption that the goal of public companies is to create value for their shareholders and owners. In law, the goals of public companies are in fact often broader than this, which makes it even harder for investors to oversee their managers.

[2]   The problem of getting managers to act in shareholders' interests has been extensively investigated over the years from a variety of different perspectives. In the 1930s Berle and Means called attention to the separation of ownership and control (Adolf Berle and Gardiner Means, *The Modern Corporation and Private Property*. New York: McMillan, 1932). There was strong academic interest in the 1970s and 1980s in how to resolve the problems this caused. 'Agency Theory' examined how shareholders as 'principals' could set up contracts that would motivate managers as 'agents' to act in their interests in the face of conflicting personal goals and different risk preferences and information. Important articles in the early development of Agency Theory included: Michael Jensen and William Meckling, 'Theory of the Firm: Managerial behavior, agency costs and ownership structure'. *Journal of Financial Economics*, 1976, Volume 3, Issue 4, pp. 305–360; Eugene Fama, 'Agency problems and the theory of the firm'. *Journal of Political Economy*, 1980, Volume 88, Number 2, pp. 208–307; Eugene Fama and Michael Jensen, 'Separation of ownership and control'. *Journal of Law and Economics*, 1983, Volume 26, Number 2, pp. 301–325; Kathleen Eisenhardt provides a useful summary of the Agency Theory literature up to the end of the 1980s in Kathleen Eisenhardt, 'Agency Theory: An Assessment and Review'. *The Academy of Management Review*, 1989, Volume 14, Number 1, pp. 57–74.

[3] Quoted in Andreas Ortmann, 'The Nature and Causes of Corporate Negligence, Sham Lectures, and Ecclesiastical Indolence: Adam Smith on Joint-Stock Companies, Teachers, and Preachers'. *History of Political Economy* Summer 1999.

[4] A non-executive director typically also chairs the compensation (or remuneration) committee of the board.

[5] Non-executive directors may of course lack the ability to add value for other reasons. A board should include at least some members with industry expertise. But many of the boards of banks that suffered in the 2008 financial crisis clearly didn't fulfil this criterion. On the board of Lehman Brothers, whose collapse triggered the crisis of 2008/2009, were a theatrical producer, a retired rear admiral in the US Navy, and the former CEOs of an art auction house, a telecommunications company, a computer company and an oil services company. Not one of the non-executive directors – investors' main representatives – had in-depth experience in mainstream investment banking. UBS lost over CHF 20 billion in 2008, but unlike Lehman Brothers was considered 'too big to fail', and was therefore rescued by the Swiss government. At the time their non-executive directors were a lawyer and a number of current and former CEOs from companies in a wide range of industries: automobiles, chemicals, oil, computers, railway engineering and market expansion services – but none with a prominent executive career in financial services. Corporate governance of public companies is difficult to get right, but there is no need to make it any more difficult than it need be.

[6] Derek Higgs, 'Review of the role and effectiveness of non-executive directors'. January 2003.

[7] Although we do believe lack of time available to be a serious problem, there is a need to take this self-evaluation by non-executives with some caution. If asked what your personal weaknesses are, you may well, consciously or subconsciously, try to give an answer that keeps your true weaknesses hidden. Lack of time is, in that respect, a good answer because it is a weakness inherent in the role and does not reflect on non-executives personal qualifications to do the job.

[8] Most non-executive directors, particularly in Europe, have a career background as managers, not as investors or investor representatives such as fund managers. Their natural inclination is to side with the concerns of managers when these diverge from those of shareholders. Analysis of board communications provides one interesting indication that they are indeed often preoccupied by management rather than shareholders' concerns. CE Asset Management AG, a Swiss asset management firm, analyzed the language in chairman's letters to shareholders in the annual reports of over 100 US and European public companies. Management concerns such as growth, strategy, sales, quality, and processes were each mentioned by over half of all these companies, yet no individual issue of specific concern to shareholders, such as financial policy, dividends, share price or share price development, was mentioned by more than 10 per cent. Investors can overcome some of the weaknesses of the public company approach by prodding boards to add directors with a background as investors, investment bankers or even private equity fund managers.

[9] In many countries non-executives are therefore largely remunerated with a fixed fee or attendance fees or with company stock but not, for example, with options.

[10] *Harvard Business Review*, September–October 1989.

[11] *Bild am Sonntag*, 17th April 2005. See also 'Die Namen der "Heuschrecken"' ('Naming the "Locusts"'). *Stern*, 28th April 2005.

[12] 'Locust debate'

[13] Nicholas Lemann, 'Transaction Man: Mormonism, Private Equity, and the Making of a Candidate'. *New Yorker*, 1st October 2012.

[14] Some investors do in practice get help from managers of funds – just as some public company investors invest via mutual funds – but this is not a must.

[15] But see the textbox 'Making use of persistence?' in this chapter.

[16] In practice there are provisions made to replace the fund manager in case of breach of fiduciary duty and sometimes, usually based on a supermajority of limited partners' votes, without cause. The fund manager is however, to the best of our knowledge, very seldom indeed replaced during the life of the fund. The effectiveness of provisions to change the fund manager is seldom put to the test.

[17] The problem for private equity investors may in practice be the reverse, in contracting with a large fund management firm, investors may want to make sure that the fund management team promised does not change. When investors contract with a fund management firm they may introduce a 'key man' clause into the contract to ensure that enough of the particular individuals that they want to manage the fund actually do so.

[18] Some funds distribute profits to the fund manager on a deal-by-deal basis, sometimes before the fund ends, rather than a single profit-sharing distribution at the end for the fund as a whole. But this approach worsens the risk mismatch problem described below.

[19] In many private equity funds, the fund management contract sets a minimum hurdle for the annual rate of return for investors on their investment in the fund, below which the fund manager is not entitled to any share of fund profits. The hurdle rate set is typically substantially lower than the rate of return investors actually expect on their, usually highly leveraged, fund investment, but is still substantial – eight per cent is common these days. The substantial hurdle rate induces the managers to aim for better than mediocre returns. Yet the high rate also encourages greater risk-taking, because managers receive no profits at all if returns are low. To prevent risk-taking further, firms could lower their hurdle rate, and in fact one major private equity firm, KKR, has traditionally not required its funds to achieve a minimum rate of return in order for the manager to receive a share of the profits (see John Jannarone, 'No Fee Ride at KKR Despite Push'. *Wall Street Journal Online*. 9th August 2010). A low or absent performance hurdle better aligns managers and investors because managers have more to lose from 'bet the company' decisions that can result in not even a low level of profits. On the other hand, eliminating the hurdle rate can create other problems. Fund managers might hold on longer to fund investments, in the hopes of finally netting a small return – rather than return the money to investors early. It may also be argued that eliminating the hurdle rate will encourage the fund manager to invest funds in businesses even if there are no business investment opportunities likely to yield a high return.

[20] A rough and unreliable estimate on our part, based on looking at returns for a sample of funds, would be that only about 5 per cent of large diversified funds have historically had a significantly negative return over their full life.

[21] Kara Scannell, 'Telecom Firms' Hang-Ups Cloud The Record of a Buyout Expert'. *The Wall Street Journal*, 8th May 2001.

[22] Dan Milmo, 'Terra Firma scales down to face the future: EMI debacle forces Guy Hands to have a rethink. Private equity firm decides to cut back on its staff'. *The Guardian*, 18th May 2011.

[23] There is considerable debate about the true comparison of returns to investors between private equity and public companies. We have complete information on the returns of public companies on the public market, but not so complete for private equity funds. Some studies show private equity doing, over the long term, a little better; some show private equity doing a little worse. To make the comparison more difficult, it is also unclear what the required rate of return for an investment in private equity should be in relation to that for a stock-market investment. A rule of thumb in talking to investors in private equity buyouts is that, to be at par, considering the supposed greater risk in private equity and the lack of liquidity, private equity should achieve a return three hundred to five hundred basis points more than an investment in a public company. However, there are also a minority, mostly academics, who contend that private equity does not need to earn a higher return for investors at all, as it constitutes a different asset class and diversifies investors' risk. Steven N. Kaplan and Per Strömberg, in a June 2008 NBER research paper, *Leveraged Buyouts and Private Equity,* provide a good summary of much academic research into private equity buyout returns and a useful list of references to academic papers on the issues. Robert M Conroy and Robert S Harris in 'How good are private equity returns?', in the *Journal of Applied Corporate Finance*, Volume 19, Number 3, Summer 2007, pp. 96–108, provide another good summary of research. It is too early to look at comparisons post financial crisis as many of the funds to be examined have not, at the time of writing in 2013, sold all their investments. Arguably, comparisons, when they can be made, will need to take account of the fact that private equity buyouts generally do not focus on the hard-hit banking sector.

[24] Gregory Zuckerman and Amy Or, 'Bain Capital Lowers Its Fees'. *The Wall Street Journal Online*, 15th July 2011.

[25] This problem is much more acute in venture capital than in buyout funds, but buyout funds may also be substantially oversubscribed.

[26] Thanks to Thomas Kubr at Capital Dynamics, a leading asset management firm focusing on private equity investments, for pointing this out to us.

[27] On this and the following points in this paragraph, see Christophe Rouvinez, 'Top Quartile Persistence in Private Equity'. *Private Equity International*, June 2006.

[28] And, but to a much lesser extent, the top managers of the companies in the private equity portfolio.

[29] The high fee structure in private equity is probably in part the result of high growth rates in the industry over the past two decades. As the industry matures, the gap between compensation levels in private equity and public companies is likely to fall. But we expect fund managers and their operating company executives to continue to do better, relative to investors, than their counterparts (non-executive directors and company executives) in public companies.

[30] See 'Clayton, Dubilier & Rice: Engineers of a different kind, A buy-out firm that really does focus on operational improvements'. *The Economist*, 22nd June 2013.

[31] 1999/2000, figures for year previous to buyout not publicly available.

[32] Figures from Wincor Nixdorf IPO document and annual reports.

[33] Andrew Bulkeley. 'Goldman, KKR cash out of Wincor'. *The Deal.com*, 28th January 2005.

[34] In recent years when profits have fallen, private equity investors were no longer in control of the business, so we cannot, of course, know if the business might not have performed better if they had continued to be responsible for its management.

[35] A 2010 study by Ernst and Young for the British Venture Capital Association suggests that debt accounts for (using round numbers) about 60 per cent of the enterprise value of a typical European private equity buyout but only 20 per cent of the enterprise value of a comparable public company. This comparison is not entirely fair as the ratio for private equity is measured here, as is typical (presumably because the information is more easily available), at time of acquisition. Private equity firms traditionally use the profits and cash flows of the companies they have acquired to pay down debt rather than to pay dividends. They also strive to increase the enterprise value of the companies they have acquired. Consequently, over the life of private equity ownership, private equity owned firms have a much lower level of debt in relation to their enterprise value than on acquisition. Nevertheless, even after making adjustments, one may confidently expect to find that private equity owned firms use considerably more debt than public companies.

[36] As public companies have focused their business portfolios, they have also reduced their financial leverage. In contrast to governments, public companies now have more cash and less debt than for a very long time. Net debt as a percentage of shareholder equity has fallen from around 80 per cent in the mid-1990s to closer to 40 per cent in 2011. About one-third of European public companies are debt free. As of December 2011, the 1100 non-financial corporations rated by Moody's were sitting on record gross cash balances of $1.24 trillion (see Richard Milne and Anousha Sakoui, 'Corporate finance: Rivers of riches'. *Financial Times*, 22nd May 2011).

[37] Private equity funds better align the interests of investors and managers in using more debt to finance businesses. But there is a way to give public company shareholders more say on the finance policy of their companies. An annual 'say on payout,' in analogy to the 'say on pay' and covering company financial policy and dividend policy, might be considerably more valuable to shareholders than a 'say on pay.' It would encourage managers to adopt the financing policy that shareholders want. Reducing cash, increasing debt and increasing dividends might even reduce the need for investors to resort to private equity buyouts to exploit opportunities for additional leverage.

[38] See Per Strömberg, 'The New Demography of Private Equity. The Global Economic Impact of Private Equity Report'. World Economic Forum, 2008.

[39] The 'enterprise value' of a company is the sum of the market value of shareholders' equity and of the company's interest-bearing debt.

[40] 'HCA I.P.O. Takes Tarnish Off Mega-Buyouts'. *New York Times Dealbook*, 10th May 2010.

[41] RJR Nabisco was $31 billion in 1989, less than HCA in absolute terms but more when inflation adjusted.

[42] All financial data based on HCA Holdings Inc. SEC filings unless otherwise stated.

[43] Of course, an individual instance of superior profit growth does not prove that buyout investors can always find a way to grow profits faster. However, while there is no proof, there are now quite a number of studies that suggest that buyout firms, in the particular type of situations they target, can often generate superior profit growth, see for example BVCA Annual Report on the performance of Portfolio Companies, III, copyright Ernst&Young 2010, or O. Gottschalg, E. Talmor and F. Vasvari. 'Replicating the Investment Strategy of Buyout Funds Based in the United Kingdom (UK) with Public-Market-Investments' also for the BVCA.

[44] The HCA buyout made a good return for investors also because the funds paid an acquisition premium over the market price of only 18 per cent. RJR Nabisco's premium, by contrast, was close to 100 per cent,

and it achieved an internal rate of return of only 2.8 per cent before management fees (George P. Baker and George David Smith, *The New Financial Capitalists: Kohlberg Kravis Roberts and the Creation of Corporate Value*. Cambridge University Press, 1998).

[45] It may be helpful to note here that units (shares) in Blackstone, KKR and other now publicly traded US private equity firms are units in fund management firms. They are not units in the funds managed. As fund management firms, Blackstone and KKR continue to manage private equity funds of limited life that are not traded on the market. They are not now managing holding companies making investments of indefinite life. From the point of view of fund investors, there is no change in what they are investing in as a result of Blackstone or KKR becoming public companies. There are tax issues involved in these private equity firms going public but they are different. Publicly traded partnerships are 'normally' treated as corporations for tax purposes and need to pay corporate taxes. Publicly traded US private equity firms make use of a controversial provision that allows them to continue to be treated as partnerships for tax purposes. As partnerships, they are not subject to corporate taxes.

[46] The value of buying-to-sell for investors in a diversified business portfolio was also the theme of Felix Barber and Michael Goold, 'The Strategic Secret of Private Equity'. *Harvard Business Review*, September 2007.

[47] In some jurisdictions, private equity funds also have important tax advantages over public companies. Unlike conglomerates, private partnerships do not pay corporate taxes, and these taxes on capital gains have made it harder for conglomerates to sell businesses at a profit. When General Electric, for example, buys a business and sells it at a profit, it pays tax on the capital gain at the normal rate of corporate tax. This difference is not offset by differences in personal tax for investors. Conglomerates can avoid these taxes if they spin off the business as a separate quoted company, but these and other workarounds limit their flexibility in selling relative to private equity. Since 2002, most European countries (but not the United States) have eliminated corporate tax on capital gains on sales of subsidiaries. Conglomerates such as Melrose PLC have made something of a comeback here, usually following a model similar to private equity buyout funds. But because of the limited-life advantages of private equity, a level tax playing field is unlikely to be enough to make conglomerates significant vehicles for most investors. Observers have also pointed out that fund partners make most of their money through the carried interest in fund profits, which are treated as capital gains taxed at a lower rate than ordinary income. But governments usually treat conglomerate executives' income from share options, quite similar to carried interest, as capital gains as well.

Chapter 9

Sharing Business Ownership

Getting non-routine work done for you is a major challenge. At the beginning of the book, we advised that responding to this challenge meant treating your key employees and suppliers as 'partners' in the business. But now that we have looked at many examples of collaboration problems and solutions, what does that really mean?

The fundamental problem with non-routine work is that it is difficult to precisely specify what you – the business owner – want. So you must give the people and companies doing this work a significant amount of discretion. In effect, you must share some of the entrepreneurial responsibilities that come with ownership with your partners – they have to take critical decisions that materially affect the business outcome. In Chapter 8 we looked at private equity, an extreme case, where managers take overall decision-making responsibility from investors. Partners may take on other ownership responsibilities as well: provide critical assets and capabilities, and share in the business risk. Think of the franchisor providing the brand and concept to franchisees, or the small venture-capital-backed companies providing R&D know-how to Big Pharma firms.

If collaboration with your partners means that you rely on them to take on some of the responsibilities of ownership, then your collaboration will likely involve sharing the rewards of ownership as well – the profits from the business, or at least the revenues. We see this happening more and more.

Now if it looks like a duck, swims like a duck, and quacks like a duck, then it probably is a duck. If you are sharing the owner's responsibilities with partners, and you are sharing the owner's rewards as well, you are sharing the business ownership as a whole. In the case of private equity this is clear enough. The financial investors and the private equity firm are partners in the private equity fund. Partners are effectively sharing in the ownership in many other collaboration designs we have looked at, just not so obviously. In many cases that's because we tend to equate owning a business with owning a company – a legal entity – and there is no legal entity in which partners share ownership. But a business is an activity, not a legal entity. Producing and selling cars is a business, not General Motors Company. General Motors Company is just a legal entity – a 'legal person' – that carries on a business of producing and selling cars. Collaboration designs may rely on contracts,[1] rather than companies, to share the responsibilities and rewards of business ownership shown in Figure 9.1.

Figure 9.1 The elements of business ownership

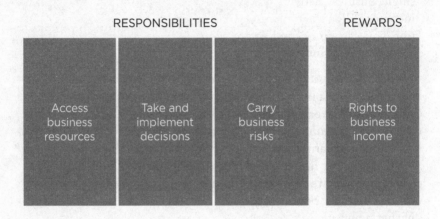

McDonalds and McDonalds' franchisees share ownership in the business of producing and selling McDonalds hamburgers, and they set up contracts to do so directly. There is no intermediate legal entity in which they share ownership. An alliance between a big pharmaceutical company and a small biotech firm effectively shares ownership in the business of developing a new drug, without forming a joint venture or other new company.

The idea of sharing ownership in a business without a legal entity takes a bit of getting used to. But it is real. Each of the major European airlines now has a commercial arrangement with a partner airline in the US, in which revenues (and in some cases profits) are shared. These arrangements are typically referred to as 'joint businesses'. A senior airline executive told us that managers new to the company are at first a bit puzzled by the term – 'What do you mean it is a joint business?

There is no joint-venture company is there?' But they soon get comfortable with the language because it accurately describes how alliance partners are working together.

Because this ownership sharing focuses on contracts not companies, it's harder to describe and analyze it. There are far more ways of setting up contracts – legally binding agreements – than setting up companies. But that gives you the flexibility to be much more creative in setting up collaboration. You can go beyond simply separating responsibility for different business activities and allocating them to whoever is best able to take each activity on. You can allocate different responsibilities for a single business activity to different parties and share the business income to align their interests. To gain further benefits from specialization you can go beyond Adam Smith's 'division of labour' and use contracts to engineer a sophisticated 'division of ownership' as well.[2]

We have already described several examples of de facto ownership-sharing agreements, but in this chapter we look at them explicitly. How do you share profits or revenues to motivate partners to take on these ownership responsibilities – providing resources, taking and implementing decisions, and carrying the business risks? In this chapter we first look briefly at sharing business income to access resources and to share risks. These are issues we have not focused on so far in the book but which offer some interesting opportunities. We then focus on the greater challenge of sharing business income to motivate partners to take and implement decisions in your interests. We introduce some new examples and revisit some old ones from an ownership-sharing perspective.

While we focus in this chapter on contracts to share business income and ownership directly, we also look at joint-venture companies. Together with the wide range of ownership-sharing contracts and entities described in earlier chapters, we can therefore provide a broad overview of ownership-sharing tactics. Figure 9.2 lists a number of collaboration designs that share ownership, both contractually and through companies. In addition to these standard 'name' designs, there are far more that are tailor-made to provide collaboration solutions for individual companies and their partners.

Figure 9.2 Some collaboration designs that share business ownership

DESIGNS	INDUSTRY APPLICATION
Contracts/partnerships	
• Venture capital	• Biotech, hi-tech
• Private equity buyouts	• Undermanaged basic businesses
• R&D Alliances	• Pharmaceuticals
• Network Alliances	• Airlines
• Risk-and-revenue-sharing partnerships	• Aerospace (jet engines)
• Franchising/licensing	• Hotels, restaurants, luxury goods
• Production sharing contracts	• Oil exploration and production
• Public Private Partnerships	• Infrastructure, public services
• Pain-gain-sharing Alliances (projects)	• Engineering, construction, mining
• Options/warrants/restricted shares	• Start-ups/top executives
Companies	
• Public companies	• All industries
• Mutuals, Credit Unions, Raiffeisen	• Banking and insurance
• Cooperatives, Associations	• Dairy, utilities, professional sport
• Joint ventures	• All industries

Accessing business resources

When it comes to resources for your business, simply paying market prices may work poorly. That's especially true for critical resources – those that few other partners can provide and which will have a substantial impact.[3] Instead, both sides will want to consider sharing business income, particularly where there is uncertainty about just how much the resource will be worth.

If you don't have enough information to assess how much a resource is going to be worth – such as a patent, a brand, or an oil reserve – you and the resource owner won't find it easy to agree on a fair price. The best way to price the resource may be to share the income gained from using it in your business. A pharmaceutical company with a strong sales and distribution network in a country, but a weak drug portfolio, will want to take on a drug patented by a company that lacks this network. Neither side can readily predict how well the drug will do, so it's easier for the owner to license the drug to the distributor for a royalty on sales rather than for a fixed fee.

In some cases a company will share ownership simply because it has no alternative. Start-up companies have to be especially creative in making these arrangements, as they have very limited cash to pay for the resources they need. Indeed, their only tradable resource is often the promise of future earnings. What is more, they often depend on being able to access resources from large companies to get established. Priceline.com's entry into the online airline ticket business is a case in point. A vital element of Priceline.com's success depended on the agreement it was able to set up with Delta Airlines, shown in Figure 9.3.

In 1998, Delta was the first major airline to sell tickets on Priceline.com. Other major airlines, cautious about selling via a start-up on the Internet, then a new sales channel with which they had little experience, had turned Priceline down.[4] Delta negotiated Priceline.com warrants worth approximately 10 per cent of the new company in exchange for making their tickets available for sale on Priceline. Both sides benefitted. Two years later, after Priceline's IPO, Delta recorded pre-tax profits of $1 billion from the move. Priceline's founder, Jay Walker, pointed out that 'These guys took a brilliant risk in joining with an unknown Internet company . . . They said if they were going to do it they wanted to participate on the equity side.'[5] Walker needed at least one major airline in order to make the business work, and that gave Delta enormous leverage and a rightful share of the rewards.

Concerns if you must share decision-making

Suppliers of critical resources may not be satisfied with simply receiving a share of the business income. They may also want to make some of the decisions for the business. While letting Priceline sell their tickets, Delta demanded limits on Priceline's ability to offer tickets from other airlines[6] – which did happen once the start-up established itself.

The constraints were not, as it turned out, enough to present a serious problem for Priceline, but it's easy to see how they could have done so. If Priceline had favoured tickets from Delta over those from other airlines, then the business would not have been as attractive to consumers. But Delta could have decided it gained more from its preferential status than it lost in lower value for its Priceline shares. In sharing ownership, you must be careful to see where your interests diverge and protect the business accordingly.

Figure 9.3 Delta provides some critical resources to Priceline's e-commerce business

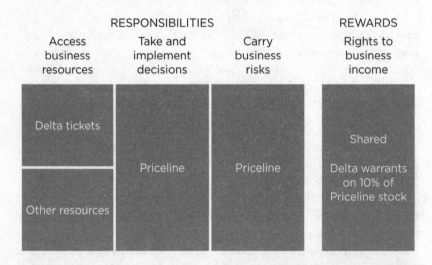

Constraints from working with for-profit companies are clear enough, but you may also need resources from political entities. Oil exploration companies, for example, are always looking for new fields to exploit, but many of these are owned by national governments in developing countries. These governments, with their corresponding national oil companies, often lack the skills and resources to tap their oil reserves directly. Nor are they willing to simply sell these rights, not only because there may be great uncertainty about their value, but also because of political backlash if they sell a most valuable national asset. So an exploration company may share the profits from these fields with the government in exchange for full operational rights to exploit the field. These arrangements can work well, but governments pursue non-commercial as well as commercial objectives, and usually impose corresponding constraints.

Oil production sharing contracts were pioneered in Indonesia and have been used in Malaysia and elsewhere.[7] The exploration company makes all operational investments, while the national oil company retains the rights to the lion's share of the oil produced and hence the profits from the business, as shown in Figure 9.4. Besides profits, governments typically seek to use their rights to impose constraints on the contractor's work programme to build the skills of the national workforce. Contractors usually have to increase the share of local people employed as managers or technical specialists by the contractor.

Figure 9.4 National oil company provides critical resources to and sets constraints on work of oil multinational

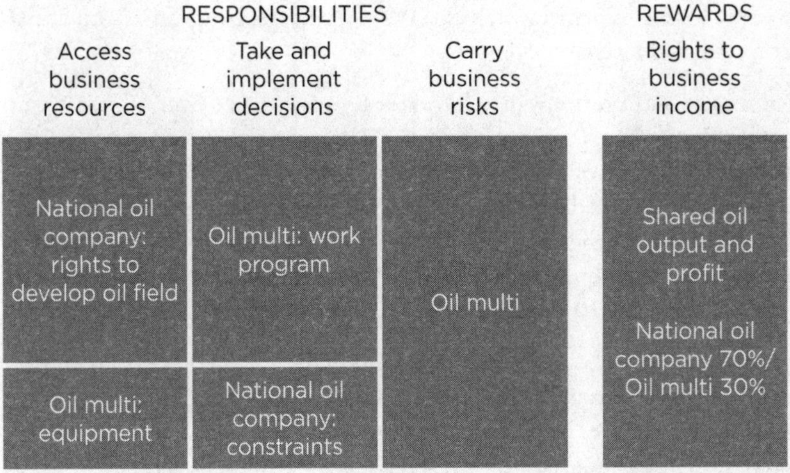

RESPONSIBILITIES			REWARDS
Access business resources	Take and implement decisions	Carry business risks	Rights to business income

National oil company: rights to develop oil field

Oil multi: work program

Oil multi

Shared oil output and profit

National oil company 70%/ Oil multi 30%

Oil multi: equipment

National oil company: constraints

If local managers and specialists are poorly qualified, the national oil company and the contractor have an awkward conflict of interest. Here it may help to describe in more detail what the contractor is required to do to help with these broader objectives – perhaps provide more training programmes, for example. But a description that sufficiently limits how the government can intervene may not be possible. Qualifications of managers and specialists are to some degree a matter of judgement.

Before committing to collaboration, the oil exploration company has to decide if the government's broader objectives are sufficiently at odds with narrower commercial objectives to create serious problems. The company should also assess how much leverage it has to convince the government to weaken or modify the kinds of constraints in question.

Carrying business risks

In especially risky industries, you may want a partner to take on some of your risk, and often that requires sharing business income. The very act of sharing income itself is a small way of sharing risk. When banks pay bankers with profit-sharing bonuses instead of fixed salaries, that helps to reduce the volatility of profits.[8] But while bankers' bonuses help to reduce the volatility of bank earnings, they don't help to limit losses. Working with external suppliers, companies can transfer more of the risk.

Commercial aircraft engines have a long lifecycle of over 40 years, and profitable revenues are back-ended. Manufacturers need three to five years and billions of dollars to develop an engine. Series production of the engine then starts and may continue for 20 years or more. But sales are not particularly profitable. The high margins come largely from spare parts, maintenance, repairs and other services, and these revenues may continue for 10 or more years after production stops.[9]

With this profile of cash flows, even a successful engine development may take 10 years to reach breakeven, and a failed one is exceptionally costly. Rolls Royce's RB211 engine did so poorly in 1971 that the company fell into bankruptcy and had to be rescued by the British government.[10]

Rolls Royce and General Electric, the two biggest manufacturers, have accordingly adopted risk- and revenue-sharing with suppliers as shown in Figure 9.5. Risk- and revenue-sharing partners[11] (RRSPs) together take on approximately 30 per cent of the risk on a new engine development with GE. That means they take responsibility for activities that represent 30 per cent of engine programme costs throughout the engine lifecycle. They then receive 30 per cent of the corresponding revenues. They deliver engine parts and other work outputs with the target cost agreed, and are paid only when GE is paid. So their cash-flow profile matches GE's, and they help finance the programme and share in the risk.

Figure 9.5 Aircraft engine OEM works with suppliers who act as risk and revenue sharing partners

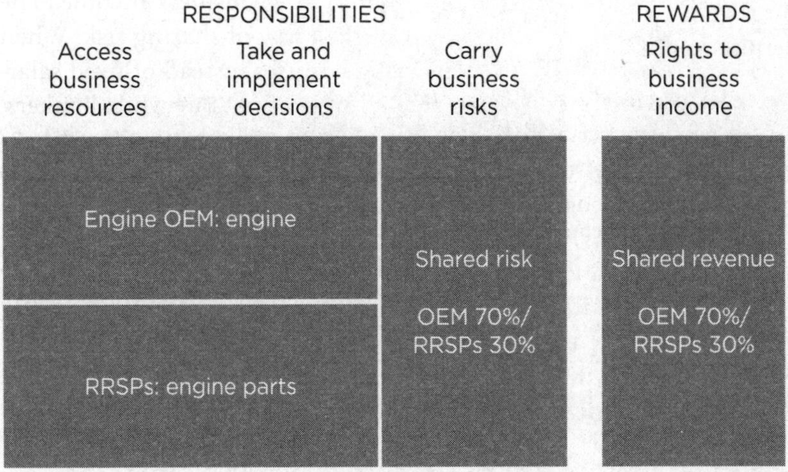

RESPONSIBILITIES			REWARDS
Access business resources	Take and implement decisions	Carry business risks	Rights to business income

Engine OEM: engine

RRSPs: engine parts

Shared risk

OEM 70%/ RRSPs 30%

Shared revenue

OEM 70%/ RRSPs 30%

Risk- and revenue-sharing partnerships limit programme risks and diversify the sources of finance for aircraft engine companies. Sharing business income with those doing the work as a way of sharing the business risks is most interesting in highly risky businesses such as the development of aircraft engines. You want to spread the risk as widely as you can. In some circumstances, working partners may also be more prepared to share in the risk than financial investors. They are interested in the work and can influence the business outcome.

Motivating partners to take and implement decisions

The most common reason for sharing ownership – and the most complex – is to motivate employees, suppliers and other business partners to take and implement decisions on your behalf. It has become a core option for getting non-routine work done. By sharing business income and ownership, you align your partners' interests with your own, and this is helpful when you can't direct and control the work or define the output you need. Sharing business income gives your partner a powerful incentive to do what you want. As we have discussed throughout the book, the approach works well in many situations despite its pitfalls.

We saw this clearly with financial investors in Chapter 8. Many businesses perform better for their financial investors when overseen by private equity partners, with a direct stake in the profits as shown in Figure 9.6, than when overseen by directors of a public company with little if any stake.[12] Private equity in turn also shares ownership of the individual companies with operating executives more than public companies do. Within companies, sales agents and employees are often compensated and motivated by receiving a commission or bonus related to the business income they generate. Many 'creative workers', such as designers, authors or musicians, are compensated in this way too.

Figure 9.6 Private equity firm partners take key decisions and independent financial investors carry risks in fund

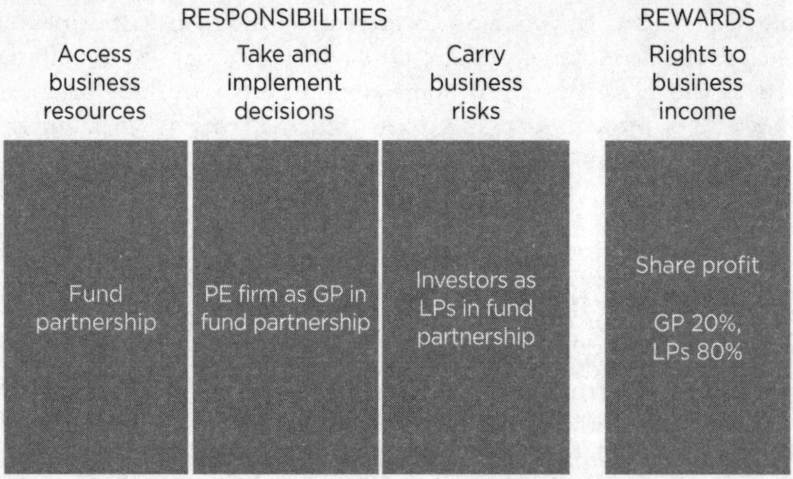

RESPONSIBILITIES			REWARDS
Access business resources	Take and implement decisions	Carry business risks	Rights to business income
Fund partnership	PE firm as GP in fund partnership	Investors as LPs in fund partnership	Share profit GP 20%, LPs 80%

Companies are increasingly sharing ownership to motivate not just individuals but also companies to take and implement decisions. Reversing the oil exploration example earlier, let's take the perspective of the national government that would like to commercialize its oil reserves. By sharing ownership of exploration and development with the outside exploration company – rather than simply paying a fee for a service – the government motivates the exploration company to optimize results.

Figure 9.7 Contractor in construction alliance provides resources for and shares decisions and risks with client

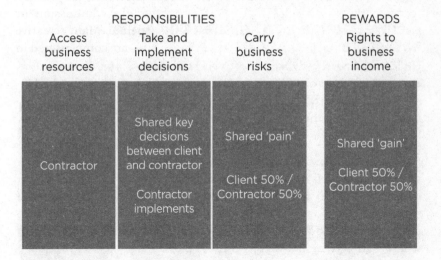

RESPONSIBILITIES			REWARDS
Access business resources	Take and implement decisions	Carry business risks	Rights to business income
Contractor	Shared key decisions between client and contractor Contractor implements	Shared 'pain' Client 50% / Contractor 50%	Shared 'gain' Client 50% / Contractor 50%

You can even effectively share ownership with a partner without sharing your business income from customers. When your contractor's work affects your costs but you can't measure its influence on your customer revenue, you can't find an income stream well aligned with the value your partner's work creates. So sharing your customer income may not help motivate your partner to create more value for you. But if you can reach a broad agreement with the contractor on the output you want, you may be able to agree a target cost to produce it. You can then share with your partner the risks and rewards of the job coming in under or over the target costs you set.[13] That is the approach used in the pain-and-gain sharing alliances we discussed in Chapter 4. In a pain-and-gain sharing alliance, the business in which you share ownership can be seen as simply the business of producing the output you want.

Pain-and gain-sharing gives both sides an incentive to actively seek out or accept changes that will reduce project costs – both share ownership of the net gains or losses relative to the target. The contracting firm must be willing to pay a share of any overruns. Although it has been closely involved in setting reasonable targets, the client is also paying a share of overruns and, as shown in Figure 9.7 above, both sides must agree to any changes in specifications. Once the preliminary specifications and target costs have been set, there is a high degree of alignment between client and contractor, even if the specifications of the work evolve during the project.

A clever design as a source of competative advantage

Understanding the dynamics of ownership is essential to designing effective collaboration – and with it, competitive advantage. The US residential real estate brokerage industry shows this in action. The industry has seen three major shifts in competitive advantage, all driven by changes in the design of collaboration.

Early leaders in the industry, such as Coldwell Banker, began by owning and operating their own brokerage branches. The first shift, starting in the 1970s, was to franchising under Century 21. As with fast-food restaurants, brokerages could share their brand with franchisees and rapidly expand the branch network at low cost. A bigger network meant scale advantages in branding and the real estate database. From there, firms experimented with collaboration one level down, between the franchised brokers and the self-employed real estate agents. The agents bring buyers and sellers of residential properties together and make their living by earning commission income on sales of properties. Traditionally, they split this income with the brokers who provide them with services such as office space, training, systems support and the brand and property database that helps them market their services. A common ratio has been 60 per cent for the agents and 40 per cent for the brokers. Brokers need to set up a remuneration system that helps to grow and retain a network of high-performing agents.

Re/Max gained share in the market in the 1980s and 1990s by moving away from ownership sharing and giving all the commission to agents, who paid a fixed monthly fee for brokerage services. This design attracted high performing agents, who had rightly felt they were paying too much for the broker's services as a percentage of their high commissions. However, over the past decade Keller Williams has become the new market leader with a system that is effectively positioned between the traditional split commissions and the fixed brokerage fee. Although Re/Max's fixed fee brings in the best agents, it discourages new agents who initially might not earn enough to pay the relatively high fixed fees, which makes it hard for brokers to grow. Keller Williams charges agents about 30 per cent of the sales commission but with a cap on the annual commission fee charged. That way agents starting out don't pay high fixed fees, yet the stronger agents get to keep a greater share of the income from their high volume of sales.

Figure 9.8 Keller Williams agents share responsibilities, commission and profits with Keller Williams brokers

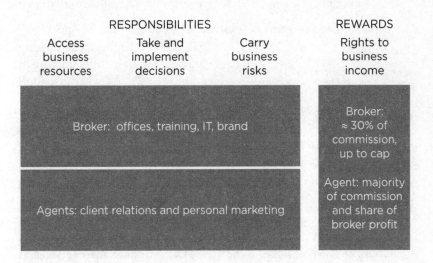

But Keller Williams has innovated further by having the franchise brokers share ownership directly with agents (see Figure 9.8.). In addition to keeping 70 per cent or more of the commission on sell-ing properties, agents share in the profits of the brokerage branch – close to half on average. But agents don't get profits according to sales they themselves generate – that's what the commissions are for. Instead, branches (or 'market centres' as they are called at Keller Williams) distribute the income according to another goal: building and retaining the brokerage's network of agents. Every Keller Williams' agent is sponsored by another agent, the one considered most responsible for that new agent joining. Sponsors receive a profit share linked to the commissions generated by the agents that they sponsor – and eventually a further share linked to the commis-sions from agents sponsored by the agents they sponsor. The link goes on down through seven levels of a 'sponsoring tree'[14], as shown in Figure 9.9. Sponsoring agents have a powerful incentive not only to recruit new agents, but also to mentor them in an ongoing way so they stay and succeed.

Figure 9.9 How Keller Williams profit share is distributed

Of the profit share earned by a Keller Williams agent...

...these people	...can receive this %
1st level sponsor (agent's sponsor)	50%
2nd level sponsor (sponsor of 1st level sponsor)	10%
3rd level sponsor (sponsor of 2nd level sponsor)	5%
4th level sponsor (sponsor of 3rd level sponsor)	5%
5th level sponsor (sponsor of 4th level sponsor)	7.5%
6th level sponsor (sponsor of 5th level sponsor)	10%
7th level sponsor (sponsor of 6th level sponsor)	12.5%
1st to 7th level sponsors	100%

Agents can continue to receive their profit share if they move to another market centre and even after they retire. The profit share is substantial – one agent we talked to was able to finance a child's college education from it.

Keller Williams brokerages do not just share profits with agents, they also involve top performing agents, via Agent Leadership Councils, in managing the market centres. Since top agents receive a substantial share of the market centre profits, they have a clear incentive to help the market centre perform. The results are convincing – 95 per cent of Keller Williams' offices make a profit – a substantially higher percentage than in most franchise businesses.[15] Keller Williams' approach is unusual and sophisticated – it requires a consistent accounting system across the entire US network to administer it, easier for a brand expanding organically than by acquisition. It has enabled Keller Williams to expand more rapidly than its competitors over a sustained period.[16] A well designed system of sharing business ownership can be a source of sustained competitive advantage.

The main challenges in sharing ownership by contract

Income-sharing contracts can work well, but should still be checked against the 10 requirements framework. They can suffer from many of the same troubles discussed for more prosaic collaboration with employees or suppliers. If you can't set goals to measure your partner's performance and align rewards with performance to prevent awkward conflicts of interest, gather the information to be able to specify favourable terms, or preserve your own bargaining power, then you have to adjust your collaboration design.

Setting goals and measuring partner's performance

When you share ownership with partners, the business income itself can serve as a proxy for your partner's performance. This is especially helpful when you can't provide detailed direction about output or monitor your partner's work – such as with a general manager.

But, for sharing business income to suitably motivate your partners, you need to find an income stream in your business sufficiently closely aligned to the value your partner helps to create. It must also be sufficiently simple to calculate, so your partner understands what to do. If the rewards are long term, you should have no management discretion in measuring the income stream – partners should trust the measure used and have no concerns about receiving the rewards promised if they achieve the goals set.

Some difficulties are easy to see, some are more difficult to spot. Strategy consultants and advertising agencies may work independently with little detailed direction, but unlike salesmen or business general managers, have no income stream that reliably measures their performance. But other difficulties are hard to spot. Measuring a salesman's contribution by the revenue he generates will ignore his contribution to building a team and helping others to generate revenue for you. You can measure this year's profit in the general manager's business unit, but you can't tell if she achieved it at the cost of lower profits in the future.

Profits depend on costs as well as revenues. If you and your partner are active in a range of business activities, how do you measure your respective shares of costs? Setting up an agreed basis of cost measurement and an auditing procedure may be expensive and difficult. And how do you ensure your partner uses the best resources they have available and carries out the work at the lowest possible cost?

Suppose you run a European airline and have a joint business with a US airline to share profits on transatlantic routes. What is to stop you putting old aircraft on the joint business routes and reserving new aircraft with better fuel efficiency for other routes elsewhere on your network? To align interests, you can decide to share revenue only, so costs are not an issue. Some airlines do this and it is standard practice in franchising. Another way to prevent your partner gaming you on costs is to impose constraints on how your partner does the work. You may, for example, require your airline partner to fly the joint routes using a particular type of plane. Or you may negotiate target costs for the work and then share revenues in proportion to the target costs agreed, as in the risk- and revenue-sharing arrangements for aircraft engines.

Each industry faces specific challenges and needs customized solutions. If we return to real estate, Keller Williams' arrangement nicely accounts for the various dynamics involved. It starts with the annual commission income the agent generates on real estate sales, but this income ignores the agent's work to help recruit and coach other agents. The brokerage might have rewarded agents for the number of new agents recruited, but then they would have lacked incentive to support retention as well. It could reward agents according to the annual sales from agents they recruited, but then the original agents would not also encourage the new agents to go out and recruit over time. Keller Williams' profit-sharing ingeniously integrates all these issues in an elaborate formula that gets around teaming and timing problems. The percentages of the profit-sharing an agent contributes that go to sponsors at different levels is somewhat arbitrary. But the formula is free of managerial discretion, and agents can readily calculate what they are likely to get in the long term: young agents can look forward to substantial payouts many years in the future. Few performance bonuses, particularly for people at lower and middle levels in a workforce, successfully encourage such long-term thinking about the business.

Aligning rewards with performance

Sharing an income stream that reflects your partner's performance will not be enough to align interests if your partner can't carry the business risk. As discussed for bankers and CEOs in Chapters 6 and 8, managers who share in the business income but not in losses will be tempted toward risky behaviour. They reap rewards from success but see disproportionately fewer losses from failure. But you can require the managers to invest in the business for which they are responsible. A little investment should go a long way to curb a manager's risk appetite because managers are less able to diversify their risks.

If your business is quite risky, however, and you can't require enough investment to balance against these risks, you can set constraints on partners' behaviour to prevent them from destroying value. But as we saw with financial services in Chapter 6, it is hard to motivate an organization to enforce such constraints. Rogue traders in investment banks, and insurance salesmen who sell improper policies, tend to get away with it because their employers enforce these constraints in a halfhearted way.

You should aim for constraints that are easy to set up and require little monitoring to enforce. Those used in private equity funds and discussed in Chapter 8 are a good example: broad diversification of investments, separate limited liability for each business investment, and critical decisions taken by investment committees of several people rather than just one person.

Specifying favourable terms

When setting up an income-sharing contract, you want to ensure not only that you align your partner's interests with yours, but also that you get favourable terms. Assessing whether you have favourable terms with an income-sharing contract is tricky.

The criteria are clear enough. To get favourable terms you should first gain from collaboration relative to your alternatives.[17] A European airline will form an alliance on transatlantic routes with a North American airline only if the code-sharing collaboration with that partner delivers better results than going it alone or working with another airline.[18] Second, you should see whether you get a good share of the combined gains from collaboration. But when the rewards of collaboration are a share of the income, you don't know about these gains until you know the results of the business. It's often hard to predict these results or to assess alternatives. When you share business income to gain access to scarce business resources – such as the rights to develop an oil field or the rights to sell Delta airline tickets – you do so precisely because it is difficult to know how much the resources will be worth, and because you have no close alternatives.

Capturing a good share of the value

When all parties take on a similar mix of entrepreneurial responsibilities, it can be straightforward to agree what constitutes a good and fair share of the business rewards for all parties. Both the manufacturers and suppliers for aircraft engines have roughly similar activities – providing resources, making and implementing decisions, and carrying some risk. So sharing rewards in proportion to the share of responsibilities taken on seems appropriate. But when the nature of the entrepreneurial responsibilities different parties take on is quite different, what constitutes a 'good share' of the gains is a matter more of opinion than fact. What share of the Priceline stock should Delta have received for providing access to the critical airline tickets, what share should Priceline management have received for the decisions that made the business a success, and what share should Priceline investors have received for carrying the risks? When parties take on such different entrepreneurial responsibilities, it is hard to compare their value and determine fair shares of profits.

One way to think about your bargaining strength is to go back to a point we made in Chapter 8: the money needed to carry business risks is a commodity, but access to resources such as the rights to develop an oil field, or the decisions needed to manage a private equity fund, are far from commodities. So the parties providing distinctive resources or handling decisions tend to receive the more favourable share of business income.

But there are wide variations in the bargains struck when sharing income. The norm in private equity is for fund managers to get 20 per cent of the fund profits, while investors carrying the risks get 80 per cent. But Bain Capital, which has a strong track record and claims to invest sufficiently in business analysis and management to reduce the riskiness of its funds, takes 30 per cent. And, when private equity firms go public with an IPO, fund managers subsequently get closer to 10 per cent than 20 per cent. Shareholders in publicly-quoted private equity fund managers, such as KKR or Blackstone, get to keep a substantial share of the fund profits that used to go to the fund management team.[19]

Making good trade-offs between creating and capturing value

When you set up an income-sharing agreement, there is no one right answer to the question of who should get what share of the income. But rather than jump into comparing the returns going to each partner, start with how your proposed agreement will affect the business. If a powerful income-sharing agreement results in the business outperforming, a wide range of income shares may all produce a good deal for everyone. You can help ensure this by sharing only the outperformance of the business to a benchmark, as they often do in private equity.[20]

If you set up a clever agreement that strongly motivates your partner or creates strong synergies and helps you both outperform, you can afford to be generous. Consider the best available alternatives for you and your partner and how much they are worth, along with the share of the income that seems reasonable for the contribution you will make. Get the benchmarks you can for similar income-sharing agreements. But think of all this just as the first step to exercising your judgement.

Designing an income-sharing agreement with favourable terms is a strategic challenge, not an operational problem with a single-point solution. But this has its advantages, because it allows for creativity. Sometimes taking less may even give you more. Keller Williams has prospered with its income-sharing agreement even though it gives agents a better deal than elsewhere. Brokerage profits are highly sensitive to the number of productive agents working in a branch, and the arrangement has boosted this number so much as to pay for itself.

Preserving your bargaining power beyond the end of the contract

Income sharing agreements initially help to get around bargaining power problems when you outsource the responsibility for investing in critical assets or building critical capabilities. That is part of their appeal. But you must be aware of bargaining power problems re-emerging later on.

As discussed in Chapters 2, 3 and 4, when you rely on partners to provide critical resources, they may gain too much bargaining power with you. The problem occurs when a partner has critical assets or capabilities for a business in which you have invested before you have agreed what you will pay for the work for which these assets or capabilities will be needed. You are locked in to getting the work done by your partner but you haven't agreed the price for it.

You want to get around this problem by paying for the work with a share of your business income. You can then agree what you will pay upfront before you decide to invest in the business. For this tactic to succeed, your business income should be a reasonable measure of the value your partner provides. As described in Chapter 3, and represented in Figure 9.10, franchisees agree upfront to pay the franchisor a fixed share of their restaurant revenues in return for the right to use the brand and concept. Sharing in franchisees' revenues both secures access for franchises to the use of the brand and concept and motivates the franchisor to do a good job in further developing them to increase franchisees' restaurant sales. It does this even though the franchisees can't tell the franchisor what work they want done to develop the brand and concept.

Figure 9.10 Fast food franchisees share responsibilities and revenues with franchisor

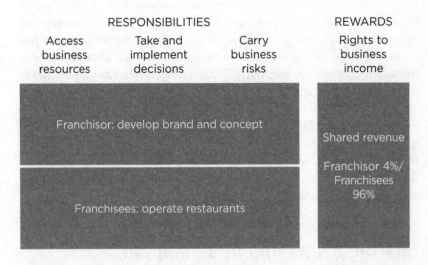

But what about when your contracts end, and your partner's resources remain critical to your business success? Fast-food franchisees avoid this problem by setting contracts long enough for them to fully amortize their investments in buildings, equipment and décor. So they risk little if the franchisor insists on tougher terms for renewing the contract. But what if both you and your partner have assets and capabilities that are of indefinite life? If the value of what your partner can offer you is growing faster than the value of what you can offer your partner, then there is trouble brewing.

As we saw in Chapter 7, Roche relied on Genentech to research and develop drugs that Roche would then commercialize. In return, Genentech received a share of the revenues from sales of the drugs developed – similar to the revenue-sharing contract in franchising. But Genentech's R&D assets and capabilities were of high value to Roche after the end of this contract. If Roche had not invested to buy out independent shareholders in Genentech in 2009, Genentech would have had considerable bargaining power in renewing the commercialization contract with Roche.[21]

What you can do about bargaining power problems as a result of outsourcing investment depends on your objective in outsourcing. If you were outsourcing in order to limit your own investment in the business, you may have to resign yourself to your partner receiving most of the gains from the arrangement. You can't have your cake and eat it.

But maybe your real objective in outsourcing was to make it easier to motivate managers to create value? If so, you can look for ways to do that without outsourcing the responsibility for investing in critical assets and capabilities – and thereby surrendering bargaining power. Roche's motivation in selling and floating a minority share in Genentech in 1999 was arguably to create a more independent and entrepreneurial environment for R&D there. Outsourcing R&D to a smaller, more focused company helped measure R&D performance and offer more powerful performance rewards to managers. Giving tradable rights to royalties on drugs in development to key in-house R&D employees, also described in Chapter 7, might make that possible without outsourcing asset investments and losing control of R&D capabilities.

Sharing ownership of a company

So far we've discussed examples that involve setting up contracts to share business ownership directly. These collaboration designs have gained widespread use only recently, mostly since the 1950s. The familiar approach to sharing business income involves partners sharing business ownership indirectly, via joint ownership of a company that then owns the business, such as a public company with many shareholders, a dairy cooperative with many farmers as members, or simply a joint venture between two or more companies.[22]

Benefits from scale

Setting up companies to own businesses brings many benefits. Companies have unlimited lives, offer limited liability to shareholders,[23] and make it easier to transfer the responsibility for fulfilling contracts. But perhaps the key collaboration benefit of setting up companies to own businesses is that it makes it possible to share ownership and do things on a bigger scale. A public company with many investors provides a critical mass of risk capital for bigger investments than would be possible from merely using contracts between various parties.

Cooperatives, which restrict company ownership to a group of peers, not only achieve scale in their operations, but also protect the interests of the peers who set them up from the monopoly bargaining power that a high scale independent company would exercise. Milk processing and distribution, for example, which are highly scale-intensive activities, have traditionally been local monopolies. As we have seen in Chapter 5, a dairy cooperative lets farmers outsource their milk processing to a processor without surrendering bargaining power to an independently-owned entity.[24]

But problems with collective decision-making

But sharing ownership to permit scale of operation also creates new collaboration problems. The difficulties of collective decision-making drive the corporate governance problems for public companies discussed in Chapter 8, and the innovation problems for consortia discussed in Chapter 5. The advantages from scale of shared ownership of companies have to be balanced against the problems of shared decision-making that they can bring with them.

Benefits from permanence

Setting up a joint-venture company is a good way of ensuring that you will be able to capture the long-term value of providing critical assets or capabilities for a business. It gives you a right to a share in business income for an unlimited period. It also enables you to retain some control over the business in which your assets and capabilities will be used. But unless one or the other party sells their shares, it locks partners into collaborating forever. If the partners' contributions to the business do not stay in balance over time, problems will arise.[25]

But problems if partners' contributions drift out of balance

Tesco Personal Finance was a joint venture set up in 1997 between Royal Bank of Scotland, a major UK banking group, and Tesco, the UK's largest food retailer. As shown in Figure 9.11, both partners contributed resources critical to the business during its start-up phase. RBS developed the personal finance products, handled the processing, and supplied the technology. Tesco contributed an ability to advertise and promote products to their large retail customer base. Leveraging off this strong combination of capabilities, Tesco Personal Finance was a remarkable success. 10 years after its creation, the joint venture had more than five million customers and profits before tax of over £200 million.

But by that point the relationship between RBS and Tesco had lost its balance. Tesco's brand and other resources were all the more critical, as it had gained share in food retailing. It had also built up a strong online home shopping business as well as a strong customer loyalty card.[26] These were two important new platforms for winning personal finance customers and gaining additional revenues from existing personal finance customers. Tesco's customer connections were a truly distinctive resource of long-term value to the business, but RBS' distinctive contributions were fading. The joint venture had given Tesco enough know-how about financial services to set up a more conventional outsourcing contract for the services RBS provided. By 2007, the joint venture effectively depended far more on Tesco than on RBS. A year later Tesco bought RBS' share of Tesco Personal Finance[27] and simply contracted with them for financial product processing as an outsourced service.

Figure 9.11 RBS and Tesco both provide critical resources and share decisions, risks and profits in joint venture

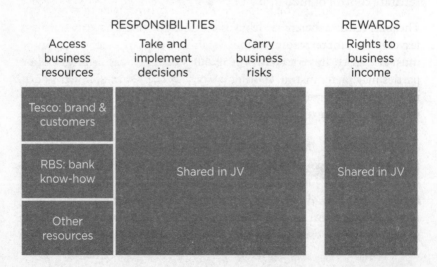

Partners in a joint venture need to think from the outset about how balanced their contributions are, how this balance may shift over time, and what they will do about it. If contributions do become unbalanced over time, the partner whose contributions become dominant is likely to want to buy out the other partner. Tesco was fortunate that 2008 was in the middle of the financial crisis and RBS needed the cash from sale, so it was relatively easy to agree on terms.

It's advisable to provide for joint-venture termination when establishing the company, but there is no easy way to do this. A common provision gives each joint-venture partner the opportunity to buy out the other, with a procedure to determine the highest bidder that then takes over the venture completely. But this approach works poorly when one partner's contribution dominates, as there is then really no choice in deciding which party will sell out. So a fallback provision for involving third parties in determining an appropriate price can be helpful.

Joint-venture companies promise to provide a vehicle for successful long-term collaboration between parties with complementary assets and capabilities for a business. But they are falling out of favour because they struggle to deliver. A joint venture sets up a permanent mechanism for taking and implementing decisions and for sharing business risks, but it all too often doesn't secure permanent access to critical business resources. Essential assets and capabilities remain instead under the separate control of individual joint-venture partners.

The joint venture therefore locks parties into collaborating long term but leaves important terms and conditions of their collaboration open. These must be settled by contracts on the side. When too much is left open, parties may prefer instead to simply focus on setting up long-term – but usually not evergreen – contracts. That gets many of the benefits of a joint-venture company and avoids a messy joint-venture divorce.

Conclusions

Collaboration strategies that share business ownership are becoming increasingly important and widely used. They can help you to access scarce resources with a value that is hard to assess, to carry business risks, and, most important, to motivate partners to work in your interests when you find it hard to clearly specify what output you want or to direct and control the work.

Sharing ownership is a valuable and powerful collaboration strategy, but there are special challenges in meeting several of the 10 requirements. First, to avoid setting up *awkward conflicts of interest*, you must *set goals and constraints to measure performance* such that you reward your partner with a share of an income stream that does a good job of aligning your interests. To fully *align rewards with performance* you must also make sure your partner has skin in the game and is subject to constraints that prevent excessive risk taking. Second, *specifying favourable terms* will not be a simple matter. It is not just about negotiating a high share of the income you jointly create. You may be better off being generous if it will motivate more partners to work with you and create more value. Third, you must be sure you have enough *bargaining power* when the contract comes to an end, and that you can take measures to protect yourself if your partner acquires critical resources for the business at a faster pace than you do. This is a particular concern if you are committed to maintaining a long-term relationship in a joint-venture company.

Sharing business ownership directly by contract is the best way to gain benefits of specialization. Contracts make it possible to flexibly divide up business responsibilities so that parties can focus just where they have competitive advantage. Sharing business ownership via ownership of a company provides less flexibility but can also be useful, especially in gaining benefits of scale – a public company to finance a bigger investment, or a cooperative to avoid the need to buy from a third party monopolist. Sharing company ownership also effectively helps you capture the full benefits of an early contribution to a business. You can lock in your right to the profits for an indefinite period even if you later make no special contribution.

If you share company ownership to gain benefits of scale, you may face problems of collective decision making with your partners. Collective decision-making is liable to cause particular problems in businesses where you want fast decisions, such as about the direction of new product development required to stay ahead of competitors. To make shared responsibilities effective, you need to be sure that the decision-making process will work well for the business you are in.

Before you decide to share ownership, you must be sure you can master these special challenges. If you can't and you get it wrong, you may end up motivating your partners to do the opposite of what you want, as some banks did with bonuses for their traders and dealmakers in the lead up to the financial crisis. Or you may struggle to take important decisions to move the business forward, which was the problem Nokia faced in their Symbian joint venture with other leading handset manufacturers to develop mobile phone operating systems.

But if you get ownership sharing right – as Keller Williams did in setting up their profit-share incentives, as Subway's founders did in setting up their franchise chain, as Delta did in agreeing to work with Priceline to sell their airline tickets, or as banks did in setting up new trading platform consortia to compete against established stock exchanges – you will create a powerful collaboration advantage. Working with the 10 requirements for successful collaboration and the tactical checklists that we have developed throughout the book will help you get it right.

---

[1] To share business ownership, these contracts should be legally binding and not merely management agreements that delegate responsibility or promise rewards that remain discretionary.

[2] Readers may be asking themselves 'How does sharing business ownership relate to the 10 requirements framework for collaboration?' Ownership sharing is simply a third mode of setting up agreements with partners – not as employees with resource contracts, not as suppliers with output contracts, but as joint owners of the business activity with shared responsibilities and rewards. Our framework, after all, lumps employees and suppliers together as partners, so all we're doing is just expanding the category of partners. And all the 10 requirements apply just as much to partners sharing ownership as to employees or suppliers with whom you set up more traditional agreements. When you set up contractual agreements to get the work done, you are establishing how you divide and share business ownership. With a contract to pay for resources, especially an hour of an employee's time, you retain business ownership. You pay to access business resources and thereby fulfill one of your responsibilities as a business owner. With a contract to buy an output for a fixed price, you transfer all ownership of a part of your business to your supplier – the ownership of the business of producing the output. Your supplier is responsible for accessing all business resources, taking decisions, and carrying the risks in producing it. What you pay for producing the output is the reward for doing the business, and your supplier has the right to it. With an income-sharing agreement, you share ownership for all or part of your business. But this can play out in many different ways, depending on how your contracts divide the responsibilities and rewards for achieving the goals you set.

[3] If few other partners can provide what you need, you may be facing a monopolist. We discussed possible ways around the monopoly problem in Chapter 5, but we will discuss some rather different situations in this chapter. In these situations, if you want to do the business, you must simply set up the best commercial agreement you can with the partner that controls the critical resource you need. Sharing business income can be a good way to do it.

[4] Martha Brannigan and Carrick Mollenkamp, 'Heard On The Street: Delta's Priceline.com Stake Presents Challenge'. *Dow Jones Business News*, 14th June 1999.

[5] Scott Thurston, 'Delta hits Internet jackpot for working with ticketing site, airline holds a stake now valued at $1.48 billion'. *The Atlanta Constitution*, 2nd April 1999.

[6] See Note 4.

[7] Tengku Nathan Machmud, *The Indonesian Production Sharing Contract, An Investor's Perspective*, Kluwer Law International, 2000, and Daniel Johnston, *International Petroleum Fiscal systems and Production Sharing Contracts*, PennWell Books, 1994 are two useful books on the history of oil production sharing contracts.

[8] Assuming of course, as we discussed in Chapter 6, that profit-sharing bonuses do not lead bankers to take more risk!

[9] See, for example, John Gapper, 'Only the brave can make jet engines'. *Financial Times*, 20th February 2006.

[10] 'Rolls-Royce: Britain's lonely high-flier'. *The Economist*, 10th January 2009.

[11] For a more extensive description of how risk and revenue sharing partnerships work see 'The Power of Partnerships: A Rolls Royce case study'. The Times 100 Business Case Studies: http://businesscasestudies .co.uk/rolls-royce/the-power-of-partnerships/risk-and-revenue-sharing-partners.html#axzz2d4sSfbwH or the lengthier academic article by Kyle Mayer and David Teece, 'Unpacking strategic alliances: The structure and purpose of alliance versus supplier relationships'. *Journal of Economic Behavior & Organization*, Vol. 66 (2008), 106–127.

[12] But, as we pointed out in Chapter 8, Private Equity and Public Companies are horses for courses and Private equity is by no means always the better solution for investors.

[13] This approach is similar to defining a performance target for a company manager and then offering the manager a bonus for achieving the target, with a higher bonus for outperforming and a lower bonus or no bonus for underperforming. The company manager might even be judged based on achieving the same targets as an external contractor, for example, on spec, on cost completion of a project. With a company manager, it is easy to see why you might want to share the pain and gain of under- or outperformance using the approach of a target bonus. You want to reward performance, but the company manager can't carry the full financial risk of things going wrong, so you could not agree with the company manager to carry out the project for a fixed price. But with a large external contractor capable of carrying the risk, you can do this. So it is less common and only makes sense when it is difficult to clearly specify the output you want from the work and transfer the full financial risk. Although similar to a pain-and-gain sharing contract with an external contractor, target bonuses are often discretionary – the manager has no legal right to the reward – so it is less appropriate to consider that they include an element of shared ownership.

[14] See the Keller Williams 2009 White Paper on 'Profit Share'.

[15] http://redcareers.com/hudsonvalley/blog/keller-williams-crushes-profit-growth-and-productivity-records-for-2013.php downloaded on 12th March 2014.

[16] For further background on Keller Williams, the Keller Williams profit-sharing scheme and the US real estate brokerage market, see, for example: 'Keller Williams Profit Share White Paper', KWU Writing and Research, Keller Williams Realty Inc. 2009; and 'Keller Williams Realty A and B'. Stanford Graduate School of Business, Cases HR 29A and HR29B, prepared by James N Baron, David F Larcker, and Bryan Tayan.

[17] The book *Getting To Yes* by Roger Fisher and William Ury of the Harvard Program on Negotiation describes how assessing the value of the best alternative to a negotiated agreement (BATNA) can help in negotiating a good deal. *Getting to Yes*, Penguin Books 2011. First published by Houghton Mifflin Company in 1981, revised edition by Roger Fisher, William Ury and Bruce Patton.

[18] In the specific context of an airline alliance, revenue or profit sharing also requires anti-trust immunity, which in turn requires the prospective partners (hitherto competitors) to demonstrate that the collaboration is in the interests of the consumer.

[19] When a private equity firm, previously a private partnership, IPOs to become a public company, the firm can continue to act as a fund manager for private equity funds. It is the fund management firm that IPOs to go public, not the funds it manages.

[20] A private equity fund manager typically gets 20 per cent of the profit on the fund, but subject to investors receiving a minimum percentage return on their investment. With this arrangement, there is a 'catch-up' for the fund manager as returns on the fund rise above the hurdle rate for investors. Suppose the hurdle rate is 8 per cent p.a. Below this rate of return on the fund, the fund manager receives no share of the profits. As the return rises above 8 per cent p.a., all the additional profit goes to the fund manager until the fund manager catches up and receives 20 per cent of the fund profits. If returns rise further, above 10 per cent p.a. with an 8 per cent hurdle rate, then 80 per cent of the additional profit goes to investors and 20 per cent to the fund manager.

[21] These concerns about how the balance of bargaining power between partners develops over time are also present in joint-venture companies. We look at the issues in that context later.

[22] John Micklethwait and Adrian Wooldridge, *The Company*, Modern Library, 2005, is a valuable and entertaining short history of public companies, which became widespread in business only with readily available charters of incorporation and limited liability in the nineteenth century.

[23] Introducing limited liability for shareholders is generally beneficial but creates acute problems of awkward conflicts of interest in financial services businesses with little equity. Sharing company ownership of financial services companies between customers can help to solve these problems of awkward conflicts of interest as well as solve problems of monopoly bargaining power. If the customers own the insurer or the bank, then one way or another, as owners or customers, they suffer the losses if the company takes too much risk. Customer ownership eliminates conflicts of interest between a bank or insurance company's shareholders and its customers when shareholders have limited liability. Ownership forms such as building societies, credit unions, Raiffeisen Banks and mutual insurers can make a contribution to solving some tricky problems in financial services. This has probably not been sufficiently recognized by governments who have done little to ensure their good governance in the long-term interests of their customers or to prevent their conversion to become public companies.

[24] Chapter 5 described how, if an intellectual property (such as a software product) is an important industry platform, you can contract to obtain it with an open source licence to prevent the supplier of the platform gaining too much bargaining power. This is an alternative to the user community setting up a cooperative or consortium joint venture. In effect, you put the platform product into common ownership. The question then arises of how to motivate people or companies to reliably further develop the product with sufficient speed and to sufficient standards. One approach is to rely on donations of time and money by the user community, as is the case for the Linux operating system for PCs, and another is to rely on the side-benefits of controlling development being sufficient to motivate a single party to take on the development task and give the work away for free, as is the case for the Android operating system developed by Google for smartphones.

[25] There are few collaboration problems if joint-venture partners transfer control over all the critical assets and capabilities that they have for the new business into the joint-venture company. But in this case the joint-venture company becomes an independent business and not a vehicle for partners who independently control critical resources and capabilities for the business to collaborate.

[26] 'Tesco's £950m buy out of RBS'. *Daily Post* (Liverpool), 29th July 2008.

[27] See note 26.

Chapter 10

Collaboration Strategy

In this final chapter we sum up our main ideas and recommendations and consider their broader implications. We address these thoughts not just to business owners and executives, but also to individuals, governments and any non-commercial organizations that want to get non-routine work done. We consider the underlying trend toward creative collaboration designs, especially the sharing of ownership, that has important ramifications for society as a whole.

The key ideas

We have argued that setting up right to get things done is both increasingly difficult and increasingly vital for business success. Implementing market and competitive strategy is no longer a simple matter of, for example, investing in additional production capacity to gain market share or rolling out a well-established retail store concept to new sites. More and more, it means creatively carrying out new product development, marketing, selling, trading, and deal-making, or managing major projects that draw on a variety of expertise. For these non-routine tasks, it is difficult to specify precisely what you want done. And if you can't provide sufficient direction, it's hard to select and motivate your partners. So companies are stumbling in getting what they want from employees and suppliers.

In fixing problems, the emphasis is often on improving management and leadership – addressing problems when collaboration is already underway. But if collaboration isn't set up right in the first place – if the collaboration strategy is faulty, the best leaders will simply burn themselves out trying to improve matters. Our focus has been on how to develop a good collaboration strategy, set things up right and so make implementation as easy as possible for business owners and their managers.

To have the best chance of developing a good collaboration strategy, you must address issues early on. Instead, companies tend to first focus on their market and competitive strategy, then on the partners to help them implement it, and only after that on the agreements to motivate their partners. But if you can't specify what you want, you're going to struggle to motivate your partners to serve your interests – so much so that you may end up having to drop an otherwise attractive plan because you cannot get it satisfactorily implemented.

As businesses become more specialized and non-routine tasks more important, companies need to think differently about how to get the work done and adopt innovative solutions to collaboration problems. Patterns are emerging and we can see some important trends in collaboration design. The new collaboration challenges and trends have important broader implications for developing business strategy and building competitive advantage.

The process for developing a collaboration design

Figure 10.1 outlines the process for developing a collaboration design that we have advanced and used throughout the book.

Step 1

The first step in the process is to come up with an initial draft design for collaboration. You can go about this using the traditional sequential approach, starting with your customer value proposition and how to achieve competitive advantage in delivering it. You will want to focus in-house on activities where you intend to have competitive advantage, and to outsource other activities. You will motivate in-house employees by directing and controlling their work and paying them for the use of their resources. You will motivate external suppliers by paying them to take on all risk and responsibility for producing the specified work outputs that you want.

But if you can't effectively direct and control your employees, or precisely specify the work outputs you want from your suppliers, setting up agreements in this way may not produce the desired results.

Figure 10.1 The process for developing a collaboration design

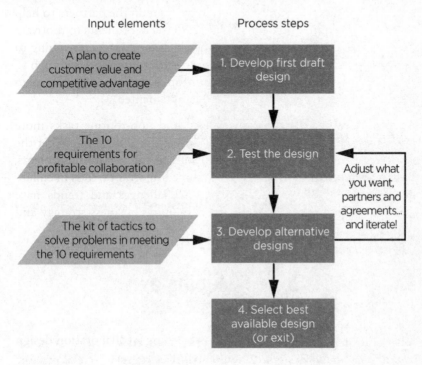

Step 2

So, once you have your first draft design, you test it with the 10 requirements framework used in the book – and shown again in Figure 10.2 below. The 10 requirements will allow you to assess whether or not you can set up robust agreements to motivate your partners. In the areas where you cannot establish good agreements, check that your partners will not face awkward conflicts of interest or gain too much bargaining power.

Step 3

If your first draft design does not meet the 10 requirements – most likely because you can't set up agreements to motivate your preferred partners to do what you want on favourable terms – you will need to consider alternatives. Throughout the book, we have developed an extensive set of tactics for addressing problems in meeting different

Figure 10.2 The 10 requirements for profitable collaboration

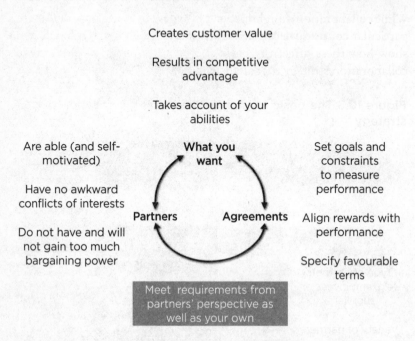

collaboration requirements. You can use these tactics to help you come up with alternative designs. When it is difficult to set up collaboration to meet the 10 requirements, you need a tailor-made design, and you should expect many iterations. Modifying the design to meet one requirement is likely to cause problems in meeting others.

Step 4

When you have considered a number of alternative designs and are reaching diminishing returns, you should choose the best available design. If you can't clearly specify the output you want from the work, no design will be perfect. The question is whether you can find one that is, all things considered, good enough. If no design is good enough, you will need to consider selling or liquidating the business.

We provide a more detailed description of the overall process – a process user's guide – including an overview of the full set of tactics for solving problems at the end of the book.

The big trends in collaboration design

While collaboration designs depend heavily on a company or industry's particular context, we can describe some big trends emerging. We can show how these affect the basic choices to be made in developing a collaboration strategy that are listed in Figure 10.3.

Figure 10.3 The basic choices in developing a collaboration strategy

Offer to customers

Extent of responsibility transferred to partners for delivering the offer

How to gain ability to fulfill own responsibilities

What you want

Type of partners (e.g. employees or suppliers)

Type of goals set as basis for rewards

Variety of partners

Sharing of business risk

Partners

Agreements

Separate or link planning and doing

How to measure partners' performance

Organization of partners

Constraints on how results may be achieved

Partner ownership (e.g. co-op, inc.)

Commitments to partners

Information exchanged

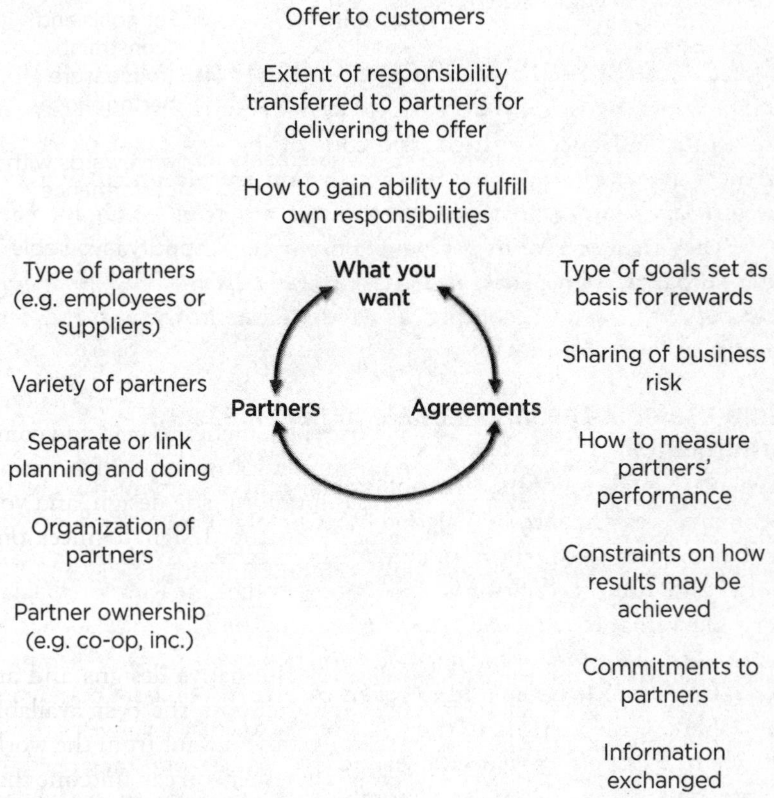

What you want: more specialization and focus

To build competitive advantage, companies are increasingly seeking to further specialize and more sharply focus their investment of time and money on a limited range of activities. Their aim is to do what they are advantaged in doing and *transfer the entrepreneurial responsibility* for everything else to external partners who can do it better. *More and more activities are being outsourced.*

But with the growth in non-routine tasks and specialization, companies and their managers are finding it difficult to transfer as much responsibility as they would like. They are left with more responsibility for specifying and supervising work than they can easily handle. To *gain the ability to fulfil their own responsibilities*, they are being *forced to innovate in their choices of partners and agreements.*

Agreements: more sharing of business ownership

As it becomes increasingly difficult to either define the precise outputs you want in advance, or direct and control the work as it proceeds, partners are acting more autonomously and are often simply given the *goal of helping to generate business income* – a part of which, increasingly, they then receive in payment. Employees, suppliers and other external partners are *sharing in entrepreneurial responsibilities – including risks and rewards* and becoming, as we discussed in the last chapter, co-owners in the business.

More use of secondary markets to help measure performance

If you set your employees or suppliers the goal of helping you create income, it is essential to find a good measure of the income your partner helps create. In the short- or even medium-term, customer revenues and profits often do not provide a good enough measure of a partner's performance. *Agreements increasingly rely on market valuations of companies or assets, before and after the work, to measure partners' performance* – CEOs and R&D engineers get stock options, or asset managers get a share of the increase in the value of the assets they invest in. To be able to make effective use of secondary markets, you may need to outsource the work to small entrepreneurial firms with shares whose value have a better line of sight with the performance of the key managers that you wish to reward.

Setting constraints becomes almost as important as setting goals

As income sharing becomes more common, managing risk and *incorporating constraints into contracts becomes a bigger concern*. Even when you have a good measure of your partner's performance, sharing income with your partner may not sufficiently align your interests – partners with greater upside than downside may be tempted to take risks that destroy value. To deal with this problem, you can and should set some constraints on how your partner goes about helping you generate income.

Franchisors, for example, typically set strict guidelines for the use of their brand; deviating from the standard Burger King menu might be profitable for an individual Burger King franchisee in a specific market, but it reduces the consistency of the brand promise and destroys value for other franchisees and for Burger King.

Your commitments to suppliers matter as much as their commitments to you

When partners share ownership, they become mutually dependent for their success. The customer must work to help the supplier succeed just as much as the supplier must work to help the customer succeed. *Commitments are no longer one way from the supplier to the customer*. It is more important *to meet requirements from your partner's perspective*. To get commitments from the supplier, the customer must make commitments in return, as in alliances, franchising, and ERP installations. When you and your partner are truly collaborating and making reciprocal commitments, business processes stretch seamlessly across company boundaries, so there is *a need for a much greater exchange of information* between you.

Partners: more variety of partners and more dependent relationships

How we categorize 'partners' depends on the type of agreement we set up with them to get the work done. When you are not sharing entrepreneurial responsibility for getting the work done, there are just two types of agreement: payment for resources, usually employees' labour resources, if you want to retain responsibility for the work; or payment for the output, usually to an external supplier, if you want to transfer responsibility for it.

But companies are increasingly sharing the entrepreneurial responsibilities, and the number of these ownership-sharing agreements is unlimited. So there will be *a much greater variety of types of partner:* employees, suppliers, licensors, franchisors, fund managers, risk- and revenue-sharing partners, and of course alliance partners of many different kinds.

Greater variety of specialized partners working more closely together

With greater specialization of companies and personal skills, *a greater variety of types of partners must unite to get the work done.* To put together the right mix of skills, teams stretch across company boundaries. Clients and contractors work closely together and share information and decision-making.

When so many different parties work together to produce a joint output, relationships need to be organized not just between employees in the company hierarchy, but also between different suppliers, and between suppliers and employees. For example, when utilities choose to work so closely with suppliers in framework alliances that they staff projects on a 'best person for the job' basis, they must also agree how a supplier manager supervising a utility employee will help determine the employee's annual bonus.

More dependent relationships require checks and balances

Companies are becoming more dependent on their partners. To gain the benefits of specialization they are transferring more responsibility to suppliers for providing business critical assets and capabilities. And they are transferring more responsibility to suppliers or to employees for taking critical decisions. But companies don't want to become any more dependent on individual partners than they have to. So they will also work with *a greater variety of partners, not just because they need the right mix of skills, but also to avoid becoming too dependent on any one partner.*

They will ask several partners to work on similar tasks in order to maintain competition among these partners. They will second source or insist on employees teaming up to serve clients, and they will work with partners to check up on their other partners. Taking on additional partners can help to counterbalance the primary partner's greater leverage in the relationship. For example, when banks rely for their profits on traders working relatively autonomously and with powerful performance incentives, they must build up an independent cadre of specialized risk managers to prevent traders from taking too much risk.

More advice

More generally, both the uncertainty involved in taking decisions about how to carry out non-routine tasks that require specialized know-how, and the desire to avoid dependence on partners with awkward conflicts of interest, have led to a *rapid growth in 'advisory business'*. Consulting of various forms – from business strategy and IT to HR or benefits consultants for pension funds – has become a major global industry growing at a double-digit rate over decades.

Special types of partners to manage (monopoly) industry platforms

As industries become more specialized, participants rely more on *common platforms* to coordinate all the different parties offering products and services. These assets need to be *owned by the industry community – by a cooperative or association* – or be made freely available to all to prevent a platform provider with a monopoly gaining too much bargaining power. *For intellectual property, open source 'copyleft' licensing* provides an attractive new alternative to a traditional industry cooperative.

The implications for strategy and competitive advantage

These new collaboration challenges and designs driven by the growth in non-routine tasks and specialization have profound implications for developing strategy and building competitive advantage as we outline below.

Business strategy becomes more personal

No longer is it enough to consider if the strategy is right for the company. It must be right for the person in charge of getting things done. This has always been the case, but people are now much more likely to need specialist qualifications to define what needs to be done and to monitor and control the work accordingly.

General managers will not have an even balance of all the different specialist skills needed to get all types of non-routine work done. Hence what they decide to get done should take account not only of what might create most value for their company but also of what they will be best at overseeing. An executive with deep experience in managing large IT projects will want to be more ambitious in these investments than someone without. A pharmaceutical company, whose executive team is weak on research expertise but strong on legal or financial expertise, will be more likely to go outside and rely on acquisitions and alliances for new product development. Companies should therefore build the personal skills of executives, and the types of strategy that they will find easy to implement, explicitly into their strategy development.

Collaboration strategy becomes an important source of competitive advantage

The greater salience of collaboration means that companies now have more ways to achieve competitive advantage. Keller Williams' elaborate profit-sharing agreements with real-estate agents have given them an advantage over other residential brokerage brands in building a loyal and motivated team. Private equity funds have grown rapidly and profitably in their target markets based on a collaboration design that provides high-powered, transparent and well-aligned incentives for investors, private equity partners and operating company managers. The trick is to get all the key decision-makers to be highly motivated to carry out the activities needed to implement the agreed business strategy.

Owning superior assets or contracting to employ a team of people with superior skills gives you the potential to do the work better or cheaper. It gives you competitive advantage of a traditional kind – a resource advantage. But when setting up to get things done becomes a complex task, a resource advantage is no longer enough. It is what you make of your potential that counts. To succeed, you must be able to motivate your partners to do what you want on favourable terms. By setting up to do that well, you can achieve a competitive advantage of a new kind – a collaboration advantage. With the growing importance of non-routine tasks, that is becoming increasingly critical.

Shifting the strategic focus to your business system as a whole

When you share your income with partners providing hard-to-specify outputs, you need to think about the competitive advantage of the broader business system in which you operate. This business system – you might call it an ownership network – includes you and all the partners that share income with you. In franchising, this network may include the franchisor, franchise development agents, and all the franchisees. For an electric utility, it could be the utility and contractors bound together in long-term framework alliances. For an airline, it is their airline network alliance partners.

Your network's advantage lies not just in its resources – people and materials – but also in how well it uses these resources. And that depends on the agreements you and other partners have set up to motivate each other. The competitive advantage of the utility's ownership network, for example, therefore depends not just on the resources that the utility and its contractors bring to the table, but also on how well the pain-and-gain sharing contracts between client and contractors tie into longer term framework agreements between them focused on continuous improvement – and how well the interests of the various parties in the network are aligned over time. Your network's collaboration advantage will be just as important as its resource advantage.

If your industry depends on one or a few suppliers of a key platform, such as a smartphone operating system, you need to include that platform in your business system. You should work out which platform is likely to prevail over time and see if you can get a good deal now. If a platform supplier is likely to gain excessive bargaining power, you'll want to pursue community ownership of the platform with your peers or other tactics.

Aiming to fill the most attractive role within the business system

Of course, it is not enough to know how well your business system will perform as a whole. You want to know how well you and your company will perform within it. That means understanding the attractiveness of the different roles in the system – and going after the most attractive role. The attractiveness of the role you have within a business system depends on which responsibilities you take on and whether you have distinctive advantages in doing so. In private equity, for example, are you an investor, a private equity firm partner, or an operating executive in a fund-owned company? What share of any system outperformance will you and other parties get? Not all parties profit equally from the strength of a business system. In private equity, it is usually the partners in the private equity firms that profit the most, not the executives or investors, but they also have the greatest responsibilities to oversee the investment portfolio.

Within a business system, owning or controlling critical resources – assets or capabilities – is what determines the share you capture of any system outperformance relative to your partners. In restaurant franchising, for example, the franchisor captures much of the outperformance because of its ownership of the brand and concept. There are scale effects in brand building, and restaurant brands and concepts are distinctive. A restaurant brand and concept is effectively an industry platform, albeit one likely to have competitors. Individual franchisees with particularly good restaurant sites or a particular talent at managing restaurants may do very well, but scale effects are much smaller for them, so they face more competition from potential franchisees. So we can expect franchisees as a whole to achieve average returns. Superior returns accrue to companies that are focused on activities where they have distinct advantages, and that are able to leverage those advantages in working with partners in their business system.

Greater opportunity to earn profits while others put up the money

We often think of the business owner as the person or group that provides the risk capital. That is indeed what it takes to become the legal owner of a public company. But carrying the risks is just one of the responsibilities of ownership. Owners must also be able to provide access to critical business assets, as well as take and implement business decisions, and these are the abilities that now drive competitive advantage. Risk capital is money, which is a commodity; but having preferential access to critical resources – patents, brands, property, plant, equipment, and people – is distinctive. How well you take and implement decisions then determines what you make of any competitive advantage you have. If you make good decisions, you will build advantage; if not, your advantage will gradually fade.

When you rely on partners for resources or decision-making, or both, you depend on them for achieving superior returns in your business system. That gives them leverage to gain a larger share of those returns. So you will aspire to control the use of the critical resources and to become highly competent in taking and implementing decisions about how to use them. You would like to get partners to do everything else: provide access to lesser resources, use them to help meet the system's goals, and provide the capital to carry the risks.

Clearly you will not always be able to meet this high aspiration. But some – Doctors' Associates, the owners of the Subway brand and concept, and the partners in successful private equity firms, such as Bain Capital or TPG – have come pretty close to doing so. They have control over the critical resources and the skills to use them. They put up relatively little of the risk capital needed in the business. And they reap handsome returns for their highly focused work.

Collaboration for other constituencies

Throughout the book we have focused on issues of setting up collaboration in commercial businesses. The perspective we have taken has been largely that of business owners, managers or investors. But the key challenge we have been discussing, setting up to get non-routine work done, is not just an issue for commercial businesses and those involved in them.

Setting up collaboration in non-commercial settings

The problems in getting building work carried out in the home, though on a smaller scale, are not so different from those involved in a large construction project for a commercial company. Designing and installing a new IT system to serve a government department has many parallels with the same work for a corporation. It is just as important for individuals, governments and non-profit organizations to think through how they intend to set up collaboration to get things done. Indeed, because of public accountability, the problems governments face in getting things done are probably better known and documented than those in companies. The US government's struggles in setting up a national online health insurance marketplace, Berlin's setbacks in building its new airport, and the UK National Health Service's cancellation of a national patient database have all been prominent news items and the subject of major public enquiries.

Governments and non-profit organizations face the toughest challenges

In setting goals and constraints and measuring performance, governments and non-profit organizations face the toughest challenges. They lack the revenue indicators that show customer value created and the profit markers that demonstrate competitive advantage. In most cases the beneficiaries of government or non-profit services don't directly pay for the services they receive, and it is difficult to conclusively measure the value of services to beneficiaries in other ways.

Governments are not good at running businesses – it's not their core competence. So they sensibly prefer to outsource as much of the work as possible and transfer management responsibility wherever they can. But the difficulty of setting goals and measuring performance makes it even more difficult for a government to transfer full management responsibility for an activity than for investors in a commercial business. When shareholders in a public company transfer management responsibility to the CEO, or investors in a fund transfer management responsibility to the fund's managers, they need to provide few instructions. Shareholders and limited partner investors in commercial enterprises can motivate their managers to make a profit simply by agreeing to share the profit made. Governments providing services for free can't offer partners a share of business income to motivate them, so they have to provide partners more instructions about what to do.

Despite the acute difficulties they face in setting goals, governments and non-profit organizations are increasingly defining the outputs and outcomes they want and paying to get them, rather than simply paying for people's time and other resources used to do the work. Not surprisingly, goals set for measuring performance frequently lead to awkward conflicts of interest that provide a field day for the political opposition.

For example, in a hospital, it's easy to measure the number of surgical operations carried out – and that's a rough and ready measure of value created. So the German government since 2004 has agreed payment to hospitals at a standard determined rate per operation. But in many cases, whether an operation is necessary is a matter of judgement. Operations on the spine to eliminate back pain are increasingly popular, but are far more expensive than a regimen of rest and exercise that might get the same benefit. Since 2004, the annual number of spine operations to relieve back pain in Germany has more than doubled. Does this indicate progress in operating techniques, a better level of healthcare or simply a lucrative revenue opportunity for hospitals? Some hospitals have even paid doctors personal bonuses for the number of operations they carry out.[1]

To complicate matters, in many of the health and other social services that governments and non-profit organizations provide, personal relationships are part of the value provided. But it is easier to measure whether an elderly person in care has been washed or had their dinner, than to determine whether he or she has been cheered up by conversation with a caregiver. When measuring performance, there is a risk of focusing on the mechanical and measurable, dehumanizing the work and reducing its value.

Because it is so difficult to measure value created, it is crucial that governments and non-profit organizations balance quantifiable goals with constraints. Just as investment banks rely on a risk-management function to minimize awkward conflicts of interest, governments need something similar to oversee hospitals' decisions on surgeries or their treatment of patients. No government would relish its practices being compared to an investment bank, but the comparison is apt nevertheless.

The broader issues for society

Since Adam Smith's time, setting up collaboration between parties specialized in carrying out different types of work – the 'division of labour' – has been recognized as the key driver of business productivity and growth in the economy. The growing success of collaboration designs that share business ownership between parties – private equity, franchising, alliances and others – suggests that a sophisticated 'division of ownership' will continue this trend. It does so, as we discussed in Chapter 9, by permitting greater specialization of entrepreneurial responsibility. The different responsibilities of an owner – providing resources, taking and implementing decisions, and carrying risks – are distributed to whomever is best able to take each on, with the income shared accordingly to align their interests. So collaboration designs that involve sophisticated division of ownership should be valuable to society in further promoting specialization and productivity growth.

However, this division of ownership not only has the potential to enhance productivity and growth. It also has some rather profound broader consequences for society – some good and some bad. Preventing the undesirable consequences will pose a major challenge for governments as they set taxes, laws, and regulations for business.

Talented individuals will capture greater value

When people and companies share ownership in the sophisticated ways described in this book, we enter a post-capitalist society in which a substantial share of business profits no longer goes to the providers of risk capital. It goes instead to those providing critical resources for the business, or taking and implementing critical decisions. A sophisticated division of ownership creates attractive opportunities for the owners of critical resources such as brands, oilfields or development land. They can, thanks to a shared ownership approach, motivate others to do the work to exploit the resources they own, while still keeping a good share of the profits.

More importantly for society, a sophisticated division of ownership creates opportunities for talented individuals to capture more value from the talent they have in taking and implementing decisions. Suppose you excel at strategy development, and you'd like to get the most value from your skills. You can aspire to become a Chief Strategy Officer in a public company. You will then be working in a corporate hierarchy, where your personal performance will be hard to measure. You will have influence but not be fully responsible for strategy decisions. You may report to the CEO but not be a member of the top executive management team. You may have little ownership in the business in which you work.

Alternatively you can join a strategy consulting firm and aspire to become a partner. You then have ownership in your firm. Your firm can develop a reputation for good work. You will capture some of this value, and so you will likely do financially rather better than as an employee in a large company. But your strategy consulting firm is carrying out a service for other companies. It is still not fully in control of whether its recommendations are implemented.

The best way to capitalize on your talent may be to become a partner in a private equity firm. You go out and persuade investors to invest in your fund, and you put your strategy recommendations into practice. You don't have to get your hands dirty with the operational management – you hire executives in the funds companies to do that. But now you have a large measure of control over the businesses whose strategy you develop – and your strategy's performance is fully measurable via the performance of the fund itself. Your talent is leveraged by limited partners' money and by a considerable amount of debt. If you really do have talent and your strategies are successful, you have set up collaboration in a very favourable way. Many former strategy professionals have joined private equity firms and made a great deal more money there than they ever could have in a public company or a consulting firm.

Government policies on collaboration may unnecessarily widen the gap

Because these sophisticated forms of collaboration allow individuals to leverage their talent, they contribute to the increasing spread in income and wealth between the top 10 per cent in society and everyone else, and that is becoming a critical issue.

Dealing with this issue is a job for governments as they establish and adjust the legal and tax frameworks supporting collaboration. The more collaboration designs share ownership, the more sophisticated government needs to be in setting the ground rules. So far, as we discuss below, governments have actually made things worse, unnecessarily accentuating the spread in income and wealth as a result of division of ownership.

Tax loopholes in shared ownership

Sharing business ownership makes it more difficult for governments to set fair tax rates. Rewarding highly paid executives with an ownership stake in the business they manage gives them a variety of opportunities to reduce their tax rates. For example, both personal tax and corporate tax usually distinguish between just two basic types of income – ordinary income and capital gains. People and companies pay ordinary income tax on their regular business or work income, and capital gains tax when they sell assets that they own. Where do you put an executive's income from grants of stock options, or a fund manager's carried interest in the fund's profits? These incomes are driven by capital gains, but the payment is a reward for doing the work. Should these payments be taxed at the rate for capital gains, at the rate for ordinary income, or at some other rate? Mostly they end up being taxed at the usually favourable capital gains tax rate. So some of the people who earn the most from their work end up paying the lowest taxes. Warren Buffet famously said that he paid taxes at a lower rate than his secretary.[2] To prevent this division of ownership further widening the gap between the haves and have nots, governments need to be more sophisticated in taxation.

Subsidized risk capital that favours bankers

Risk capital has become progressively cheaper in recent decades, to the point where it has become a commodity that talented individuals can leverage to maximize their rewards. But governmental actions have made risk capital even cheaper than it should be.

Bankers' bonuses, which let them share in banks' profits but not their losses, are widely perceived to be the cause of the excessive risk taking that led to the financial crisis of 2008. But it turns out that bank shareholders have had a similar incentive to take on too much risk. Governments have allowed banks to have only three or four per cent of their total capital in the form of equity, and bank shareholders to have limited liability. So if a bank makes heavy losses and goes bankrupt, shareholders don't pick up the full tab. Depositors and lenders pick up the residual losses, unless a government considers the bank too big to fail and rushes in to guarantee customer deposits. This gives especially the megabanks an incentive to lend aggressively, which in turn gives artificially cheap risk capital to talented individuals throughout financial services. Not just the bankers themselves, who can trade in risky instruments, but also the private equity managers and real-estate developers – who can then pocket the gains. If taxpayers weren't shouldering the additional risk, the financial services industry's risk tolerance would be better aligned with that of society as a whole. As it is, the people who make the decisions get too much of the cake when things go well, while the taxpayers get too little recompense for underwriting the major losses.

From this perspective, high bankers' bonuses have been a consequence of a deep-seated problem in the way governments set up collaboration in financial services that encourages too much risk taking. Since the financial crisis of 2008, governments have been working to make corrections. Unfortunately, the current collaboration design in financial services is so broken that this is an exceptionally difficult task. It is not just bank managers and shareholders that have the wrong incentives; almost all other financial services stakeholders have the wrong incentives too. Consumers know that their deposits are guaranteed by the government so they can choose the bank that offers them the highest interest on their deposits without fear of losing their money. This encourages banks to take too much risk to compete for deposits. Rating agencies paid by the companies whose credit they rate have an incentive to rate them leniently. Governments themselves, struggling to make their debt payments, overstate their own creditworthiness by zero rating government bonds for the purpose of calculating bank equity ratios. How do you get to a good collaboration design for the financial services industry? Alas, 'don't start from here!'

It is crucial for the success of the whole economy that governments master the skills involved in setting up business collaboration, not just for contracting but equally importantly in taxing, legislating, regulating and supervising business. They need to understand the full range of tactics available and make good trade-offs. But that is the subject of a different book.

Conclusions

Increasingly, intelligent machines are taking over the routine tasks and the tasks left for us to do are non-routine. For non-routine tasks, it is more difficult to set up to get the right work done. That makes the ability to set up collaboration to motivate employees, suppliers, and other partners to do what you want a central issue – in business and more broadly in society. Throughout the book, we have dealt with the problem in a business context. But this is a universal problem. Everyone should have a framework for how to address it.

In practice they don't have any framework in place. When it is difficult to set things up so people and companies do what you want, you need a substantially new frame of reference for thinking about the problems and coming up with solutions. The new framework we propose in this book for thinking through the problem is certainly not rocket science, but it is not in common use. In fact, it is so different to the usual way of thinking about things that it requires new terms to describe it: 'partners' to cover all the employees, suppliers and other business partners, such as fund managers or franchisees, that you may rely on to get work done; and 'sharing business ownership' to cover all the relationships in which parties contract, in a legally binding form, to share the responsibilities and rewards in the business. It also requires a sharper understanding of the wide range of possibilities for managing business responsibilities and rewards – how these can be divided and distributed in new ways so you can capture the benefits of specialization and get work done by able partners while motivating them to do what you really want.

Setting up collaboration to get non-routine work done for you on favourable terms is never going to be easy. But having a simple process for developing your collaboration strategy, a framework delineating the requirements for success and a set of tactics for meeting them can help you, whoever you are, to do it better.

---

1 See, for example, Esther Langmaack, 'Wie viel Medizin braucht der Mensch?' ('How much medical treatment do we really need?'). *Hörzu*, 15th February 2013.

2 Tom Bawden, 'Buffett blasts system that lets him pay less tax than secretary'. *The Times*, 28th June 2007.

Summary of the Process for Developing a Collaboration Design

With greater specialization and non-routine work, the way you set up collaboration to get work done is becoming an important and difficult challenge for business owners and managers. This book has developed a powerful analytical process for developing a collaboration design to meet this challenge. It addresses what you want from partners to implement your market and competitive strategy; the type of partners you can work with – employees, suppliers and co-owners; and the agreements – binding contracts and informal understandings that you establish with these partners to motivate them. Chapter 1 introduced and outlined the process, and subsequent chapters developed and applied it to a wide variety of sectors and situations. We here summarize the entire process as a compact guide for those who have read the book and are looking to apply the process in their own organizations.

The process has four key steps in it, as shown in Figure S.1. The steps are:

- Develop a first draft collaboration design
- Test the design, using the 10 requirements framework to diagnose potential problems
- Develop alternative designs, using the tactics checklists for dealing with problems, and considering radical alternatives if needed
- Select the best available design that emerges and make it your collaboration strategy

Figure S.1 The process for developing a collaboration design

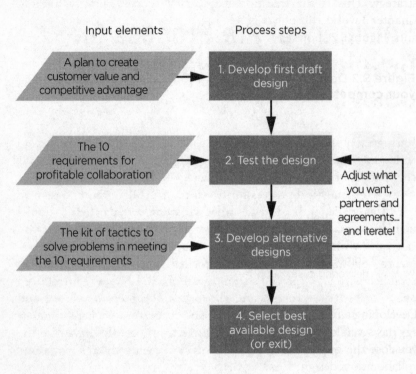

Step 1: Develop a first draft collaboration design

How you get to a first draft is not critical. Any problems with your first draft collaboration design will be shaken out in steps 2 and 3 in our process. The key is to have something to start with.

If you are already in business and working with partners, you can start with the design that you are currently using. Or you may consider alternative designs prompted by what other companies are doing, by articles or reports of what has worked well elsewhere, or simply by an intuitive feel for how you could improve things.

If you are starting up a new business, or you want to undertake a more thorough review of your current set up, you can develop a first draft collaboration design systematically from your market and competitive strategy. This is the traditional approach to collaboration design. Chapter 3 works through this step in some detail for fast-food restaurants. Figure S.2 shows how to proceed.

Figure S.2 Developing a first draft collaboration design from your competitive strategy

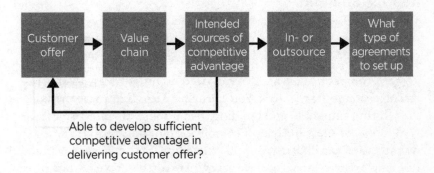

Able to develop sufficient
competitive advantage in
delivering customer offer?

Developing a first draft design to fit your market and competitive strategy has several advantages. After all, if you copy what others have done, you lose the opportunity to gain a competitive advantage from your collaboration design. Chapter 3, in examining fast-food restaurants, showed that rivals with different business strategies developed quite different designs. Subway outsourced almost everything, while Starbucks kept many activities in-house. Your strategy may prompt you to consider innovative ways of dividing up and outsourcing responsibilities. You still need to test your design with our framework, but systematically coming up with a first draft from your market and competitive strategy should reduce the further work you need after testing.

The customer value proposition determines the business activities

Your market strategy determines how you propose to create customer value. This, in turn, determines the value chain you need, including what resources will be required,[1] what work will need to be done, and how much capital will be at risk. Fast-food restaurants require a brand and restaurant concept, some real estate (sites), fixtures and fittings for each site, food and supplies, and people to do the work in developing the brand, purchasing food and supplies, and running the sites. Since your personal capabilities are limited, you will need help from partners in creating this customer value proposition. So you will need to start by laying out the value chain for the business to deliver your customer offer.

Competitive advantage drives choices of partners and agreements

Your competitive strategy lays out how you expect to achieve competitive advantage, which in turn drives what to do in-house and what to outsource.

To gain competitive advantage, you need exclusive access to superior resources for doing the work. You can achieve this by owning the assets or by hiring employees and building the in-house capability to get the work done, or most likely by a combination of both. So for these key resources and capabilities, you will generally want to own the assets and hire employees to carry out the work. Where you don't seek competitive advantage, you can leave it to others to own the assets and take the responsibility for getting the work done.

For a chain of fast-food restaurants, we said competitive advantage would likely come from the brand and concept. You would therefore want to own these yourself, and carry out at least some of the brand and concept development work in-house. For other parts of this work you might rely on suppliers such as advertising agencies. But you will feel comfortable relying entirely on outside parties for most other components of the restaurant chain value proposition, since these activities offer little competitive advantage now or in the future. See the textbox 'What is critical for building competitive advantage?'

What is critical for building competitive advantage?

Not all assets and capabilities offer equal potential for building competitive advantage in a business, and you may not need to own or fully control them to gain advantage from their use.

The assets or capabilities that create advantage should be distinctive and in short supply. For example, you must have office space for the employees working to help you develop your brand, but you don't need to own your office building, as this is an easily obtained resource. However, if you are running a department store, retail space is critical, and there may be few suitable properties downtown. If you rent and do not own your department store property, you are quite vulnerable at the end of the lease, as the landlord may have many other uses for the space. For this reason most department stores often do own their buildings, especially for their downtown flagship locations.

As for assets and capabilities specific to your business, which cannot be used for anything else, these will certainly be distinctive and in short supply. It is risky to rely on partners to provide them unless you contract from the start to get what you want from them over their full useful life. If you can't do that, you may prefer to own the asset but outsource the work. For example, you might own the mould for producing a distinctive bottle cap but outsource the production of the caps.

Assets tend to have finite lives, but capabilities, such as skill in pharmaceutical research, do not. With good management, the more you use a capability, the better it gets as you go down the experience curve. So outsourcing distinctive capabilities is particularly tricky if you want to capture a good share of the value from their use.

If you don't need the full scope of an essential asset or capability for your business, owning it fully may not be necessary. You can devise an exclusive contract to use an asset or capability only in a limited way. You might license a brand or a patent for a specific territory or industry, or you might contract for exclusive use in your industry of a consultant's advanced data mining capability. However, as we discuss in Chapter 9, when you do that, your partner may demand payment with a share of the income from your business rather than a fixed fee. After all, these distinctive resources and capabilities drive your competitive advantage, so your partner may feel entitled to share the value arising from that advantage.

By holding assets and carrying out work in-house only where you can build distinctive strengths, you will be able to leverage your investment of time and money. Collaboration designs that allow you to focus on your key sources of competitive advantage and outsource everything else have the potential for exceptional profitability, as Apple in electronics and Subway in fast-food restaurants clearly demonstrate.

Competitive advantage also determines the type of agreements you want with partners. Where you have a competitive advantage, you will pay for the resources you need, retain the business risk, and capture the rewards. That means paying your employees for their time – the resource capacity they provide. Where you do not have a competitive advantage, you will transfer to the supplier all the risk and responsibility involved with the desired output, in exchange for a fixed price.

Complications in coming up with a first draft based on market and competitive strategy

If you aren't sure whether you can properly motivate a supplier, or control the work of an employee, we suggest going ahead anyway, in a first draft, with whatever partner and type of agreement makes sense on the grounds of competitive advantage. The problems you already see will come out fully in testing the design in step 2, and in step 3 you can address how to deal with them.

You may also find that competitive advantage is not clear-cut, or that considerations of competitive advantage don't clearly determine what to do. To have a clear-cut competitive advantage, you should have a superior ability to take on one or more of the three entrepreneurial responsibilities for an activity:[2] accessing needed resources – both assets and people, taking and implementing decisions, and carrying the risks. And you should not have a significant disadvantage in any of these.

Different parties may be separately advantaged in taking on specific responsibilities for the same activity. You may be good at carrying the risks, while a partner can better handle the decision side. Chapter 3 explains how McDonald's Corporation outsources the management of restaurants to franchisees, but provides the financing – carrying a share of the risks for many of these franchisees, especially first-timers. Likewise, Chapter 9 describes how a national oil company owns and therefore has advantaged access to the resources of a local oil field, but relies on a multinational oil company to develop the oil field and extract the oil, because the multinational oil company is advantaged at taking and implementing decisions and carrying the risks of exploring for and producing the oil.

Where competitive advantage is not clear-cut, you may want to divide up the business responsibilities, and then, to align your partner's interest with yours, also share the corresponding business income. For example, when providing risk capital for store investment, McDonalds' Corporation charges franchisees a percentage of their store revenues. In the same vein, to develop the oil field, the national oil company sets up a production-sharing contract that shares the profits from the oil produced with the exploration company.

When different parties are advantaged at taking on different entrepreneurial responsibilities for a single activity, you should, in step 1, make a first attempt at allocating responsibilities to whoever is best able to take each on and share business income to align interests. Sharing income may not be enough to align your partners' interests with yours, so testing the design in step 2 to see if it does will be critical.

Step 2: Test the design to reveal potential problems

You're now ready to test your initial design for collaboration, using the 10 requirements framework see Figure S.3.

What you want

If you developed the draft based on your market and competitive strategy, you have already satisfied the requirements to create *customer value* and achieve *competitive advantage*. But it is worth checking these requirements again, since they are a vital starting point. As for the third requirement, that what you want *takes account of your abilities*, this means that the executives in charge of collaboration should have access to the resources and capital needed to carry out the work involved. They should also have the skills to identify suitable partners and set up effective agreements to direct and motivate them, as shown in Figure S.3. Managers often lack these skills when dealing with non-routine and complicated activities such as installing a new ERP system, developing new pharmaceutical products, or doing investment banking deals. As a senior manager designing collaboration, you need to make an honest assessment of whether you personally have the skills to make your design work well.

Figure S.3 The 10 requirements for profitable collaboration

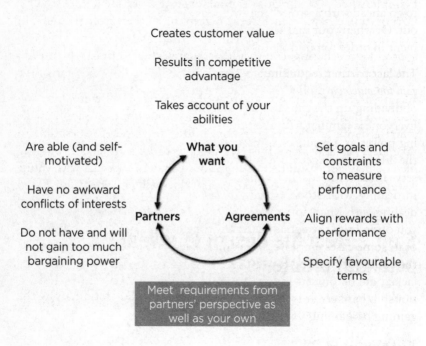

Partners

Your first draft set up, based on your market and competitive strategy, should identify partners that are *able to provide the help you want and sufficiently self-motivated* to carry the work out professionally and competently. The requirement is usually easy to meet provided there is a wide range of possible partners to choose from. Picking a new supplier for a standard component or hiring a new production line employee should present few problems. But the requirement is harder to meet if the needed capabilities are rare and it's hard to tell in advance whether candidates possess them, as we saw in Chapter 7 with leading-edge product development.

A further requirement that your draft may not cover is that partners should have *no awkward conflicts of interest* that will undermine their motivation. Most people would rather play golf or go to a movie than work, but paying them for their time removes most of this kind of conflict of interest. An awkward conflict is one that persists despite this payment, such as when you hire a supplier to help you decide whether to go ahead with a project that this supplier would likely help you carry out. Or when your marketing director advocates expanding his department in order to build up his empire and advance his career.

The last partner requirement is that partners *should not have and will not gain too much bargaining power.* This requirement relates to the problem of dividing up the cake in ways that leave you with a satisfactory slice. Everyone is familiar with the problem of suppliers with strong bargaining power as a result of some unique assets or position; and likewise, the difficulties in getting a good deal when there is little competition to serve industry needs. In Chapter 5, we discussed the problems of banks in dealing with stock exchanges and of computer manufacturers in dealing with Microsoft to acquire the Windows operating system. But you often miss the equally serious problems that arise when suppliers, or in some cases employees, become difficult to substitute only during the course of working for you, and so gain bargaining power that they lacked at the outset. From ERP implementation consultants to relationship bankers, it is important to anticipate problems with partners gaining bargaining power and to devise agreements to mitigate them.

Agreements

It is often in relation to agreements that your draft design will need the most modification and refinement. Do your agreements *set clear goals to measure performance*? If not, you'll face ambiguity about what help is wanted and whether it has been satisfactorily provided. Chapter 4 highlighted the specification problem in the garment, automobile and construction industries. When you can't specify the output you want before you start working together, suppliers face awkward conflicts of interest and may acquire increasing bargaining power as the collaboration progresses. Similar problems arise with employees who need a good deal of autonomy to perform well, as we saw in Chapters 6 and 7 in discussing traders in investment banks and managers of pharmaceutical R&D.

Giving your partner the simpler goal of helping you create business income and then sharing this income – revenue, profits, or the increase in share value – may avoid the need to provide precise directions. But income-sharing contracts succeed only if based on clear and agreed ways of measuring the income created by the work. Performance measurement is a serious practical problem, not least because your partners will be tempted to manipulate measures to increase their rewards.

Even with good measures, you may still face problems in *aligning rewards with performance* if poor performance cannot be sanctioned. Traders in investment banks, who typically share in the profits but not so much in the losses, may well take on too much risk.

To avoid misalignment problems, particularly when working with income-sharing contracts, it is crucial that agreements *set constraints* on how goals may be achieved. Franchise contracts, for example, need to include constraints on the minimum level of advertising investment in the brand. If they do not, franchisors will be tempted to under spend, as they typically receive a share of franchisees' revenues, not their more ad-dependent profits.

Finally, the agreement should *specify favourable terms* for you. This, of course, is hard with a partner holding a great deal of bargaining power. But you can also risk unfavourable terms if you lack the information to know what payment is fair. How much should it cost to build this facility? What is a reasonable price to make this garment? How generous do I need to be to attract and retain key staff? These sorts of questions are vital in putting in place good agreements, and you need to organize the capabilities to give the right answers to them – or else you will not profit from the collaboration as much as you should.

The partner's perspective

The last requirement recognizes that partners will want the collaboration to be profitable for them too, and so should be looking at a similar set of requirements from their perspective. You will therefore need *to meet the requirements from your partners' perspective as well as your own*. This is particularly important where you have to provide resources or carry out activities for your partner to succeed, as with the internal staff to assist an ERP system integrator committed to install the system for a fixed price. Not only will you want to commit to providing certain resources, but you may also need to reassure the partner that you will limit the change-orders.

Step 3: Develop alternative designs for dealing with problems

Now that you have identified the problems, you need to find tactics to mitigate or resolve them. Sometimes the tactics become obvious once you see the problem and you review the basic choices in setting up collaboration, shown in Figure S.4. You had hoped, for example, to outsource an activity, but the bargaining power problems with suppliers are so great that you realize you need to bring the work in-house.

When solutions aren't so clear, you may need to get at the problem indirectly, by moving elsewhere in the framework. If you are concerned that *agreements* to pay performance bonuses are leading traders to take too many risks, you can change the nature of *what you want* from your partners by hedging more of the risks taken on. Or if you can't measure the performance of your R&D to set up motivating *agreements* with R&D managers, you may decide to change the type of *partners* you work with and outsource R&D to small focused development companies whose market prices provide a currency to measure managers' performance.

The checklists of tactics presented throughout the book capture the indirect as well as the direct approaches. They list the most important alternatives in making choices, but in devising and testing alternative designs, you will need to take account of trade-offs between meeting different requirements. A tactic to solve a problem in meeting one requirement may raise new problems in meeting another. So the process of developing and testing possible alternative designs is iterative. When you come up with a new design you need to test it against all 10 requirements afresh.

Solving more complex problems may require considering radical alternatives that have not been tried before. The pain-and-gain sharing alliances discussed in Chapter 4 were a radical alternative when first introduced to build oil platforms in the North Sea. Keller Williams' profit-sharing scheme discussed in Chapter 9 is still a radical alternative for rewarding real-estate agents. Radical alternatives can be high return. Testing them against the 10 requirements helps to reduce their risks.

Choices of what you want and agreements

Many of the basic choices to be made when setting up collaboration, particularly choices of what you want and agreements, map directly onto the 10 requirements and need little commentary, as shown in Figure S.4

Figure S.4 The basic choices in developing a collaboration design

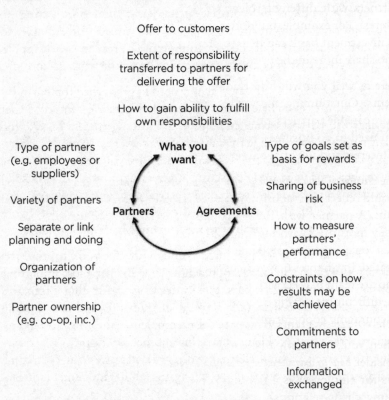

Offer to customers

Extent of responsibility transferred to partners for delivering the offer

How to gain ability to fulfill own responsibilities

Type of partners (e.g. employees or suppliers)

Variety of partners

Separate or link planning and doing

Organization of partners

Partner ownership (e.g. co-op, inc.)

What you want

Partners   **Agreements**

Type of goals set as basis for rewards

Sharing of business risk

How to measure partners' performance

Constraints on how results may be achieved

Commitments to partners

Information exchanged

Choosing partners

The issues involved in choosing partners map less directly onto the 10 requirements, but it is still fairly easy to see how different choices can help meet requirements. The *type of partners*, the *variety of partners you work with*, and *whether you take separate partners for the planning and doing phases of a project*, can all help ensure that your partners have the proper ability, do not face awkward conflicts of interest and do not gain too much bargaining power.

Working with a greater variety of partners can help you find those with the proper abilities when it is difficult to do so, as in the 'open innovation' discussed in Chapter 7. Working with more partners with similar roles, through second-sourcing, can also maintain competition and prevent partners gaining too much bargaining power. Introducing new partners with different roles can help prevent awkward conflicts of interest. For example, building a separate risk management function in an investment bank can help to prevent excessive risk-taking by traders who share more in the upside than in the downside of the deals they do.

Here as well you will find trade-offs in meeting the different requirements. Outsourcing the work to suppliers may help you work with more capable partners, but because they control other assets and people you need to do business, you are more likely to face awkward conflicts of interest and unequal bargaining power.

The choice of *which specific partners you work with*, employees or suppliers, should reflect their ability and also their self-motivation to do what you want. A partner with the right personal characteristics may be more easily motivated without financial incentives – less tempted to pursue their own interests or demand an unreasonable share of the value created. In Chapter 6, we discussed how Egon Zehnder hires employees who are team players with a high sense of professionalism to overcome the difficulty of setting up incentives for personal performance without discouraging cooperation.

When you, as a company, contract with many partners, you need to consider *how to organize the relationships between partners*. The need to do this for employees is a familiar topic in organization design, such as asking client relationship managers to team up. Not only does this bring more ability to bear for client needs, but it also helps prevent managers from gaining bargaining power by 'owning' certain clients. Usually less attention is paid to organizing relationships between suppliers and employees, or relationships among suppliers, but this is becoming a critical issue. In framework alliances, for example, 'best person for the job' principles can result in employees supervised by a manager from a supplier who also recommends their bonus. Franchisors can encourage franchisees to form a buying cooperative, to avoid the awkward situation of the franchisors doing the purchasing and potentially setting a high mark-up. As the dominant player in a business system, you can influence how your partners cooperate.

Placing restrictions on the *ownership of your partner*, such as by working with a supplier owned jointly with your peers like a mutual, cooperative or association, can help remove awkward conflicts of interest or address bargaining power problems. Such a supplier should be self-motivated to do what you want, and even if it does raise prices, you'll receive the benefits in dividends.

The partner's perspective

The need to meet requirements from partners' perspective as well as your own is a distinct factor in setting up profitable collaboration. Except in extreme cases when you may need to change your basic strategy, you meet partners' requirements largely through your choice of agreements – for example, by committing more internal staff to assist an ERP systems integrator.

Checklists of tactics for solving problems

The checklists of tactics developed in Chapters 4 to 8 describe the indirect as well as the direct approaches to finding solutions to problems and list alternatives in making choices about how to set up collaboration. They summarize the results of our research and experience in a wide range of sectors and cover solutions to all the common problems that we have encountered. Combining a number of familiar tactics can lead to a quite creative collaboration strategy for solving problems. For convenience, we've collected all the tactics in an Appendix to this process summary.

The figures used throughout the book cover all of the 10 requirements with two exceptions. We left out how to create customer value, a topic so large it could fill another book. Sometimes difficulties in setting up collaboration may cause you to revise your customer value proposition. But whether a customer offer creates value is independent of how you set up collaboration to deliver it. We have also left out a figure on setting up collaboration for competitive advantage. But we have covered this critical issue extensively in Chapter 3 in our discussion of step 1 in the process. The tactics figures on 'setting goals and constraints to measure performance' focus on setting goals, but other figures point out where constraints will be needed to avoid collaboration problems.

We have included a figure on meeting requirements from your partners' perspective, but with far less detail than those for other requirements. It offers a few basic moves, but the tactics for meeting requirements from your own perspective may all be used to meet partners' needs rather than your own.

The issues for which we offer checklists of tactics to help solve collaboration problems and their numbers in the Appendix are:

1. Ensuring you have the needed ability to get what you want
2. Finding partners able to help you innovate by taking an 'open' approach
3. Harnessing partners' self-motivation
4. Avoiding or managing awkward conflicts of interest
5. Preventing a partner gaining bargaining power with your company
6. Preventing a partner gaining bargaining power with your industry
7. Mitigating problems in setting goals for the output of the work
8. Mitigating problems in measuring individual or team performance
9. Addressing timing problems in measuring performance
10. Aligning rewards with performance measured
11. Acquiring the information to specify favourable terms
12. Meeting requirements from partners' perspective

The tactics checklists provide ideas for how you might deal with tricky collaboration design problems that you face. For example, suppose you are entering into an outsourcing relationship. You can see that your supplier is likely to acquire increasing knowledge of your needs and your organization, and may also invest in assets specific to your needs. You may well conclude that the supplier will gain bargaining power. Checklist 5 in the Appendix suggests that there are several tactics to consider in order to prevent a partner gaining bargaining power with your company, including:

- Owning more of the assets critical to the business
- Setting up a second source supplier
- Finding ways of maintaining a credible threat of changing supplier
- Doing more of the work in-house
- Offering the supplier a long-term relationship subject to performance
- Finding ways to prevent small changes in specifications leading to price renegotiation
- Insisting on good formal documentation of work being done

Chapter 4 shows how such tactics, particularly in combination with the complementary tactics in Checklist 11 in the Appendix that help in negotiating favourable terms, can help you address the challenges.

The other checklists in the Appendix give guidance on problems related to other requirements for setting up profitable collaboration. Together, these checklists are not so much a set of simple standard recipes as a way of stimulating ideas about how to resolve your specific issues.

Successful collaboration also depends on good management and leadership, but we focus on the initial set up. If you don't set things up well, often no amount of good management and leadership will bring success – you will just burn yourself out trying to make things work. It is far better to prevent problems from occurring, than to struggle to fix them when you have many fewer degrees of freedom. Where others emphasize good management and especially leadership to improve collaboration, we shift the balance to focus on setting things up right in the first place.

With greater specialization and non-routine tasks, competitive advantage depends as much on creative collaboration to get full value from resources – financial, human and other resources – as gaining access to these resources. This is a main theme throughout the book and we give it a particular focus in Chapters 9 and 10.

Step 4: Select the best available design

The final step is to consider your options, select the best available design and implement it.

Choosing among alternative designs

Overcoming problems with your first draft design usually leads to a variety of alternative designs, with a delicate balance in choosing between them. If you use an alliance approach for a major construction project – choosing your contractor early, agreeing on target costs and sharing pain and gain – you have strong alignment between client and contractor in executing the project and strong incentives for the contractor to meet the target costs. But because you settle on the contractor before finalizing your specifications, you can't use competitive pressure to drive favourable terms for target costs. When setting up collaboration is difficult, you must make difficult trade-offs and you need to choose the best available design in the light of these.

If you are not starting from scratch but changing an existing collaboration design, your strategy will need to consider the often substantial costs of transition. This is especially the case in bringing work in-house. Rather than building the assets and capabilities from scratch, you may well prefer to acquire your current partners. But there is no guarantee they will sell at a price you consider reasonable. The more partners you need to buy out, the greater the difficulties you are likely to face. For example, Obi, the leading home improvement retailer in Germany, has been buying out franchisees to own more stores and do the work in-house, but many franchisees have preferred not to sell. They enjoy being entrepreneurs and are reluctant to become managers or simply investors with a minority stake.[3] Relations between Obi and its franchisees have been difficult, and one of the largest has jumped to another chain.[4]

So if you are considering a radical change, you may prefer to proceed incrementally. Rather than outsource all their research and development overnight, big pharmaceutical companies have moved over a decade to build up a network of external R&D firms in parallel to their in-house work. A transition plan to a new collaboration set-up will be critical, and difficulties in getting there from here may sometimes change the balance of attractiveness toward squeezing more from an existing design instead.

Business exit as a last resort

By now you should have at least one acceptable design that can be implemented at a reasonable cost. But in some cases intractable problems persist regardless of the tactics employed, however radical. To avoid the inevitable problems with implementation, you need to consider exiting the business. This is clearly not a desirable option or one to take lightly, but it may be the best way forward. In investment banking, UBS, RBS and other large banks decided to downsize or exit large parts of their operations.[5] The intractable problems of setting up bonus agreements and other aspects of collaboration to prudently manage risks undoubtedly contributed to these decisions.

Conclusions

Non-routine tasks and increasing business specialization make getting work done for you a greater challenge. Big, costly mistakes in setting up collaboration to get the work done are common, but new collaboration designs that rise to the challenge also create important new business opportunities.

The process we have described is a practical approach to developing a collaboration strategy to meet this new challenge, helping avoid mistakes and seize opportunities. The traditional process of choosing what type of partners to work with and what agreements to put in place to motivate them based on considerations of market and competitive strategy remains a valuable first step. It is a good way of coming up with an initial draft collaboration design. But allocating business responsibilities to whoever has a competitive advantage in taking them on – the essence of the traditional process for choosing whether to do the work in-house with employees or outsource to external suppliers – is not enough if you can't motivate your preferred partners to do what you want on favourable terms. So you also need, in a second step, to test your design to see if it meets these motivational requirements. The third step in the process gets you to think through the key choices in collaboration design in order to address the problems you identify. It offers a set of practical tactics to help you come up with a better solution, integrating considerations of ability and motivation. Finally, in a fourth step, you need to assess the trade-offs between the alternatives and choose a collaboration design, taking into account the costs of changing from your current set-up.

As setting up profitable collaboration becomes more complex, a clear, systematic and iterative process for developing a collaboration strategy is essential to avoid mistakes. It is all too easy to overlook one or more of the 10 key requirements and so design a fatally flawed set-up. And it is difficult to remember that the tactics to deal with one problem may have consequences elsewhere which need to be thought through and taken into account. The analytical, structured process for developing a collaboration strategy that we propose in this book should also help managers come up with more profitable and innovative collaboration designs. It's all about enabling you and your company to specialize in what you do best while getting the help you need to succeed.

---

[1] Both balance sheet assets and human resources.

[2] The three entrepreneurial responsibilities are: access business resources, take and implement decisions, and carry the business risks.

[3] Mathias Vogel, 'Wie wo was will Obi? Managementfehler und Umsatzschwäche sorgen beim DIY-Riesen für Verdruss. Unternehmenschef Sergio Giroldi muss verhindern, dass ihm Franchisenehmer von der Fahne gehen' ('What is Obi up to? Management mistakes and poor revenues cause frustration at the DIY giant. CEO Sergio Giroldi must stop franchisees leaving the brand'). *Lebensmittel Zeitung*, 19th June 2009.

[4] 'Alle unter einem Hut; Auf dem hart umkämpften Heimwerkermarkt wollen zwei neue Partner die Region auffrischen. Ein Gespräch über unternehmerische Freiheiten, Folgen für die Kunden und einen bevorstehenden Kraftakt' (Getting together; two new partners want to liven things up in the region in the hard fought DIY market. A conversation about entrepreneurial freedom, the consequences for customers and an impending major move'). *Süddeutsche Zeitung*, 28th June 2013.

[5] See, for example, Dana Cimilluca, David Enrich and Sara Schaefer Munoz. 'Banking Cuts Reflect New, Leaner Era'. *The Wall Street Journal Europe*, 13th January 2012.

Checklists of tactics to meet the 10 requirements for profitable collaboration

1. Ensuring you have the needed ability to get what you want

2. Finding partners able to help you innovate by taking an 'open' approach

3. Harnessing partners' self-motivation

4. Avoiding or managing awkward conflicts of interest

5. Preventing a partner gaining bargaining power with your company

6. Preventing a partner gaining bargaining power with your industry

7. Mitigating problems in setting goals for the output of the work

8. Mitigating problems in measuring individual or team performance

9. Addressing timing problems in measuring performance

10. Aligning rewards with performance measured

11. Acquiring the information to specify favourable terms

12. Meeting requirements from partners' perspective

1. Ensuring you have the needed ability to get what you want

Adapt the customer offer
to match your skills and
resources

Set up agreements that
transfer more responsibility
to partners

Invest to acquire more of the
needed skills and resources

For further information see Chapter 2, page 22, where we introduce our discussion of how collaboration design must take account of your personal abilities using the example of designing and installing an ERP system.

2. Finding partners able to help you innovate by taking an 'open' approach

Create an open business
platform that partners can
plug into

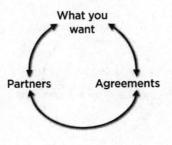

Adopt more 'open'
sourcing policy:
look 'outside' for
ideas and ready-
made solutions to
problems

**What you
want**

Avoid reinventing
the wheel (e.g. by
rewarding speedy
work)

Partners   **Agreements**

Employ managers to
make 'unexpected
connections' inside
and outside the
company

Use 'prize
competitions'
to find partners
with solutions to
problems

Let several partners
work on the same
problem

Share business
revenues with
product developers
who use your market
platform

For further information, see Chapter 7, the section 'Choosing partners',
page 155, where we discuss open innovation in the context of developing new consumer products and new pharmaceutical drugs.

3. Harnessing partners' self-motivation

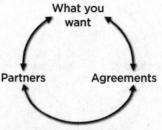

Clearly communicate the
company's value creation
goals and how these will be
achieved

Hire partners with
personal goals
strongly aligned with
the company's goals

**What you
want**

Set clear personal
goals

Make the link
between company
goals and personal
goals

Hire partners with
strong professional
values

Partners   **Agreements**

Provide sufficient
resources and avoid
too many constraints

All tactics shown are
to meet partners'
requirements

Build team spirit

For further information see Chapter 7, the section 'Choosing partners'
starting on page 158, where we discuss issues of harnessing partners'
self-motivation, taking the example of employees in pharmaceutical
R&D.

4. Avoiding or managing awkward conflicts of interest

Focus on activities you have
the specialist skills to direct

Set up early indicators of
performance

Take separate
contractors for
planning and doing

**What you
want**

Offer partners
a long-term
relationship subject
to performance

Hire 'professional'
contractors

Partners   **Agreements**

Share business
income with partner

Take additional
advisor to help plan
projects/propose
favourable terms

Share pain/gain
of deviations from
agreed goals

Do more of the work
in-house

Use non-compete
clauses/ 'golden
handcuffs'

Establish separate
performance control
function

Reward partners for
teaming-up

For further information see Chapter 4, the section 'When you want help deciding what you want and then doing it', page 83, where we discuss awkward conflicts of interest with suppliers, taking the example of engineering and construction projects. See also Chapter 6, the section 'The challenge of investment banking', page 138, where we discuss awkward conflicts of interest with employees.

5. Preventing a partner gaining bargaining power with your company

Own more of the assets
critical to the business

Second source

Otherwise maintain
the credible threat of
changing supplier

**What you
want**

Offer partners
a long-term
relationship subject
to performance

Do more of the work
in-house

Partners   **Agreements**

Prevent small
changes in project
specifications
leading to price
renegotiation

Make employees
work in teams, not
independently

Specify good formal
documentation

Establish succession
plans

For further information see Chapter 4, the section 'Not ready to decide what you want done', page 69, where we discuss problems of suppliers gaining too much bargaining power, taking fashion retailing and automotive industry examples. See also Chapter 6, the section 'The challenge of investment banking' and 'Awkward conflicts of interest and bargaining power', page 138, where we discuss problems of client relationship managers and other employees gaining bargaining power.

6. Preventing a partner gaining bargaining power with your industry

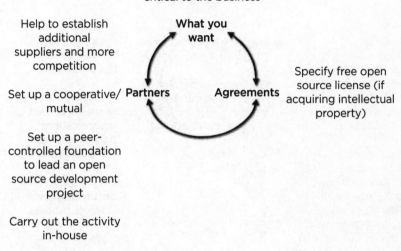

Own more of the assets
critical to the business

Help to establish
additional
suppliers and more
competition

**What you
want**

Set up a cooperative/
mutual

Partners

Agreements

Specify free open
source license (if
acquiring intellectual
property)

Set up a peer-
controlled foundation
to lead an open
source development
project

Carry out the activity
in-house

Encourage
government
regulation and
supervision

For further information see Chapter 5, starting on page 99. The chapter is entirely devoted to this issue. We discuss it, taking examples from professional sports, utilities, stock markets, dairy farming, and operating systems for computers and mobile phones.

7. Mitigating problems in setting goals for the output of the work

Adapt your offer to make it
easier to define the output
you want

Invest more time in defining
the output you want

Outsource a complete
process so need to
define only a 'functional
specification'

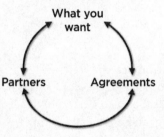

Take partners to
help you decide the
details of what you
want to do, who
have a skill set and
experiences that plug
any gaps in your own

Direct and control
the work

Use 'briefing/back-
briefing' process
to communicate
strategic intent

Pay for combined
provision of output
and resource
capacity

Set-up income-
sharing agreement to
motivate partner and
limit your risk

Problems in setting goals for the output of the work are the central theme in the book and we discuss them in all chapters. For further information see particularly Chapter 4, the section 'When you want help deciding what you want' , page 78. We there discuss problems in setting goals for suppliers, taking examples from the consumer products industry. See also Chapter 6, page 118, where setting goals to be able to direct the work is the main focus of our discussion of problems in working with employees.

8. Mitigating problems in measuring individual or team performance

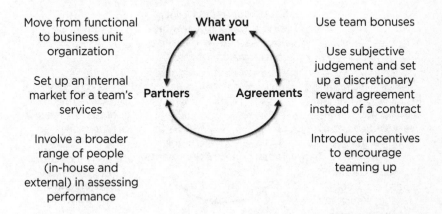

Move from functional to business unit organization

Set up an internal market for a team's services

Involve a broader range of people (in-house and external) in assessing performance

What you want

Partners

Agreements

Use team bonuses

Use subjective judgement and set up a discretionary reward agreement instead of a contract

Introduce incentives to encourage teaming up

For further information see the beginning of Chapter 6, page 115, where we take a broad perspective on problems of performance measurement for employees. See also Chapter 6, the section 'The challenge of investment banking' and 'Problems in measuring individual performance', page 127.

9. Addressing timing problems in measuring performance

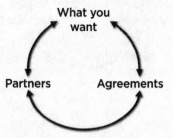

Set up contracts to sell, hedge, insure or guarantee value of assets as basis for performance rewards

Add independent in-house partners to develop and manage early indicators of performance

Add external partners to buy, hedge, insure, or guarantee asset values

What you want

Partners

Agreements

Make partners wait to receive rewards until performance can be measured

Use early indicators to help measure performance

For further information see Chapter 6, the section 'The challenge of investment banking' and 'Problems in quickly measuring performance', page 131. See also Chapter 7, section 'Establishing agreements', page 160 and subsequent sections where we consider timing problems in performance measurement at greater length, taking a pharmaceutical R&D example. We discuss timing problems in measuring performance for CEOs and business general managers in Chapter 8, section 'Publicly-held companies' and 'No reliable objective measure of performance for all shareholders', starting on page 182, and the section 'Private equity', page 189.

10. Aligning rewards with performance measured

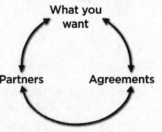

Exit high-risk business segments

Diversify mix of business

Own business via multiple legal entities

Retain personal decision-making power over decisions that may destroy value

Add independent cadre of managers to manage risks and prevent unwanted risk-taking

What you want

Partners

Agreements

Make partner invest

Offer longer term rewards

Lower fixed and increase variable compensation

Use team (or company) performance to set rewards

Cap performance rewards to limit partner's temptation

Set up constraints to limit risk-taking

For further information see Chapter 6, the section 'The challenge of investment banking', from page 133. See also Chapter 8, the section 'Private equity', from page 190.

11. Acquiring the information to specify favourable terms

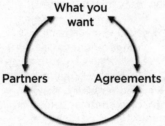

Build your own goal-setting/
cost-estimating capability

Use competitive bids

Specify output, even
if not yet precisely
known, so as to
later only negotiate
changes

Add a third party
assessor to help
set demanding
standards

Demand continuous
improvement

Establish
'frameworks'
for information
exchange

Use open book
accounting

For further information see Chapter 4, the section 'Not ready to decide what you want', from page 72, and also 'The automotive industry: a more difficult challenge', from page 76.

12. Meeting requirements from partners' perspective

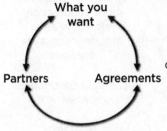

Let partners take on more or fewer entrepreneurial responsibilities so they are less locked in to working with you

What you want

Partners

Agreements

Reassure partners that they will get the help they need to meet your goals (this may require commitments from you to your partners)

If partners will need to pay you to get the help they need to meet your goals, reassure partners that they will get the help they need on sufficiently favourable terms

This checklist shows basic tactics only. For further information in the context of a discussion of designing and installing an ERP system, see Chapter 2, the section 'Generating the 10 requirements', page 29, and the section 'Improving your likelihood of profitable collaboration', page 35. For a further discussion, taking the example of setting up a chain of fast-food restaurants, see Chapter 3, section 'Factoring in partner motivation with the 10 requirements', 'Meeting requirements from your partners' perspective' and 'Why Starbucks owns rather than franchises its stores both page 60'.

Index